The Plight of Indian Dalits

The Plight of Indian Dalits

Vidya Devi

MD Publications Pvt Ltd
New Delhi
www.mdppl.com

Published by :

MD Publications Pvt Ltd
'MD House', 11, Darya Ganj
New Delhi - 110 002
Phone : +91-11-41563325 (Customer Service)
+91-11-41562846 (Editorial)
E-mail (orders): contact@mdppl.com
Website: www.mdppl.com

ISBN: 978-81-7533-184-6

Published and Printed by Mrs. Rajni Gupta on behalf of **MD Publications Pvt Ltd** at Times Press, New Delhi.

Contents

PREFACE

The Indian society has a long tradition of caste system. In this caste hierarchy the dalits have always been the most deprived section of population. The word 'Dalit' in Marathi literally means 'broken'. First used by Jyotiba Phule, the term was later popularized by Dalit leader Dr. B. R. Ambedkar to reflect the situation of the millions of Dalits within South Asia, who are systematically and institutionally deprived of their civil, political, economic, social and cultural rights in every aspect of life. Treated as untouchables, the Dalits occupy the lowest position in this abhorrent social system.

The Indian caste system has a tradition of social segregation, which works on the principle of purity and pollution. Though the Indian caste system is historically linked to Hinduism, it is also followed by Muslims, Sikhs and Christians in the country.

Of late there have been many efforts from government and other many reformers of the society to abolish this tradition. The social, economic, political and religious disabilities and discriminations to which hitherto depressed classes were subjected got initial efforts by social reformers towards removal of inequalities and overall amelioration of conditions of these people. This book traces the historical background of this tradition, efforts to remove this and the present condition of dalits in Indian social system.

I am very grateful to Mr. Pranav Gupta, Director, MD Publications Pvt Ltd, New Delhi who has readily expressed his acceptance and supported me fully for completing this book.

Vidya Devi

1

Caste System in India

The Indian caste system describes the social stratification and social restrictions in the Indian subcontinent, in which social classes are defined by thousands of endogamous hereditary groups, often termed as *jâtis* or castes. Within a jâti, there exist exogamous groups known as gotras, the lineage or clan of a person, although in a handful of sub-castes like Shakadvipi, endogamy within a gotra is permitted and alternative mechanisms of restricting endogamy are used (e.g. banning endogamy within a surname).

The Indian classes are similar to the Iranian classes (*"pistras"*), wherein the priests are Athravans, the warriors are Rathaestha, the merchants are Vastriya, and the artisans are Huiti.

Although generally identified with Hinduism, the caste system was also observed among followers of other religions in the Indian subcontinent, including some groups of Muslims and Christians. The Indian Constitution has outlawed caste-based discrimination, in keeping with the socialist, secular, democratic principles that founded the nation. Caste barriers have mostly broken down in large cities, though they persist in rural areas of the country. Nevertheless, the caste system, in various forms, continues to survive in modern India strengthened by a combination of social perceptions and divisive politics.

There is no universally accepted theory about the origin of the Indian caste system.

GENETIC ANALYSIS

A 2002-03 study by prominent authors concluded that the "Indian tribal and caste populations derive largely from the same genetic heritage of Pleistocene southern and western Asians and have received limited gene flow from external regions since the Holocene." Studies point to the various Indian caste groups having similar genetic origins and having negligible genetic input from outside south Asia. However, a 2001 genetic study, led by Michael Bamshad of the University of Utah, found that the affinity of Indians to Europeans is proportionate to caste rank, the upper castes being most similar to Europeans. The researchers believe that the Indo-Aryans entered India from the Northwest and may have established a caste system, in which they placed themselves primarily in higher castes." Because the Indian samples for this study were taken from a single geographical area, it remains to be investigated whether its findings can be safely generalized.

An earlier 1995 study by Joanna L. Mountain et al. of Stanford University had concluded that there was "no clear separation into three genetically distinct groups along caste lines", although "an inferred tree revealed some clustering according to caste affiliation". A 2006 study by Ismail Thanseem et al. of Centre for Cellular and Molecular Biology (India) concluded that the "lower caste groups might have originated with the hierarchical divisions that arose within the tribal groups with the spread of Neolithic agriculturalists, much earlier than the arrival of Aryan speakers", and "the Indo-Europeans established themselves as upper castes among this already developed caste-like class structure within the tribes." The study indicated that the Indian caste system may have its roots much before the arrival of the Indo-Aryans; a rudimentary version of the caste system may have emerged with the shift towards cultivation and settlements, and the divisions may have become more well-defined and intensified with the arrival of Indo-Aryans.

The Indian classes are similar to the Iranian classes (*"pistras"*), wherein the priests are Athravans, the warriors are Rathaestha, the merchants are Vastriya, and the artisans are Huiti.

A 2006 genetic study by the National Institute of Biologicals in India, testing a sample of men from 32 tribal and 45 caste groups, concluded that the Indians have acquired very few genes from Indo-European speakers.

VARNA AND JATI (CLASS AND CASTE)

According to the ancient Hindu scriptures, there are four "varnas." The Bhagavad Gita says varnas are decided based on Guna and Karma. Manusmriti and some other shastras mention four varnas: the Brahmins (teachers, scholars and priests), the Kshatriyas (kings and warriors), the Vaishyas (traders), and Shudras (agriculturists, service providers, and some artisan groups). Offsprings of different varnas belong to different *Jâtis*. Another group excluded from the main society was called Parjanya or Antyaja. This group of former "untouchables" (now called Dalits) was considered either the lower section of Shudras or outside the caste system altogether. Passages from scriptures such as Manusmriti indicate that the varna system was originally non-hereditary.

Several critics of Hinduism state that the caste system is rooted in the varna system mentioned in the ancient Hindu scriptures. However, many groups, such as ISKCON, consider the modern Indian caste system and the varna system as two distinct concepts. Many European scholars from the colonial era regarded the Manusmriti as the "law book" of the Hindus, and thus concluded that the caste system is a part of Hinduism, an assertion that is rejected by many Hindu scholars, who state that it is an anachronistic social practice, not a religious one.

Although many Hindu scriptures contain passages that can be interpreted to sanction the caste system, they also contain indications that the caste system is not an essential part of Hinduism. The Vedas place very little importance on the caste system, mentioning caste only rarely and in a cursory manner. In the Vedic period, there was no prohibition against the Shudras (which later on became the low-castes) listening to the Vedas or participating in any religious rite.

In *Early Evidence for Caste in South India*, George L. Hart stated that "the earliest Tamil texts show the existence of what seems definitely to be caste, but which antedates the Brahmins and the Hindu orthodoxy". He believes that the origins of the caste system can be seen in the "belief system that developed with the agricultural civilization", and was later profoundly influenced by "the Brahmins and the Brahmanical religion". These early Tamil texts also outline the concept of equality. Saint Valluvar has stated "pirapokkum ella uyirkkum", which means "all are equal at birth". Likewise, Saint Auvaiyaar has stated that there are only two castes in the world: those who contribute positively and those who contribute negatively. From these, it can be inferred that the caste system is more of a socio-economic class system.

CASTE AND SOCIAL STATUS

Traditionally, although the political power lay with the Kshatriyas, historians portrayed that the Brahmins as keepers and interpreters of religion enjoyed much prestige and many advantages.

Fa Hien a Buddhist pilgrim from China visited India around 400 AD. *"Only the lot of the Chandals he found unenviable: outcastes by reason of their degrading work as disposers of dead, they were universally shunned... But no other section of the population were notably disadvantaged, no other caste distinctions attracted comment from the Chinese pilgrim, and no oppressive caste 'system' drew forth his surprised censure."* Yet another Chinese pilgrim Hsuan Tsang's accounts (around 600 AD) indicate that the king of Sind region was of Sudra caste. In this period kings of Sudra and Brahmin origin were as common as those of Kshatriya *varna* and caste system was not wholly prohibitive and repressive.

The castes did not constitute a rigid description of the occupation or the social status of a group. Since British society was divided by class, the British attempted to equate the Indian caste system to their own social class system. They saw caste as an indicator of occupation, social standing, and intellectual ability. Intentionally or unintentionally, the caste system became more rigid during the British Raj, when the British started to enumerate castes during the ten year census and codified the system under their rule.

The Dalits, or the people outside the varna system, had the lowest social status. The Dalits, earlier referred to as "untouchables" by some, worked in what were seen as unhealthy, unpleasant or polluting jobs. In the past, the Dalits suffered from social segregation and restrictions, in addition to extreme poverty. They were not allowed temple worship with others, nor water from the same sources. Persons of higher castes would not interact with them. If somehow a member of a higher caste came into physical or social contact with an untouchable, the member of the higher caste was defiled, and had to bathe thoroughly to purge him or herself of the impurity. Social discrimination developed even among the Dalits. Upper sub-castes among Dalits, like *dhobi, nai* etc., would not interact with lower-order Bhangis, who were described as "outcasts even among outcastes".

Sociologists have commented on the historical advantages offered by a rigid social structure, such as the caste system and its lack of usefulness in the modern world. Historically, the caste system offered several advantages to the population of the Indian subcontinent. While Caste is nowadays seen by instances that render it anachronistic, in its original form, the caste system served as an important instrument of order in a society where mutual consent rather than compulsion ruled; where the ritual rights as well as the economic obligations of members of one caste or sub-caste were strictly circumscribed in relation to those of any other caste or sub-caste; where one was born into one's caste and retained one's station in society for life; where merit was inherited, where equality existed within the caste, but inter-caste relations were unequal and hierarchical. A well-defined system of mutual interdependence through a division of labour created security within a community. In addition, the division of labour on the basis of ethnicity allowed immigrants and foreigners to quickly integrate into their own caste niches. The caste system played an influential role in shaping economic activities. The caste system functioned much like medieval European guilds, ensuring the division of labour, providing for the training of apprentices and, in some cases, allowing manufacturers to achieve narrow specialisation. For instance, in certain regions, producing each variety of cloth was the speciality of a particular sub-caste. Also, philosophers argue that the majority of people would be comfortable in stratified endogamous groups, and have been in ancient times. Membership in a particular caste, with its associated narrative, history and genealogy, would instill in its members a sense of group accomplishment and cultural pride. Such sentiments are routinely expressed by the Marathas, Rajputs, Iyers for instance.

CASTE MOBILITY

Some scholars believe that the relative ranking of other castes was fluid or differed from one place to another prior to the arrival of the British. Sociologists such as Bernard Buber and Marriott McKim describe how the perception of the caste system as a static and textual stratification has given way to the perception of the caste system as a more processual, empirical and contextual stratification. Other sociologists such as Y.B Damle have applied theoretical models to explain mobility and flexibility in the caste system in India. According to these scholars, groups of lower-caste individuals could seek to elevate the status of their caste by attempting to emulate the practices of higher castes.

Flexibility in caste laws permitted very low-caste religious clerics such as Valmiki to compose the Ramayana, which became a central work of Hindu scripture.

According to some psychologists, mobility across broad caste lines may have been "minimal", though sub-castes (jatis) may change their social status over the generations by fission, re-location, and adoption of new rituals.

Sociologist M. N. Srinivas has also debated the question of rigidity in Caste. In an ethnographic study of the Coorgs of Karnataka, he observed considerable flexibility and mobility in their caste hierarchies. He asserts that the caste system is far from a rigid system in which the position of each component caste is fixed for all time. Movement has always been possible, and especially in the middle regions of the hierarchy. It was always possible for groups born into a lower caste to "rise to a higher position by adopting vegetarianism and teetotalism" i.e adopt the customs of the higher castes. While theoretically "forbidden", the process was not uncommon in practice. The concept of sanskritization, or the adoption of upper-caste norms by the lower castes, addressed the actual complexity and fluidity of caste relations.

Historical examples of mobility in the Indian Caste System among Hindus have been researched. There is also precedent of certain Shudra families within the temples of the Sri Vaishnava sect in South India elevating their caste.

The distinctions, particularly between the Brahmins and the other castes, were in theory sharper, but in practice it now appears that social restrictions were not so rigid. Brahmins often lived off the land and founded dynasties. Most of the groups claiming Kshatriya status had only recently acquired it. The conscious reference to being Kshatriya, a characteristic among Rajputs, is a noticeable feature in post-Gupta politics. The fact that many of these dynasties were of obscure origin suggests some social mobility: a person of any caste, having once acquired political power, could also acquire a genealogy connecting him with the traditional lineages and conferring Kshatriya status. A number of new castes, such as the Kayasthas (scribes) and Khatris (traders), are mentioned in the sources of this period. According to the Brahmanic sources, they originated from intercaste marriages, but this is clearly an attempt at rationalizing their rank in the hierarchy. Many of these new castes played a major role in society. The hierarchy of castes did not have a uniform distribution throughout the country. Khatri appears to be unquestionably a Prakritised form of the Sanskrit Kshatriya.

REFORMS

There have been challenges to the caste system from the time of Buddha, and from the time of Mahavira (Jaina founder) and (still earlier) of Gosâla Maskarin.

Opposition to the system of varna ('caste') is regularly asserted already in the Yoga Upanishads (of early mediaeval date); and is a constant feature of Cîna-âcâra tantrism (Chinese-derived movement in Asom, and also of mediaeval date). The Nâtha system (likewise mediaeval) founded by Matsya-indra Nâtha and by Gorakca Nâtha, and spread throughout India, has likewise been in consistent opposition to the system of varna.

Many Bhakti period saints rejected the caste discriminations and accepted all castes, including untouchables, into their fold. During the British Raj, this sentiment gathered steam, and many Hindu reform movements such as Brahma Samaj and Arya Samaj renounced caste-based discrimination. The inclusion of so-called untouchables into the mainstream was argued for by many social reformers. Mahatma Gandhi called them "Harijans" (children of God) although that term is now considered patronizing and the term Dalit ("downtrodden") is the more commonly used. Gandhi's contribution toward the emancipation of the untouchables is still debated, especially in the commentary of his contemporary Dr. B. R. Ambedkar, an untouchable himself, who frequently saw Gandhi's activities as detrimental to the cause of upliftment of his people.

The practice of untouchability was formally outlawed by the Constitution of India in 1950, and has declined significantly since then. K. R. Narayanan, who became the President of India in 1997, and K. G. Balakrishnan (the present Chief Justice of India) have belonged to castes formerly considered untouchable.

BRITISH RULE

The fluidity of the caste system was affected by the arrival of the British. Prior to that, the relative ranking of castes differed from one place to another. The castes did not constitute a rigid description of the occupation or the social status of a group. Since the British society was divided by class, the British attempted to equate the Indian caste system to the class system. They saw caste as an indicator of occupation, social standing, and intellectual ability. During the initial days of the British East India Company's rule, caste privileges and customs were encouraged, but the British law courts disagreed with the discrimination against the lower castes. However, British policies of divide and rule as well as enumeration of the population into rigid categories during the 10 year census contributed towards the hardening of caste identities.

During the period of British rule, India saw the rebellions of several lower castes, mainly tribals that revolted against British rule. These were:

1. Halba rebellion (1774-79)
2. Bhopalpatnam Struggle (1795)
3. Bhil rebellion (1822–1857)
4. Paralkot rebellion (1825)
5. Tarapur rebellion (1842-54)
6. Maria rebellion (1842-63)
7. First Freedom Struggle (1856-57).
8. Bhil rebellion, begun by Tatya Tope in Banswara (1858)
9. Koi revolt (1859)
10. Gond rebellion, begun by Ramji Gond in Adilabad (1860)
11. Muria rebellion (1876)
12. Rani rebellion (1878-82)
13. Bhumkal (1910)

MODERN STATUS OF THE CASTE SYSTEM

In some rural areas and small towns, the caste system is still very rigid. Caste is also a factor in the politics of India.

The Government of India has officially documented castes and subcastes, primarily to determine those deserving reservation (positive discrimination in education and jobs) through the census. The Indian reservation system, though limited in scope, relies entirely on quotas. The Government lists consist of Scheduled Castes, Scheduled Tribes and Other Backward Classes:

Scheduled Castes (SC): Scheduled castes generally consist of former "untouchables" (the term "Dalit" is now preferred). The present population is 16% of the total population of India (around 160 million). For example, the Delhi state has 49 castes listed as SC.

Scheduled Tribes (ST): Scheduled tribes generally consist of tribal groups. The present population is 7% of the total population of India i.e. around 70 million.

Other Backward Classes (OBC): The Mandal Commission covered more than 3000 castes under OBC Category and stated that OBCs form around 52% of the Indian population. However, the National Sample Survey puts the figure at 32%. There is substantial debate over the exact number of OBCs in India. It is generally estimated to be sizable, but many believe that it is lower than the figures quoted by either the Mandal Commission or the National Sample Survey.

The caste-based reservations in India have led to wide-spread protests, with many complaining of reverse discrimination against the forward castes (the castes that do not qualify for the reservation). The 2006 Indian anti-reservation protests are one major example. Many view negative treatment (or hatred) of forward castes as socially divisive and just as wrong.

CASTE SYSTEM AMONG NON-HINDUS

In some parts of India, the Christians are stratified by sect, location, and the castes of their predecessors, usually this refers only to the Catholic churches, not the Protestant, and could be in reference to nasrani who were bestowed caste-like status. Presently in India, more than 70% of Christians are Dalits, but the higher caste Christians (30% by estimates) control 90% of the Catholic church's administrative jobs. Out of the 156 Catholic bishops, only 6 are from lower castes. Many Dalit Catholics have spoken out against discrimination against them by the Catholic Church. Christians in Goa are certainly likely to mention their caste in matıimonial ads. However, things are different in Kerala where the non-catholic population tend to be higher in the caste ladder.

Units of social stratification, termed as "castes" by many, have developed among Muslims in some parts of South Asia. Sources indicate that the castes among Muslims developed as the result of close contact with Hindu culture and Hindu converts to Islam. The Sachar Committee's report commissioned by the government of India and released in 2006, documents the continued stratification in Muslim society.

The Muslims too have sections of washermen, tailors, smiths, and other backward castes In modern India there have been brutal clashes amongst Muslims belonging to rival castes.

Among Muslims, those who are referred to as Ashrafs are presumed to have a superior status derived from their foreign Arab ancestry, while the Ajlafs are assumed to be converts from Hinduism, and have a Iower status. In addition, there is also the *Arzal* caste among Muslims, who were regarded by anti-caste activists like Babasaheb Ambedkar as the equivalent of untouchables. In the Bengal region of India, some Muslims also stratify their society according to 'Quoms'. While some scholars have asserted that the Muslim Castes are not as acute in their discrimination as that among Hindus, Ambedkar argued otherwise, writing that the social evils in Muslim society were "worse than those seen in Hindu society".

The nastik Buddhists too have a caste system. In Sri Lanka, the Rodis have always been despised and they might have been out-casted by the Lankan Buddhists due the absence of "ahimsa" (*non-violence*), which Buddhism heavily depends on. The writer Raghavan notes: "*That a form of worship in which human offerings formed the essential ritual would have been anathema to the Buddhist way of life goes without saying; and it needs no stretch of imagination that any class of people in whom the cult prevailed or survived even in an attenuated form would have been pronounced by the sangha (i.e. the Buddhist clergy) as exiles from the social order.*" Savarkar too believed that the status of the backward castes (e.g. Chamar) that performed non-violence only worsened. When Ywan Chwang traveled to South India after the period of the Chalukyan Empire, he noticed that the caste system had existed among the Buddhists and Jains.

The Jains too have castes in places such as Bihar. For example, in the village of Bundela, there are several *"jaats"* (*groups*) amongst the Jains. A person of one *"jaat"* cannot intermingle with a Jain or another *"jaat"*. They also cannot eat with the members of other *"jaats"*.

The Sikh Gurus criticized the hierarchy in the caste system. Where some castes were perceived by people as being better or higher than others (e.g. Brahmins being higher than others) they preached all sections of society were valuable and merit and hard-work were essential aspects of life. In Shiromani Gurdwara Prabandhak Committee, out of 140 seats, twenty are reserved for low caste Sikhs. However, the quoter system has attracted much critism due to the lack of meritocracy, where merit is considered the single most important component of winning a seat.

CASTE-RELATED VIOLENCE

Independent India has witnessed considerable amount of violence and hate crimes motivated by caste. Ranvir Sena, a caste-supremacist fringe paramilitary group based in Bihar, has committed violent acts against Dalits and other members of the scheduled caste community. Phoolan Devi, who belonged to *Mallah* lower-caste, was mistreated and raped by upper-caste Thakurs at a young age. She then became a bandit and carried out violent robberies against upper-caste people. In 1981, her gang massacred twenty-two Thakurs, most of whom were not involved in her kidnapping or rape. Phoolan Devi went on to become a politician and Member of Parliament.

Over the years, various incidents of violence against Dalits, such as Kherlanji Massacre have been reported from many parts of India. At the same time, many violent protests by Dalits, such as the 2006 Dalit protests in Maharashtra, have been reported as well.

CASTE POLITICS

Mahatma Gandhi, B. R. Ambedkar and Jawaharlal Nehru had radically different approaches to caste especially over constitutional politics and the status of "untouchables".Until the mid-1970s, the politics of independent India was largely dominated by economic issues and questions of corruption. But since 1980s, caste has emerged as a major issue in the Politics of India.

The Mandal Commission was established in 1979 to "identify the socially or educationally backward", and to consider the question of seat reservations and quotas for people to redress caste discrimination. In 1980, the commission's report affirmed the affirmative action practice under Indian law whereby members of lower castes were given exclusive access to a certain portion of government jobs and slots in public universities. When V. P. Singh Government tried to implement the recommendations of Mandal Commission in 1989, massive protests were held in the country. Many alleged that the politicians were trying to cash in on caste-based reservations for purely pragmatic electoral purposes.

Many political parties in India have openly indulged in caste-based votebank politics. Parties such as Bahujan Samaj Party (BSP), the Samajwadi Party and the Janata Dal claim that they are representing the backward castes, and rely primarily on OBC support, often in alliance with Dalit and Muslim support to win the elections. Remarkably, what is called a landmark election in the history of India's biggest state of Uttar Pradesh, the Bahujan Samaj Party was able to garner majority in the State assembly elections with the support of the brahmin community.

CRITICISM

There have been many criticisms of the caste system, both within and outside India. Criticism of the Caste system in Hindu society came both from the Hindu fold and from without.

HISTORICAL CRITICISM

Gautama Buddha and Mahavira, the founders of Buddhism and Jainism respectively, were perhaps against any kind of caste structure. Further, rejection of caste may have developed before these religions within Hinduism. Many bhakti period saints such as Nanak, Kabir, Chaitanya, Dnyaneshwar, Eknath, Ramanuja and Tukaram rejected all caste-based discrimination and accepted disciples from all the castes. Many Hindu reformers such as Swami Vivekananda and Sathya Sai Baba believe that there is no place for the caste system in Hinduism. The 15th century saint Ramananda also accepted all castes, including untouchables, into his fold. Most of these saints subscribed to the Bhakti movements in Hinduism during the medieval period that rejected casteism. Nandanar, a low-caste Hindu cleric, also rejected casteism and accepted Dalits.

Some other movements in Hinduism have also welcomed lower-castes into their fold, the earliest being the Bhakti movements of the medieval period. Early Dalit politics involved many Hindu reform movements which arose primarily as a reaction to the advent of Christian Missionaries in India and their attempts to convert Dalits to Christianity, who were attracted to the prospect of escaping the caste system.

The first "upper-caste" temple to openly welcome Dalits into their fold was the Laxminarayan Temple in Wardha in the year 1928 (the move was spearheaded by reformer Jamnalal Bajaj).

The caste system has also been criticized by many Indian social reformers. Some reformers, such as Jyotirao Phule and Iyothee Thass argued that the lower caste people were the original inhabitants of India, and were conquered in the ancient past by "Brahman invaders." Mahatma Gandhi coined the term "Harijan", a euphemistic word for *untouchable,* literally meaning *Sons of God.* B. R. Ambedkar, born in Hindu Dalit community, was a heavy critic of the caste system. He pioneered the Dalit Buddhist movement in India, and asked his followers to leave Hinduism, and convert to Buddhism.India's first Prime Minister, Jawaharlal Nehru, based on his own relationship with Dalit reformer Ambedkar, also spread information about the dire need to eradicate untouchability for the benefit of the Dalit community. Another example was the Temple Entry Proclamation issued by the last Maharaja of Travancore in the Indian state of Kerala in the year 1936. The Maharaja proclaimed that "outcastes should not be denied the consolations and the solace of the Hindu faith". Even today, the Sri Padmanabhaswamy temple that first welcomed Dalits in the state of Kerala is revered by the Dalit Hindu community.

CONTEMPORARY CRITICISM

Kancha Ilaiah, a Buddhist and professor at Osmania University is known for his polemical attacks on Hindus and the caste system and is considered an anti-Hindu by his critics. Similarly, radicals such as Udit Raj, also a Buddhist, who have attacked Hindus in polemical speeches, have achieved some popularity among evangelical Christian groups such as the Dalit Freedom Network in their criticism of Hindism. The website Dalitstan (presently taken down), once banned by the Indian government, is an example of anti-Brahmin and anti-Hindu rhetoric by Dalit extremists, allegedly supported by Christian missions.

Many Hindus point out that the caste system is related to the Indian society, and not Hinduism (as is evident by presence of caste among Indian Christians and Muslims). Hindu Nationalist organizations such as the Rashtriya Swayamsevak Sangh have actively criticized the caste system.

Some activists consider that the caste system is a form of racial discrimination. The participants of the United Nations Conference Against Racism in Durban, South Africa in March 2001, condemned discrimination due to the caste system, and tried to pass a resolution declaring that caste as a basis for the segregation and oppression of peoples in terms of their descent and occupation is a form of apartheid. However, no formal resolution was passed to that effect.

India's treatment of Dalits has been described by some authors as "India's hidden apartheid". Critics of the accusations point out the substantial improvements in the rights of Dalits (former "Untouchables") enshrined in the Constitution of India (primarily written by a Dalit, Ambedkar), which is the principal object of article 17 in the Constitution as implemented by the Protection of Civil rights Act, 1955 and the fact that India has had a Dalit, K. R. Narayanan, for a president, as well as the disappearance of the practise in urban public life.

According to William A. Haviland, however: Although India's national constitution of 1950 sought to abolish cast discrimination and the practice of untouchability, the caste system remains deeply entrenched in Hindu culture and is still widespread throughout southern Asia, especially in rural India. In what has been called India's "hidden apartheid", entire villages in many Indian states remain completely segregated by caste. Representing about 15 percent of India's population—or some 160 million people—the widely scatter Dalits endure near complete social isolation, humiliation, and discrimination based exclusively on their birth status. Even a Dalit's shadow is believed to pollute the upper classes. They may not cross the line dividing their part of the village from that occupied by higher castes, drink water from public wells, or visit the same temples as the higher castes. Dalit children are still often made to sit in the back of classrooms.

However, such allegations of apartheid are regarded by academic sociologists as a political epithet, since apartheid implies state sponsored discrimination, and no such thing exists in India. The Constitution of India places special emphasis on outlawing caste discrimination, especially the practice of untouchability. In addition, the Indian penal code inflicts severe punishments on those who discriminate on the basis of caste. Anti-dalit prejudice and discrimination is a social malaise that exists primarily in rural areas, where small societies can track the caste lineage of individuals and discriminate accordingly. Sociologists Kevin Reilly, Stephen Kaufman, Angela Bodino, while being critical of casteism, conclude that modern India does not practice any "apartheid" since there is no state sanctioned discrimination. They write that Casteism in India is presently "not apartheid. In fact, untouchables, as well as tribal people and members of the lowest castes in India benefit from broad affirmative action programmes and are enjoying greater political power."

Allegations that caste amounts to race were addressed and rejected by B. R. Ambedkar, an advocate for Dalit rights and critic of untouchability. He wrote that

"The Brahmin of Punjab is racially of the same stock as the Chamar (Dalit) of Punjab. The Caste system does not demarcate racial division. Caste system is a social division of people of the same race",

Such allegations have also been rejected by many sociologists such as Andre Béteille, who writes that treating caste as a form of racism is "politically mischievous" and worse, "scientifically nonsense" since there is no discernible difference in the racial characteristics between Brahmins and Scheduled Castes. He writes that "Every social group cannot be regarded as a race simply because we want to protect it against prejudice and discrimination".

The Indian government also rejects the claims of equivalency between Caste and Racial discrimination, pointing out that the caste issues as essentially intra-racial and intra-cultural. Indian Attorney General Soli Sorabjee insisted that "[t]he only reason India wants caste discrimination kept off the agenda is that it will distract participants from the main topic: racism. Caste discrimination in India is undeniable but caste and race are entirely distinct". Many scholars dispute the claim that casteism is akin to racism. The view of the caste system as "static and unchanging" has been disputed. Sociologists describe how the perception of the caste system as a static and textual stratification has given way to the perception of the caste system as a more processual, empirical and contextual stratification. Others have applied theoretical models to explain mobility and flexibility in the caste system in India. According to these scholars, groups of lower-caste individuals could seek to elevate the status of their caste by attempting to emulate the practices of higher castes.

Sociologist M. N. Srinivas has also debated the question of rigidity in Caste.

Pakistani-American sociologist Ayesha Jalal also rejects these allegations. In her book, "Democracy and Authoritarianism in South Asia", she writes that "As for Hinduism, the hierarchical principles of the Brahmanical social order have always been contested from within Hindu society, suggesting that equality has been and continues to be both valued and practiced."

In India, some observers felt that the caste system must be viewed as a system of exploitation of poor low-ranking groups by more prosperous high-ranking groups. In many parts of India, land is largely held by high-ranking property owners of the dominant castes that economically exploit low-ranking landless labourers and poor artisans, all the while degrading them with ritual emphases on their so-called god-given inferior status.

Matt Cherry, claims that karma underpins the caste system, and the caste system traditionally determines the position and role of every member of Hindu society. Caste determines an individual's place in society, the work he or she may carry out, and who he or she may marry and meet. According to him, Hindus believe that the karma of previous life will determine the caste an individual will be (re)born into.

On 29 March 2007, the Supreme Court of India, as an interim measure, stayed the law providing for 27 percent reservation for Other Backward Classes in educational institutions like IITs and IIMs. This was done in response to a public interest litigation — Ashoka Kumar Thakur vs. Union of India. The Court held that the 1931 census could not be a determinative factor for identifying the OBCs for the purpose of providing reservation. The court also observed, "Reservation cannot be permanent and appear to perpetuate backwardness".

2

Understanding of Dalits and Untouchability

Dalit is a self-designation for a group of people of South Asian descent traditionally regarded as untouchables or of low caste. Dalits are a mixed population of numerous caste groups all over South Asia and speak various languages. It is impossible to differentiate between Dalits and the various caste groups on the basis of phenotypes or genetics alone. The caste system is a social construct among South Asian people.

While the caste system has been formally abolished under the Indian constitution, there is still discrimination and prejudice against Dalits in South Asia. Since independence, significant steps have been taken to provide opportunities in jobs and education. Other governments in South Asia such as Nepal and Bangladesh have also implemented policies to improve the living standards of their Dalit population. In the 21st century, Dalits have begun to assert political control in populous northern states of India such as Uttar Pradesh.

The word 'Dalits' comes from the Hindi root *dal* and means 'held under check', 'suppressed' or 'crushed' — or, in a looser sense, 'oppressed'. The usage of the term "Dalit" seems to have originated from the Arya Samaj and their *dalitoddhâra* ("improvement of the downtrodden") programme. The Arya Samaj began the *All India Shraddhanand Dalitodwar Sabha* to improve the lot of Dalits.

The term was used in the 1930s as a Hindi and Marathi translation of "depressed classes", a term the British used for what are now called the scheduled castes. In 1930 there was a newspaper published for the depressed classes in Pune called "Dalit Bandu" (friends of dalits). The word was also used by B. R. Ambedkar in his Marathi speeches. The so-called Dalit Panthers revived the term in their 1973 manifesto and expounded its referents to include the scheduled tribes, Neo-Buddhists, working people, landless and poor peasant women and all those being exploited politically, economically and in the name of religion. Thus the term 'Dalit' is a broad definition, encompassing all those considered to be either similarly placed.

The terms 'Scheduled castes and scheduled tribes' (SC/ST) and 'non-caste tribes' are also used in the Indian legal system. However, in 2008 the National Commission for Scheduled Castes asked the Government to end the use of 'Dalit', calling it 'unconstitutional' and to replace it with the term 'Scheduled Caste' instead. After the order, the Chhattisgarh government ended the official use of the word. The term Harijan was coined by Mahatma Gandhi, which means "Children of God" — Hari is another name for the deity Vishnu. The usage of term 'Harijan' is objected to by Dalit activists as patronizing. In Tamil Nadu state the word 'Adi Dravida' is used, whereas in Karnataka it is 'Adi Karnataka' and in Andhra Pradesh it is 'Adi Andhra'. It means the aboriginal inhabitant of the land.

SOCIAL BACKGROUND AND ORIGIN

In the context of traditional Hindu society, Dalit status has often been historically associated with occupations regarded as ritually impure, such as any occupation involving butchering, removal of dead animals, removal of night soil (human feces) and leatherwork. One million Dalits work as manual scavengers, cleaning latrines and sewers by hand and clearing away dead animals. Engaging in these activities was considered to be polluting to the individual who performed them, and this pollution was considered to be 'contagious'. As a result, Dalits were commonly banned and segregated from full participation in Hindu social life (they could not enter the premises of a temple or a school and stayed outside the village), while elaborate precautions were sometimes observed to prevent incidental contact between Dalits and other castes. Discrimination against Dalits still exists in rural areas (where two-thirds of India's people live) in the private sphere, in everyday matters such as access to eating places, schools, temples and water sources. It has largely disappeared in urban areas and in the public sphere.

Most of the Dalits are bonded workers and many work in slave-like conditions to pay off debts that were incurred generations ago. The majority of Dalits live in segregation and experience violence, murder, rape and other atrocities to the scale of 110,000 registered cases a year, according to 2005 statistics. Common belief is that these numbers do not approach the real total of crimes committed against Dalits. Many crimes go unreported, and few registered cases ever get to trial.

Many Dalits who have converted to other religions in the past few centuries continue to retain their Dalit heritage. In the 1991 census, Dalits numbered just over 130 million and constituted more than 16% of India's population. Discrimination against Dalits is not limited to the Hindu community.

Some Dalits have successfully integrated into urban Indian society, where caste origins are less obvious and less important in public life. In rural India, caste origins are more readily apparent and Dalits remain excluded from local religious life, though some qualitative evidence suggests that its severity is in fact fast diminishing. Dalits and similar groups are also found in Nepal, Pakistan, Sri Lanka and Bangladesh. In addition, the Burakumin of Japan, Baekjeong of Korea and Midgan of Somalia are similar in status to Dalits.

GENETICS

One study found some association between caste status and Y-chromosomal genetic markers seeming to indicate a more European lineage of the higher castes; however, other studies indicate no racial and genetic differences between upper and lower castes. Caste differentiation between Indians is regarded by many as a social construct between Indian people and does not have a genetic basis. Genetic testing further indicates that as a whole, Indian genetic groups do not show a great affinity to any non South-Asian groups.

SUB-GROUPS

Dalits in North India include *Dombas, Chandalas,* leather-workers (called *Chamar*), carcass handlers (called *Mahar*), poor farmers and landless laborers, night soil scavengers (called *Bhangi*), street handcrafting people, folk artists, street cleaners, sweepers (*Chura*) and washermen (Dhobi). In South India the *Parayas, Pulayas, Malas, Madigas* are notable Dalit groups amongst many others.

DALITS AND RELIGION

Sachar Committee report of 2006 revealed that scheduled castes and tribes of India are not limited to the religion of Hinduism. The 61st Round Survey of the NSSO found that almost nine-tenth of the Buddhists and one-third of the Sikhs in India belonged to the notified scheduled castes of the Constitution while one-third of the Christians belonged to the notified scheduled tribes of the Constitution.

HINDUISM

The large majority of the Dalits in India are nominally Hindus, although some in Maharashtra and other states have converted to Buddhism, often called Neo-Buddhism. Dalits in Pakistan known as Haris are Hindus, whereas as in Sri Lanka they can be Buddhist or Hindus.

HISTORICAL ATTITUDES

The term, Chandala can be seen used in the Manu Smṙiti (codes of caste segregation) to the Mahabharata the religious epic. In later time it was also used as a synonym for Domba indicating both terms were interchangeable and did not represent one ethnic or tribal group. Instead, it was a general opprobrious term. In the early Vedic literature several of the names of castes that are spoken of in the Smritis as Antyajas occur. We have *Carmanna* (a tanner of hides) in the Rig Veda (VIII.8,38) the Chandala and Paulkasa occur in Vajasaneyi Samhita. *Vepa* or *Vapta* (barber) in the Rig Veda. Vidalakara or Bidalakar occurs in the Vajasaneyi Samhita. *Vasahpalpuli* (washerwoman) corresponding to the Rajakas of the Smritis in Vajasaneyi Samhita. Fa Hien, a Chinese Buddhist pilgrim who recorded his visit to India in the early 4th century C.E., noted that Chandalas were segregated from the mainstream society as untouchables. Traditionally, Dalits were considered to be beyond the pale of Varna or caste system. They were originally considered as *Panchama* or the fifth group beyond the four fold division of Indian people. They were not allowed to let their shadows fall upon a non-Dalit caste member and they were required to sweep the ground where they walk to remove the 'contamination' of their footfalls. Dalits were forbidden to worship in temples or draw water from the same wells as caste Hindus, and they usually lived in segregated neighbourhoods outside the main village

Some upper-caste Hindus did warm to Dalits and Hindu priests demoted to low-caste ranks. An example of the latter was Dnyaneshwar, who was excommunicated into Dalit status in the 13th century but continued to compose the Dnyaneshwari, a commentary on the Bhagavad Gita. Eknath, another excommunicated Brahmin, fought for the rights of untouchables during the Bhakti period. Historical examples of Dalit priests include Chokhamela in the 14th century, who was India's first recorded Dalit poet and Raidas, born into a family of cobblers. The 15th century saint Sri Ramananda Raya also accepted all castes, including untouchables, into his fold. Most of these saints subscribed to the Bhakti movements in Hinduism during the medieval period that rejected casteism. Nandanar, a low-caste Hindu cleric, also rejected casteism and accepted Dalits. Due to isolation from the rest of the Hindu society, many Dalits continue to debate whether they are 'Hindu' or 'non-Hindu'. Traditionally, Hindu Dalits have been barred from many activities that were seen as central to

Vedic religion and Hindu practices of orthodox sects. Among Hindus each community has followed its own variation of Hinduism, and the wide variety of practices and beliefs observed in Hinduism makes any clear assessment difficult.

REFORM MOVEMENTS

The earliest known historical people to have rejected the caste system was Gautama Buddha and Mahavira. Their teachings eventually became independent religions called Buddhism and Jainism. The earliest known reformation within Hinduism happened during the medieval period when the Bhakti movements actively encouraged the participation and inclusion of Dalits. In the 19th Century, the Brahmo Samaj, Arya Samaj and the Ramakrishna Mission actively participated in the emancipation of Dalits. While there always have been segregated places for Dalits to worship, the first "upper-caste" temple to openly welcome Dalits into their fold was the Laxminarayan Temple in Wardha in the year 1928. It was followed by the Temple Entry Proclamation issued by the last King of Travancore in the Indian state of Kerala in 1936.

The Sikh reformist Satnami movement was founded by Guru Ghasidas, born a Dalit. Other notable Sikh Gurus such as Guru Ravidas were also Dalits. Other reformers, such as Jyotirao Phule, Ayyankali of Kerala and Iyothee Thass of Tamil Nadu worked for emancipation of Dalits. The 1930s saw key struggle between Mahatma Gandhi and B. R. Ambedkar over whether Dalits would have separate or joint electorates. Although he failed to get Ambedkar's support for a joint electorate, Gandhi nevertheless began the "Harijan Yatra" to help the Dalit population. Palwankar Baloo, a Dalit politician and a cricketer, joined the Hindu Mahasabha in the fight for independence.

Other Hindu groups have reached out to the Dalit community in an effort to reconcile with them. On August 2006, Dalit activist Namdeo Dhasal engaged in dialogue with the Rashtriya Swayamsevak Sangh in an attempt to "bury the hatchet". Hindu temples are increasingly receptive to Dalit priests, a function formerly reserved for Brahmins. Suryavanshi Das, for example, is the Dalit priest of a notable temple in Bihar.

Anecdotal evidence suggests that discrimination against Hindu Dalits is on a slow but steady decline. For instance, an informal study by Dalit writer Chandrabhan Prasad and reported in the New York Times states: "In rural Azamgarh District [in the state of Uttar Pradesh], for instance, nearly all Dalit households said their bridegrooms now rode in cars to their weddings, compared with 27 percent in 1990. In the past, Dalits would not have been allowed to ride even horses to meet their brides; that was considered an upper-caste privilege."

Many Hindu Dalits have achieved affluence in society, although vast millions still remain poor. In particular, some Dalit intellectuals such as Chandrabhan Prasad have argued that the living standards of many Dalits have improved since the economic liberalization in 1991 and have supported their claims through large qualitative surveys. Recent episodes of Caste-related violence in India have adversely affected the Dalit community. In urban India, discrimination against Dalits in the public sphere is greatly reduced, but rural Dalits are struggling to elevate themselves. Government organizations and NGO's work to emancipate them from discrimination, and many Hindu organizations have spoken in their favour. Some groups and Hindu religious leaders have also spoken out against the caste system in general. However, the fight for temple entry rights for Dalits is far from finished and continues to cause controversy. Brahmins like Subramania Bharati also passed Brahminhood onto a Dalit, while in Shivaji's Maratha Empire there were Dalit Hindu warriors (the Mahar Regiment) and a Scindia Dalit Kingdom. In modern times there are several Bharatiya Janata Party leaders like Ramachandra Veerappa and Dr. Suraj Bhan.

ISLAM

Muslim society in India can also be separated into several caste-like groups. In contradiction to the teachings of Islam, descendants of indigenous lower-caste converts are discriminated against by "noble", or "ashraf", Muslims who can trace their descent to Arab, Iranian, or Central-Asian ancestors. There are several groups in India working to emancipate them from upper-caste Muslim discrimination.

The Dalit Muslims are referred to by the Ashraf and Ajlaf Muslims as *Arzal* or "ritually degraded". They were first recorded in the 1901 census as those "with whom no other Muhammadan would associate, and who are forbidden to enter the mosque or to use the public burial ground". They are relegated to "menial" professions such as scavenging and carrying night soil.

Ambedkar wrote about the Dalit Muslims and was extremely critical of their mistreatment by upper-caste Muslims, writing: "Within these groups there are castes with social precedence of exactly the same nature as one finds among the Hindus."

SIKHISM

Dalits form a class among the Sikhs who stratify their society according to traditional casteism. Kanshi Ram himself was of Sikh background although converted because he found that Sikh society did not respect Dalits and so became a neo-Buddhist. The most recent controversy was at the Talhan village Gurudwara near Jalandhar where there was a dispute between Jat Sikhs and Ravidasia Sikhs. The Different Sikh Dalits are Ravidasia Sikh and Mazhabi Sikh. Although Sikhism does not recognize the Caste System, many families, especially the ones with immediate cultural ties to India, generally do not marry among different castes.

There are sects such as the Adi-Dharmis who have now abandoned Sikh Temples and the 5 Ks. They are like the Ravidasis and regard Ravidas as their guru. They are also clean shaven as opposed to the mainstream Sikhs. Sant Ram was from this community and a member of the Arya Samak who tried to organize the Adi-Dharmis. Other Sikh groups include Jhiwars, Bazigars, Rai Sikh (many of whom are Ravidasias.) Just as with Hindu Dalits, there has been violence against Sikh Dalits.

CHRISTIANITY

Across India, many Christian communities still follow the caste system. Sometimes the social stratification remains unchanged and in some cases such as among Goan Christians, the stratification varies as compared to the Hindu system. Conversion to Christianity does not necessarily free Dalits from the bondage of the caste system.

A 1992 study of Catholics in Tamil Nadu found some Dalit Christians faced segregated churches, cemeteries, services and even processions. Despite Christian teachings these Dalit also faced economic and social hardships due to discrimination by upper-caste priests and nuns. Other sources support these conclusions, including Christian advocacy groups for Dalits. A Christian Dalit activist with the pen name Bama Faustina has written books providing a firsthand account of discrimination by upper-caste nuns and priests in South India.

Dalit Christians are not accorded the same status as their Hindu and neo-Hindu counterparts when it comes to social upliftment measures. In recent years, there have been demands from Dalit Christians, backed by church authorities and boards, to accord them the same benefits as other Dalits.

BUDDHISM

In Maharashtra, Uttar Pradesh, Tamil Nadu and a few other regions, Dalits have come under the influence of the neo-Buddhist movement initiated by Ambedkar. Some of them have come under the influence of the Neo-Buddhist and Christian Missionaries and have converted away from Hinduism into religions such as Christianity and Buddhism in what they have been told is an "attempt to eliminate the prejudice they face".

BJP Scheduled Caste Morcha president Bangaru Laxman (Organiser, 6-8-1995) accused Congress leader Sitaram Kesri, who had bracketed the Dalits with the minorities as "sufferers of Hindu oppression", of thereby showing "disrespect to [Dalit] saints like Ravidas, Satyakam Jabali, Sadhna Kasai, Banka Mahar, Dhanna Chamar and others who protected Hindus against foreign onslaughts."

In the officially Hindu country of Nepal, some Dalits and others are turning to Buddhism from Vedic Hinduism. Reasons cited are to embrace non-violence and as a response to the caste system, which has led to a substantial increase in Buddhists in the population while the number of those professing Hinduism has decreased from 88% in 1961 to 80% at present.

THE PREVENTION OF ATROCITIES ACT

The Prevention of Atrocities Act (POA) is a tacit acknowledgement by the Indian government that caste relations are defined by violence, both incidental and systemic. In 1989, the Government of India passed the Prevention of Atrocities Act (POA), which clarified specific crimes against Scheduled Castes and Scheduled Tribes (the Dalits) as "atrocities," and created strategies and punishments to counter these acts. The purpose of The Act was to curb and punish violence against Dalits. Firstly, it clarified what the atrocities were: both particular incidents of harm and humiliation, such as the forced consumption of noxious substances, and systemic violence still faced by many Dalits, especially in rural areas. Such systemic violence includes forced labor, denial of access to water and other public amenities, and sexual abuse of Dalit women. Secondly, the Act created Special Courts to try cases registered under the POA. Thirdly, the Act called on states with high levels of caste violence (said to be "atrocity-prone") to appoint qualified officers to monitor and maintain law and order. The POA gave legal redress to Dalits, but only two states have created separate Special Courts in accordance with the law. In practice the Act has suffered from a near-complete failure in implementation. Policemen have displayed a consistent unwillingness to register offenses under the act. This reluctance stems partially from ignorance and also from peer protection. According to a 1999 study, nearly a quarter of those government officials charged with enforcing the Act are unaware of its existence.

DALITS AND CONTEMPORARY INDIAN POLITICS

While the Indian Constitution has duly made special provisions for the social and economic uplift of the Dalits, comprising the so-called scheduled castes and tribes in order to enable them to achieve upward social mobility, these concessions are limited to only those Dalits who remain Hindu. There is a demand among the Dalits who have converted to other religions that the statutory benefits should be extended to them as well, to "overcome" and bring closure to historical injustices.

Another major politically charged issue with the rise of Hindutva's (Hindu nationalism) role in Indian politics is that of religious conversion. This political movement alleges that conversions of Dalits are due not to any social or theological motivation but to allurements like education and jobs. Critics argue that the inverse is true due to laws banning conversion, and the limiting of social relief for these backward sections of Indian society being revoked for those who convert. Bangaru Laxman, a Dalit politician, was a prominent member of the Hindutva movement.

Another political issue is over the affirmative-action measures taken by the government towards the upliftment of Dalits through quotas in government jobs and university admissions. About 8% of the seats in the National and State Parliaments are reserved for Scheduled Caste and Tribe candidates, a measure sought by B. R. Ambedkar and other Dalit activists in order to ensure that Dalits would obtain a proportionate political voice.

Anti-Dalit prejudices exist in fringe groups, such as the extremist far-right militia Ranvir Sena, largely run by upper-caste landlords in backward areas of the Indian state of Bihar. They oppose equal treatment of Dalits and have resorted to violent means to suppress the Dalits. The Ranvir Sena is considered a terrorist organization.

In 2008, Mayawati, a Dalit from the Bahujan Samaj Party, was elected as the Chief Minister of India's biggest state Uttar Pradesh. Her victory was the outcome of her efforts to expand her political base beyond Dalits, embracing in particular the Brahmins of Uttar Pradesh. Mayawati, together with her political mentor Kanshi Ram, saw that the interests of the average Dalit (most of whom are landless agricultural laborers) were more in conflict with the middle castes such as the Yadav caste, who owned most of the agricultural land in Uttar Pradesh, than with the predominantly city-dwelling upper castes. Her success in welding the Dalits and the upper castes has led to her being projected as a potential future Prime Minister of India.

DALIT LITERATURE

Dalit literature, forms an important, yet distinct part of Indian literature. One of the first Dalit writers was Madara Chennaiah, a 11th century cobbler-saint who lived in the reign of Western Chalukyas, who is also considered by some scholars as the "father of Vachana" poetry. Later poets of Kannada literature like Basavanna (1160), who was also the prime minister of southern Kalachuri for King Bijjala II (1130 - 1167 CE), held him in high regard. Another poet that finds mention is Dohara Kakkaiah, a Dalit by birth, six of whose confessional poems survive.

MODERN DALIT LITERATURE

In the modern era, Dalit literature received its first impetus with the advent of leaders like Mahatma Phule and Ambedkar in Maharashtra, who brought forth the issues of Dalits through their works and writings; this started a new trend in Dalit writing and inspired many Dalits to come forth with writings in Marathi, Hindi, Tamil and Punjabi.

By the 1960s, Dalit literature saw a fresh crop of new writers like Baburao Bagul, Bandhu Madhav and Shankarao Kharat, though its formal form came into being with the Little magazine movement. Dalit Voice, a political magazine which started publishing in 1981, was another force in the rise of Dalit literature in India. In Sri Lanka, Dalit writers like Dominic Jeeva gained mainstream popularity in the late 1960.

DALITS IN INDIAN CASTE SYSTEM

In the Indian caste system, a Dalit, often called an untouchable, or an outcaste, is a person who according to traditional Hindu belief does not have any "*varna*". *Varna* refers to the Hindu belief that most humans were supposedly created from different parts of the body of the divinity *Purusha*. The part from which a *varna* was supposedly created defines a person's social status with regards to issues such as who they can marry and which professions they could hold. Dalit fall outside the *varna* system and have historically been prevented from doing any but the most menial jobs. (However, a distinction must be made between lower-cast people and *Pariahs*.) Included are leather-workers (called *chamar*), poor farmers and landless labourers, night soil scavengers (called *bhangi* or *chura*), street handicrafters, folk artists, street cleaners, washermen, etc. Traditionally, they were treated as *Pariahs* in South Asian society and isolated in their own communities, to the point that even their shadows were avoided by the upper castes. Discrimination against Dalit still exists in rural areas in the private sphere, in ritual matters such as access to eating places and water sources. It has largely disappeared, however, in urban areas and in the public sphere, in rights of movement and access to schools. The earliest rejection of discrimination, at least in spiritual matters, was made as far back as the Bhagavada Gita, which says that no person, no matter what, is barred from enlightenment.

'Dalit' has come to mean things or persons who are cut, split, broken or torn as under, scattered or crushed and destroyed. By coincidence, there is in Hebrew a root 'dal' meaning low, weak, poor. In the Bible, different forms of this term have been used to describe people who have been reduced to nothingness or helplessness. The present usage of the term Dalit goes back to the nineteenth century, when a Marathi social reformer and revolutionary, Mahatma Jyotirao Phule (1826-1890), used it to describe the Outcastes and Untouchables as the oppressed and the broken victims of our caste-ridden society. Under the charismatic leadership of Dr. B.R. Ambedkar (1891-1956), this term gained greater importance and popularity. During the 1970s, the followers of the Dalit Panther Movement of Maharashtra gave currency to the term 'Dalit' as a constant reminder of their age-old oppression, denoting both their state of deprivation and the people who are oppressed. This term for them is not a mere name or title: for them it has become an expression of hope, the hope of recovering their past self-identity. The term has gained a new connotation with a more positive meaning. It must be remembered that *Dalit does not mean Caste or low-Caste or poor;* it refers to the deplorable state or condition to which a large group of people has been reduced by social convention and in which they are now living.

The Dalits are called by different names in different parts of the country. These names were given by the Caste people as expressions of contempt. They include: Dasa, Dasysa, Raksasa, Asura, Avarna, Nisada, Panchama, Chandala, Harijan, Untouchable. Each of these names has a history and background. Besides these names, there are a number of other titles or names which have been given to them at the level of the regional language. For example, Chura in Punjab (North West India), Bhangi or Lal Beghi in Hindi (North India), Mahar in Marathi (Central India), Mala in Telugu, Paraiya in Tamil and Pulayan in Malayalam (South India). These names carry within them the two-term contrast of "we-the pure" and "you-the impure". In response to these insulting labels, the Untouchables have chosen to give themselves a name and this is 'Dalit', which refers to the hardship of their condition of life. This name is a constant reminder of the age-old oppression. The term is also an expression of their hope to recover their past self-identity. If today the Dalits are reduced to a life of abject poverty and treated as polluted human beings, it is the non-dalit that must be seen as the agent of their dehumanisation. By the British, the Dalits were named 'the Depressed Classes' and 'the Scheduled Castes', in the Scheduled Caste Act of India, 1935. Mahatma Gandhi named them 'Harijans' which means 'children of God': but this term was not welcomed by the Dalits because it did not adequately describe their condition.

The issue of "Dalit" identity in social, economic and political context has become so important nowadays, that it has been affecting the thinking processes of all opinion making and decision taking authorities in India. Even though, originally, it was a social problem, now it has attained significance resulting in far-fetching consequences in deciding the future of Indian polity. The handling of "Dalit" issue is very sensitive, as it is like a double-edged weapon, which may affect the person against whom it is used and as well as the person who uses it. Moreover, it is extremely delicate to deal, as it may always has ended in emotional conflicts, leading to unexpected results. Before entering into the study of "Dalit" problem, the background of it should be understood thoroughly.

Undoubtedly, the word "Dalit" has attained the prominence, only during the last one decade or even lesser than that period. But, the political exploitation of such concept can be traced back to the Muslim and British periods. The fact that the expressions "untouchables" and "untouchability" were first coined and started to be used by the British can be seen from their Census documents. As the issue of "Dalit" involves caste and untouchability, all factors behind should also be studied with care and attention.

As the social scientists got familiarization with the expressions "untouchables" and "untouchability" through the British, the other word "caste" has been introduced to them by the Portuguese with due blessings of Europeans writers[2]. The description, explanation and exposition given to the concept of "caste" have completely distorted and even tarnished the concept of "Varnashrama dharma" of Hindu religion or Sanathana dharma. Nowadays, the "Dalit" writers have started equating even the very expression "Sanathana" with racism and fascism. Similarly the explanations given to "untouchables" and "untouchability" have contorted the social stratification of Indian society based on economic and political conditions of the traditional factors. Then comes the concept of "Dalit" and its ramifications with complications.

THE IMPACT OF OTHERS

As pointed out, prior to the advent of the British, nobody thought of "untouchability", even though such practice was definitely followed. Though, the affected communities, definitely revolted against the ill-treatment meted out, many times, they compromised with their disabilities. With the success of implanting the minority consciousness in the minds of Muslims, the British writers cleverly decided to divide the Hindu society. They recognized Muslims as a distinct entity by giving separate electorate in 1909. In the year, 1910, the Census Commissioner of India chose to divide the Hindu population into:

1. Hindus,
2. Animists, and
3. Depressed classes or untoucables.

Previously, the division was always based on religion. Of course, the Muslims also aided and abetted with the British collaborators. By pointing out the differences among the Hindus and sowing the seeds by mooting the idea that tribals were different from the caste Hindus, in their address to Lord Minto, the then Viceroy of India. B. R. Ambedkar himself has pointed out this important fact. The Muslims wantonly suggested that in calculating the numerical strength of Hindus, the tribals, animists and untouchables should be excluded. Here, it may be mentioned that initially Muslims tried to convert the High Caste Hindus, particularly, Brahmins by force, lure of power and compulsory marriages or better understood as "sham marriages". Though almost, all Muslim rulers followed this practice, it was at best during the reign of Akbar. But, the Brahmins took serous action immediately by excommunicating such families and rewriting / amending the *Dharma Shasatras*, which resulted in many sociological implications. Particularly, the latter method led to different conclusions to arrive at by the scholars in deciding the date of such works and as well as know about the ancient society of India. As they failed with the Brahmins, they turned their attention towards other castes.

The experiment with Rajaputs and other royal castes also resulted in unfavourable political and social conditions. Again, it may be mentioned that it was during this period, the practice of sati was perhaps revived or introduced. Somehow, they could not match with the business communities, as they themselves were originally engaged in commercial activities.

Thus, finally they turned their guns towards the lower strata of Hindu society. They cleverly used the Sufi movement for this purpose. Accordingly they tried some sort of "Inculturation" – methods with the new converts, which were subsequently opposed by the Muslim fundamentalists. A careful study of Jizya clearly exposes the tactics of conversion (Tabligh movements) of Muslim rulers. Anybody can even now notice that it is the lower strata of Hindu society, which strongly protects and spreads Hinduism than the higher strata, by way of visiting various temples and holy places regularly and periodically according to tradition instead of convenience, conducting festivals and performing traditional pujas in all villages.

That is why "Jizya rulers" specifically affected them, as they could not use horses for pilgrimages, wear saffron robes prominently, take their women-folk with them even though it was mandatory according to their custom and tradition, use of ghats, ponds, and other holy waters and so on. Therefore it is not all a new tactics for the Muslims to create dissensions within Hindu society by their crooked methods. Only, the change was that they used the British to perform their game.

Therefore inspired by the suggestion of the Muslims, the Census Commissioner of India in 1911 tried to differentiate Hindus and non-Hindus other than Muslims and Christians. He issued a circular with the following criteria to effect such division among those who were not 100% Hindus were included – "Castes and tribes" – which –

1. Deny the supremacy of the Brahmans
2. Do not receive the manthras from a Brahmana or other recognized Hindu guru
3. Deny the authority of Vedas
4. Do not worship the Hindu gods
5. Are not served by good Brahmans as family priests
6. Have no Brahmana priests at all
7. Are denied access to the interior of Hindu temples
8. Cause pollution (i) by touch or (ii) within a certain distance

9. Bury their dead, and

10. Eat beef and do not show reverence to the cow.

Evidently the conditions framed were rater more anti-Brahmanic than anti-Hindu as at that time they themselves wrote many books about the various facets of Hindu society. Slowly they stopped using the word "untouchability" or "untouchables" and prefer to use "exterior caste".

Then, they also used the expression "depressed castes". It is in vogue between 1920 and 1935. In Tamilnadu as early as in 1857, the expression "Adi Dravidar" was used to denote lower castes. Similar expressions "Adi Andhras" and "Adi Karanatakas" were used by their counterparts in Andhra Pradesh and Karnataka regions. Thus, though "Harijans" was the glorified term used by Gandhiji in 1933 for them, the term "Scheduled caste" was the expression first invented by the Simon Commission. However, in recent times, all caste organizations and politicians are prepared to use the term "Dalit" as there have been converted Christians and Muslims from the Hindu religion and they do not want to use the label of "Harijan" as it definitely denotes to the people of Hindu origin.

ROLE OF MEDIA

Therefore the media persons particularly the journalists with the support of Christian and Muslim lobbies preferred to use very often the adjective word "Dalit" as noun to denote SCs or Harijans. Here, they tactfully used the word to include the converts from Hindu religion to Christianity and Islam also, though legally (Constitutionally) it is incorrect. Thus, from Marathi or Hindi writings the word has been picked up and started to be used by other journalists in English dailies. Dr. Ambedkar also said to have switched over to this word, as he did not want to use the terminology of Gandhiji.

UNTOUCHABILITY IN CHRISTIANITY

In spite of the tall claims made but the Christians, the caste, racism, untouchability and other factors have been there in Christianity. The hundreds of denominations in different countries based on theology, practices, tribes etc., are the direct proof. Pope Gregory XV published a bull sanctioning caste regulations in the Christian Churches of India. Even the U. N. Commission of Inquiry (1953) into the racial situation in South Africa reported the Biblical background of inspiration for them to adopt "Apartheid" or "Christian caste system" with untouchability. Untouchability also finds its way to Bible [Joshua. 9.19]. In Ireland, there are separate streets for Roman Catholics and Protestants, as each group treats others "untouchables".

Slavery has been a divine approved system. Prasadam offered to Jehovah should not be eaten by others. They should not touch things holy to him or offer sacrifice. Bible should not be taught to others. They cannot offer incense. They should not approach the holy tabernacle i.e, the "Garba Griha" / Sanctum Sanctorum. The dishonest Christians suppress everything and try to fool the gullible SCs and STs projecting that their religion saves them. they could not save their own souls of SCs / STs with dubious methods. There are A to Z Churches with denominations (castes) running into more than 3000 depending upon the nation, language, ethnicity, culture, civilization and other factors. The matrimonial columns appearing in the newspapers and periodicals expose their hypocrisy, as the bride / groom are hunted only on the basis of "caste" and not on the "Christ"!

Crores of Rupees flow into India from abroad to convert India to Christianity. World Christian Organizations never hide this plan. After the Neogi Commission Report, they have only changed their tactics in routing the money. Political pressure at national and international levels is applied through different cannels to pump money in. only 30-40% is actually spent under the guise of charity, service, and liberation etc., whereas, 60-70% is adjusted in their manipulated accounts duly certified. They have formed their own high castes and they do not want to share profits with the new converts. They treat them just as "natives" counting numbers and sending statistical figures to parent organizations.

Thus, the discrimination persists and percolates to bottom reaching new complications and crating new social tensions. Therefore, to divert the issue, as decided by the World Council of Churches and other organizations, they set up different "research groups" to shift the blame to Hinduism and escape. After politicizing, they have tried to internationalize the issue. Whoever Indian writer, journalist or "scholar", who supports this theory, is received aboard usually USA or Germany and taken care of "Dalit Theology" is the superior theology masqueraded in mere theoretical egalitarianism to fool "Dalits" projecting Jesus as the Super Star Saviour and Christianity to solve all their social problems, suppressing all cold facts, historical truths and the past tract record of Christianity.

"Liberation Theology" is nothing but "Christian Communism" with God offered in different garb mainly advocating violence. It advocates violence, terrorism and anti-national activities in a country where it is preached. After the death of Communism and exposure of their deadly acts in Latin American countries, they have turned their attention to "Dalit Theology".

BRAIN WASHING DALITS

They adopt and adapt spurious scholarship, falsified histories, forged documents to create new hypotheses and theories. Many books have been published with much fanfare and publicity. Their mouth-piece journals publicize well about the publications. Now, they unscrupulously use the same methodology in full swing as a part of their psychological warfare with all their propaganda arms and brainwashing ammunition. These forces openly join with Communist, Muslim, "Dalit" and other banner organizations, portray the symbols of Narayan Guru, Karl Marx, E. V. Ramaswami Naicker, B. R. Ambedkar and give a rhetoric or cocktail of their philosophies and ideologies to inspire, excite and animate, ultimately brainwash them.

Invariably, Hinduism is condemned and criticized for all social aberrations and modern evils; Hindu Gods blasphemed and profaned; Hindu criptures reviled and scoffed at with sacrilege. The audience would be thrilled leading to ecstasy with clapping hands, shouting slogans, jumping and raising hands. One would be perhaps baffled to see the stage, where all opposing ideologues, religious heads and propagandists sitting together. Though they stress only upon their viewpoint without sacrificing their motive and compromising religious tenets, they would be very much united as far as abusing Hinduism, Hindu Gods and Hindu religious leaders are concerned. They mix different ideologies; quote unhistorical events; make false statements and finally, perhaps, this becomes their ideology and theology.

CASTE SYSTEM IN ISLAM

Islam too claims that it has no caste system, as it treats every Muslim equal. But, to understand it, one has to understand Islam and its basic tenets. As it is not known to everybody, generally, people believe what is told to them or what they read about Islam. They either do not want to ask questions or know about it, as they are either afraid of Muslims or feel extremely "delicate" to ask such "inconvenient" questions.

Islam treats all Muslims equal, not all human beings on the earth. Even, among Muslims, there are many different castes based on theology, interpretation of scriptures, acceptance or rejection of scriptures, mode of worship, celebration of festivals, representing religious-symbols, grave-yards, Quran book, the position of Imams, Caliphs, Prophets after Mohammed, Sufism, miracles, etc. on one side, and country, tribe, culture, tradition, heritage and other factors on the other side. For converts, all factors will be applicable. The so-called Muslims who have been classified as OBC in different denominations as follows:

Faqir, Gadihar, Hima, Karanjia, Qassar, Darzi, Kasai, Bhangi, Madari, Miriasin, Mirishkar, Momin, Mukro, Nat, Pamania, Rangrez, Sayee, Thakurai, Eafan, Defer, Gadhai, Galiva, Ghanchi, Hingora, Jat, Tari, Halarikhatki, Darban, Makrani, Mausari, Kureshi, Miana, Mir, Mirasi, Panchara, Sandhi, Patni Jamat, Turk Jamat, Waghev.Bhat, Dhar, Dooma, Hajjan, Julaha, Lohar, Lone, Kul, Kumhar, Mochi, Teli, Nal Band.Ansari, Julai, Tamboli, Beri, Chaffar band, Darzi, Dhobi, Takaras, Zargars, Mappila, Meqati, Julaha, Labbi, Ansari, Kassab, Banjara, Kayastha, Ansari, Sain.

Besides, these divisions, they have their own divisions based on the factors mentioned below:

Sunni, Kariji, Shia, Zaida, Imamia, Ismaliyya, Kojha, Bohra, Nizari, Isna Ashari, Kachi-menon, Mutazila, Murji, Wahabi, Ba'hai, Ahmeddhi, Shanusi, Sufi, and so on.

This shows the hypocrisy and double standards of Muslims proclaiming universal brotherhood, non-discrimination etc., at one end and fool the converts and accepting reservation on the basis of caste on the other hand. Therefore, converts should carefully think about the motive of the converters. Are they actually liberating them or chaining them with Islamic bondage forever? In Islam, there is no exemption, exception or relaxation, once you are declared as "Kafir", you will be hunted for persecution. To say simply, you do not like Islam, you cannot leave Islam and come out. Apostasy cannot be thought of in Islam and only death is the reward for apostates. You can blame, criticize and even blaspheme your Hindu Gods and be Hindus forever, but you cannot be a Muslim or you cannot live by blaming, criticizing or condemning Islamic Gods and Prophets.

The concept of pollution and untouchability: Quran spesks of two types of pollution and impurity – Idolatry [Sura.9, Ayat. 28] and Muslim women [II.222]. Other contaminations are drinking, traveling, sexual intercourse and Devil (Satan). kafirs are always considered as untouchables according to Quran. Kufru is the unclean status/condition. Untouchability is also ascribed to eating of carrion, blood and swine flesh [II.173]. Women are prohibited from entering mosques and pray along with men as they are polluted by menstruation periodically [Hadis]. Hadis also describes about sexual pollution and ablution. Emancipation of women-believing slaves is nly mentioned, that too in the context of marriage, but not about men-slaves. Mohammed sanctioned slavery unscrupulously to kafirs (unbelievers, heathens, pagans, non-Muslims) by Jihad (holy war) denying all human rights. Thus, the entire world is divided into Dar-al-Islam (the domain of Islam) and Dar-al-Harab (the domain of war); the humanity into momins (believers) and kairs (non-believers); kafirs are further divided into people with books (al-kitabia = Jews and Christians) and people without books (all other religions other than mentioned); they are also known as Zimmis, when they pay Jizya.

The concept of kafir depends on kufr i.e, impurity, status, unacceptable condition etc., and kafiri i.e., infidelity, heathenism, paganism etc., identified accordingly. There are many verses in Quran that they should not be allowed to come near the cities of Mecca and Medina [Surah XIX]. They should not touch anything meant for Allah. They should not read Quran and other scriptures.

The above-mentioned divisions (castes) are water-tight compartments and the accommodated new converts cannot claim all rights of Sayyid, Qureshi, Ansari, Siddhiqi, Farooqi, Osmani, Alvi, Hussaini, Jafri, Naqvi, Zaidi, Kazmi, Rizvi, Hashmi, Abbasi, Sherwani, Shirazi, Isphani, Timizi, Bukhari, Barlas, Kirmaniu, Yazdani – who trace their foreign ancestry in middle eastern, Persia or Central Asian origin. Lebbai of Tamil Nadu cannot be treated at par with Bukharis or Bohras. They cannot also think of marrying their daughters. Now, the fact is that Muslims have started matching horoscopes, giving and taking dowry and so on. Therefore, just by becoming Muslim, they cannot think of going up or getting liberated.

Thus, the "Dalits" cannot get emancipated or reach heavens, as has been proclaimed by the Islamic propagandists, theoreticians and ideologues. See the Islamic countries with Islamic law, what has been going on? Are they leading happy, prosperous and peaceful lives? Why the Islamic countries fighting with each other calling other as kafirs? Why the Ahmeddiyas and Ba'hai Muslims are persecuted and their mosques demolished declared as kafirs? Why people are starving in Islamic countries? The Indian Muslims are treated only as second class citizens in Islamic countries. The kafir-workmen are treated as bonded labourers in gulf-countries. Women who are imported into such countries as servant maids / cooks are ill-treated, starved and sexually harassed. Ameena-like girls are married and taken away. Male children are bought and sold for camel-races. The returned (run-away) men and women from gulf-countries tell their miserable and horrified stories. It is a known fact that crores of petro-dollars are flowing into India officially and un-officially. Then, why do not they spend such amount for the upliftment of Muslims? Why the Indian Muslims are kept poor, in spite of their wealth? Therefore, as this is the true position, the "Dalits" should not be cheated with their propaganda.

Now, many Islamic organizations have openly come out with documents about the conversion of India by a phased manner. The Muslim politicians also proclaim that they could convert India into Islamic before the starting of 21st century. Islamic religious leaders, Sheikhs, Politicians, and others visit India periodically under the guise of conferences, seminars, inauguration of mosques etc., and encourage the conversion process.

Converted Muslims like Abdullah Adiyar has been tempting "Dalit" leaders like Ilaya Perumal to convert to Islam. RPI leaders like Dr. Seppan with the former has started writing books making claims that "Islam is the only way for total liberation" and so on. Surprisingly, Valampuri John has also joined them contributing his mite. The books written by them are just propaganda literature and a poor category of negationism [negationism is the tactful method of concealing, eliminating or destroying the past record of Islam or Christianity by their respective writers and hence it may be defined as denial of historical crimes against humanity. It is not a reinterpretation of known facts, but the denial of such known facts.

It was revived against the Suddhi movement of Swami Dayananda Saraswati in the late 1920s. But, the conversion methodology has been in operation ever since the advent of Islam in India using all tactics. The movement has again been revived in the 'Dalit" context in the recent times with the blessings and petro-dollars of International Islamic organizations.

CAN "DALITS" GET LIBERATED BY CONTINUING AS HINDUS?

The minds of "Dalit"-Hindus know very well about the implications of converting themselves to non-Hindu religions in India. In fact, they love Hindu culture, tradition, heritage and civilization most because of their hoary past and enriched connected factors, appreciated by many scholars, philosophers, historians, sociologists and psychologists/ they have also understood that in the entire world, there have been only two civilizations in existence without break or extinction from time immemorial.

The present-day problem has definitely arisen out of the Muslim and British manipulation of Census documents, enumeration of castes and willful-mischievous exposition of varna, jati, race and other pseudo-scientific hypotheses and theories.

Unlike non-Hindus, most of the Hindus do not know about their religion, scriptures and theology, but, only stories and propaganda about the same. They talk and discuss about what they are told unlike other religions, they do not have a single scripture, single religious institution, single religious head and other stereo-types. Unlimited freedom has been given within the ambit of Hinduism to its followers whether they believe it or not. These are not drawbacks or mistakes, but perfectly in accordance with the psychological needs of man. Psychologists and sociologists have come to the conclusion that for the betterment of any society in the present day world of conflicts, the religion and psychology should go together. This is possible only in Hinduism. Unlike, the propaganda made against Hinduism, it is not suppressive and oppressive of "Dalits".

WARNING TO HINDUS

As the entire burden and responsibility lie on Hindus, they should work sincerely and honestly to remove all social inequalities and injustice. The so-called "Caste Hindus" should stop their discrimination and atrocities committed against their SC / ST Brethren. Social evils may be there in every society, but they cannot be nurtured, justified or exploited in the name of religion, politics or otherwise for the benefit of themselves.

India may be a poor country, but that does not mean only the "caste Hindus" should be rich, land owners or enjoying all the material benefits. The poor also should get their share not because they are poor, but human beings, that too, their brethren.

Urbanization, Modernization, Industrialization, Science and technological advancements have made Hindus to come close together to understand each other. There have been more and more social interactions taking place among them. The SC / ST are also educating themselves and competing equally with others exhibiting and proving their skills. They about their rights and responsibilities, but others should allow them to enjoy their rights and carry out their responsibilities. Hindus should know that Vedas do not preach caste system; do not differentiate man by colour, stature, appearance or any other factor. Hindus have always been mixed population with differing features in accordance with nature. This is same in any changing society. As Hindus have been surviving from time immemorial, in spite of the onslaughts, they should treat all of their community members equally, so that not only Hindus, even the entire nation and the world can be elevated.

ADI HINDUS

In view of the above facts, the all SCs can be called "Adi Hindus" more appropriately giving all credit, instead of Harijan, Paraiyar, Dalit, Shudra etc. the one collective group "Adi Hindus" can be given the SC status and STs are nothing but our brethren "Vanavashis" from time immemorial. They should dispense with the motivated use of "Dalit" and work for the unity and integrity of India.

TOWARDS DALIT UNITY

It is a fact that the SCs have many differences among themselves and each group working separately with suspicion on the other group. The differences observed are due to the following factors:

- Educated SCs do not treat uneducated characteristically.
- Rich SCs do not mingle with the poor groups.
- Urban SCs treat rural categories differently.
- All the above categories do not want to identify with other SCs, because of their elevated status. Many

times, they even hesitates or do not want to introduce their own mother, wife, sisters, brothers etc., to others fearing that their "caste" might be revealed. At marriage and other social gatherings, one can observe how the different groups of SCs interact/ behave with each other.

- personality cult, political links for getting favours, extra-political/caste/ religious connections for getting funds for organizing meetings, printing literature etc. "Acquired groups" do not want to reveal or share with other groups about their sources and application of funds.
- Elevated groups are afraid that other SCs may get their benefits so that their prospects may be affected / restricted in the long run. They are more interested in getting benefits to their children and wards than for other SCs.
- The "We-they" complex among the SCs themselves are very intriguing leading to unimaginable state of "untouchables among the untouchables".

Competitive spirit should be there, but not rivalry leading to social manipulations. Here only, one is told about to follow some principles based on religion or otherwise. History is replete with the causes for manipulation of castes. Therefore, we need not commit the same mistakes to increase the number of castes among the existing castes. If we continue such tactics, it is nothing but suicidal politics playing with their own brethren. Therefore, forgetting the differences, one should work for the unification, instead of diversification or differentiation. For such a unification process, the concept of "Adi Hindus" would be very much helpful. Let us our brethren think over it and come for a fruitful decision, so that the Indian society may be having prosperous future with social equity and social justice.

POLITICAL USAGE

Later, politicians also started to use this word at political meetings at villages and rural areas to attract them. As the

SCs / Harijans wanted to have a new name for them, because of changing times, they also preferred to be called as "Dalits", instead of the old names. In fact, in Tamil Nadu, they still prefer to use "Adi Dravidar", "Dravidar" and even "Paraiyar", as they have reservations about the use of Sanskrit / Hindi word "Dalit". But, as their leaders started to understand the political significance of the word, they have slowly started to accept it, and it may not be denied that the editor V. T. Rajasekhara Shetty of "Dalit Voice" popularized the word in the South in selected circles. However, the interesting feature is the over-enthusiastic usage of the word "Dalit" by the Christian organizations of various hues and colours. Muslims have also started to use it. Perhaps, Muslims of Maharashtra started to use it. Then, "Dalit Muslims" became popular with the starting of organizations with "Dalit" banner like "Dalit Muslim Suraksha Samiti" by the notorious-smuggler-turned-social worker Haji Mastan of Bombay. After the Meenakshipuram episode, some Muslims have openly started using the expression, even though most of the Muslims do not want to use it, as according to the concept of "Islam", they cannot have "Caste".

INDIAN CASTE SYSTEM

One of the more confusing mysteries of India is her caste system. The caste system, which exists already for more than 3000 years, seems to have been developed by the Brahmins (priests) in order to maintain their superiority. Eventually, the caste system became formalised into 4 distinct classes (*Varnas*).

At the top are the *Brahmins*, the priests and arbiters of what is right and wrong in matters of religion and society. Next are the *Kshatriyas*, who are soldiers and administrators. The *Vaishyas* are the artisan and commercial class, and finally, the *Shudras* are the farmers and the peasant class. These four castes are said to have come from Brahma's mouth (*Brahmin*), arms (*Kshatriyas*), thighs (*Vaishyas*) and feet (*Shudras*).

Beneath the four main castes is a fifth group, the Scheduled Caste. They literally have no caste. They are the untouchables, the Dalit, which means oppressed, downtrodden and exploited social group.

The Dalits are the collection of all the communities of India who were denied a status in the traditional caste system of India. They were considered even lower that the lowest caste, namely the *Shudras*. Gandhi coined the word "*Harijan*" or "Children of God" to collectively address this community, but over a period of time, even the word *Harijan* has been considered derogatory. The politically correct term to use is "Scheduled Castes" or "Dalit". Literally, a Dalit means an exploited person.

Although Hindu scholars dispute the relationship of untouchability to Hindu codes, the rigid caste system prevalent in India denied social status and civil amenities to a class who were poor and took up menial professions such as cleaning, and washing.

In various parts of India, it was considered unholy to even touch the Dalit (hence the name *asprushya* or untouchable), and the Dalit could not use the same public facilities (such as well, or a restaurant) frequented by the upper-castes.

Mahatma Gandhi, during his leadership of India during the 20th century, made fight against untouchability as one of the top priorities of India and implemented many programmes. Entry into temples, sharing meals with the Dalit, and voluntarily performing jobs (such as cleaning toilets) meant for the Dalit were some of these activities.

HISTORY AND ORIGIN

"*Dalit*" is the only name which the Dalits of India have given themselves. Its root word is "*Dal*", which in Hebrew means broken, crushed. The Dalit, along with the present tribals, form over 30% of India's population.

The Dalits were the original inhabitants of India and resemble the African in physical features. It is said that India and Africa were one land mass until separated by the ocean. So both the Africans and the Indian Untouchables and tribals had common ancestors. Some portion of these came to found the Indus Valley Civilization. These original inhabitants of India put up a strong fight against the Aryan invaders. However, the latter, working through deceitful means, defeated the innocent but hard-working original inhabitants who had built the world's most ancient civilization in the Indus Valley.

The original inhabitants who fought and were enslaved were kept outside village limits. They became Untouchables (Scheduled Castes). Those who fled to the forests and hills became tribals (Scheduled Tribes).

The invading Aryans were nomads, barbarians, without a civilization. It was they who enslaved women and destroyed the Indus Civilization, introducing patriarchal Gods to the previously matriarchal original peoples.

The Dalits were never completely assimilated into the Aryan (Hindu) culture. All over India, they have their own Gods, shrines, food habits and cultural identities, despite the fact that they also worship Hindu Gods. The hatred and violence constantly manifested against Dalit to the present time is a clear sign that the war between the invaders and the original sons of the soil continues even today.

The Dalits are on the verge of losing their identity due to various socio-economic and historical processes. The irony is that they have been reduced to live as second class citizens in their own land. There are some who by virtue of their descent occupy places of privilege in the social and economic hierarchy, while others are thought to be doomed to the periphery of the corroders of power and socio-economic structure. The worst of it is that these discriminatory structures are condoned, justified and legitimized by socio-religious institutions. These structures perpetuate various forms of violence on humanity. Of all forms of violence, caste and ethnicity based discriminations are the worst.

POPULATION

The total population of India's Dalit is given as 250 million, forming about 25 per cent. But this figure does not take into account the vast number of Untouchables who converted to Buddhism, Christianity, Sikhism, etc., but at the same time suffered from the stigma of Untouchability. Leaders of the

Untouchables complain that the census of Untouchables is very much suppressed by India's Ruling Class. Census is a matter of first concern in all countries wedded to "democracy" based on adult suffrage. Since politics in India has become a game of numbers, census figures assume high importance. It is the numbers that give added political weight. That is why census figures are deliberately concocted.

The main reason Dalit suffer via the census is that quite a number register themselves not as "Scheduled Castes" but as Hindus, Hinduism being designated as the country's largest single religion. That being so, census figures cannot be taken as giving a correct picture of India's Dalit or its other persecuted minorities. It is said that India's Untouchables and tribals together would form a formidable one third of the country's total population.

Since the real population strength of the non-Hindu Indians would upset the balance of power of the Ruling Class, they deliberately suppress the population figures not only of Untouchables but also of tribals, Muslims and Christians. As the Dalit are scattered in all the villages and segregated, they have no capacity to assert their rights. Almost one hundred per cent poverty and illiteracy add to their misery.

DALIT THEOLOGY

Dalit theology is a stem of Christian theology that surfaced among the Dalit caste in India in the 1980s. It shares many themes with the liberation theology, which cropped up two decades before. The unique aspect of Dalit theology lies in the fact that it believes in Jesus himself being a Dalit or an outcaste.

The etymology of the term "Dalit" can be traced back to the 19th century when a Marathi social reformer and revolutionary Mahatma Jyotirao Phule used this term to describe the "outcastes" and "untouchables" as the "oppressed and crushed victims of the Indian caste system". Dalits who represent roughly 20% of the Indian population (200 million), were considered untouchables as a result of the Hindu concept of "ritual pollution and purity". They were also landless agricultural labourers and tanners. They were debarred from using village water tanks and public roads. Temple doors were closed on them.

This Dalit concept was also within the Christians. Though Catholics of the lower caste and tribes form 60 per cent of Church membership they have no place in decision-making. The entry of colonialism made it possible for the Dalit to search for new means of protest and liberation. Some Dalit incorporated themselves into the colonial system by joining the army or by serving as apprenticed labourers in British colonies. Several views are expressed regarding the causes for Dalit conversion to Christianity. They vary from the spiritual to the socio-economic.

Dalit in post Independent India sought new avenues of liberation, which became a part of the Dalit theology. One of the best instances of this new wave of Dalit liberation movement was the Dalit Panther Movement in Maharashtra, which made popular the use of the term Dalit. Further there was a rise in the Dalit literature in 1960s. Black American Literature immensely influenced Dalit literary movements. One of the salient features of the Dalit theology is that it is a theology about the downtrodden, "the theology which they themselves would like to expound". One of the major sources of the Dalit theology is the Dalit experience of suffering and pain. The theology has a two fold function. First, it acts in harmony with the aim of liberation. This liberation is a freedom from both the religio-cultural and socio-economic bondages. The theological movements also have a lot of psychological dimensions which are of equal importance.

A Dalit is not considered to be part of the human society, but something, which is beyond that. The Dalit perform the most menial and degrading jobs. Sometimes Dalits perform important jobs, but this is mostly not socially recognised. Dalits are seen as polluting for higher caste people. If a higher caste Hindu is touched by an untouchable or even had a Dalit's shadow across them, they consider themselves to be polluted and have to go through a rigorous series of rituals to be cleansed.

In India there are approximately 240 million Dalit. This means that nearly 25% of the population is Dalit. It also means that in a country, where everybody is supposed to have equal rights and opportunities, 1 out of 5 persons is condemned to be untouchable.

In general one can say that being a Brahmin means that you are more privileged. This can imply having a good education and, accordingly, a more powerful position in the society. Being born as a Dalit you will be less off and because of less education you will have a less good job. In daily life it has a lot of consequences of being a Dalit.

Dalits are poor, deprived and socially backward. Poor means that they do not have access to enough food, health care, housing and/or clothing (which means that their physiological and safety needs are not fulfilled). They also do not have access to education and employment. With deprived we would like to underline the injustice they face in every days life. Officially, everybody in India has the same rights and duties, but the practice is different. Social backwardness, lack of access to food, education and health care keeps them in bondage of the upper castes.

The practice of untouchability was formally outlawed by the Constitution of India in 1950. However in practice, the Dalit communities are still subjected to extreme forms of social and economic exclusion and discrimination. They are not only denied access to common property (water, land) but are also denied equal opportunities in education and work. Their attempts to assert their rights are often met with strong resistance from the higher castes, resulting in massacres, rapes and other atrocities.

As the slogans of 'India poised' and 'India shining' are being shouted from every roof top in the country, here is one reality which needs to be looked at:

- According to government statistics, an estimated one million Dalit are manual scavengers who clean public latrines and dispose of dead animals
- 80% of Dalit live in rural areas and 86% of Dalit households are landless

- 60% of Dalit are dependent on casual labour.
- Literacy rates too present a bleak picture with only 37% of literate Dalit
- 3 Dalit women are raped every day
- a crime is committed against a Dalit everyday

As per 2001 census present Dalit population is 16% of total population of India i.e. around 160 million. Independent India has witnessed considerable amount of violence and hate crimes motivated by caste.

The word 'Dalit' in Marathi literally means 'broken'. First used by Jyotiba Phule, the term was later popularized by Dalit leader Dr. B. R. Ambedkar to reflect the situation of the millions of Dalit within South Asia, who are systematically and institutionally deprived of their civil, political, economic, social and cultural rights in every aspect of life. But the Dalits are now redefining the word with it their identity - Dalits are those who practice equality, believe in equality and fight for equality!

The Ruling Class of India, comprising bureaucrats, the press, professionals, industrial-landed interests, academic-cultural-religious leaders, priests (the Hindu religious police), the banking-financial sector, and a section of politicians, has successfully given the outside world the impression that Buddha's and Gandhi's land of peace and *Ahimsa* (non-violence) is wedded to the highest and the noblest ideals of truth, toleration, justice, freedom and equality. If anywhere there is a perfect working model of parliamentary democracy in the world, it is in India — the living example of socialism and secularism. India's Ruling Class, as the self-chosen representative of the Buddha and Gandhi, has successfully advertised that it never hesitated to fight against any kind of breach of human rights not only inside the country but also outside. It is in accordance with this image that India observed the International Anti Apartheid Year (1978-79) with great fanfare. The then Indian Foreign Minister, A.B. Vajpayee, went to the UN General Assembly and delivered an eloquent speech (in Hindi) on the floor of the world forum denouncing the practice of Apartheid in South Africa and other African countries as well as racial discrimination in the USA, UK and other countries. Indian Prime Minister Jawaharlal Nehru, Morarji Desai and Indira Gandhi have always been first in condemning violations of human rights in any part of the world. Since India claims to have given birth to some of the greatest saints and savants, produced the world's holiest of the holy scriptures, tons of godmen, its heart bleeds at the very sight of the slightest injustice in any part of the world. That is why cow slaughter is prohibited in India. Because cow is a sacred animal.

The outside world, therefore, knows very little about untouchability or Dalit. As the late Dr. B.R. Ambedkar, the greatest leader of the Indian Dalit, put it: "Indians have not written about Untouchables for they lack the courage and honesty, and the foreigners have avoided the subject for fear of offending the orthodox Indian masses." Christian missionaries have come out with some studies. Soviet Communist scholars have completely ignored the Untouchables, fearing the wrath of the Brahmin leadership of the Indian Communist Party. The Chinese Marxists have also maintained a studied silence on this subject.

What is the position of the Dalit inside India? Nobody has described the prevailing situation better than the once Deputy Prime Minister of India, Jagjivan Ram, who noted that differences of caste and creed in India have assumed a more terrible form than the racial conflict in the USA against which Martin Luther King fought.

Untouchability, therefore, is not a thought of as a racial problem but a mental [or cultural] problem, resulting not so much from Dalit' colour as from their cultural and historical economic, social and political circumstances. Jagjivan Ram was referring to the position of India's 80-million Dalit who are called "Scheduled Castes" in India's official documents but popularly known as "*Harijans*" (meaning the children of God), a name given to them by Gandhiji.

Even many affluent Indians living in luxury prefer to believe that untouchability nowhere exists in India. Since untouchability is a mental problem, how can anybody see it? It can't be seen but only felt. The shoe pinches only the wearer. He alone feels the pain. India's Dalit alone feels the pain of untouchability. Not others.

A familiar argument of "educated" Indians is "even the little traces of untouchability left will go once the people get educated." But, we beg to differ with this. It is the highly "educated" people who are more caste conscious than their illiterate brothers back home in the village. The universities, in addition to the political parties, the news media, etc., are all instruments of the ruling class — the Upper Castes - and are used to indoctrinate the population as a whole with its values, principles and ethics — in India's case, the values, principles and ethics of Hinduism. Each and every Indian is influenced by the dominant Brahminical ideology — even the Dalits, who are the most oppressed by it.

Centuries of indoctrination and miseducation by the upper castes have produced and perpetuated literate but politically ignorant generations of Dalit youth. These Dalit have been brainwashed into accepting the commercial lifestyles, attitudes and interests fed to them by the Hindu media. They have become victims of a psychological war aimed at keeping them divided, politically ignorant and disorganized. The effect has been to make them view the world through the eyes of their oppressors, accepting their oppression and exploitation as the natural order of things. They have taken on their enemy's ideology as their own, and are thus manipulated into working in the interest of the enemy, who exploits their labour and robs them of their resources. This ideology tells them to get rich quick. To make money by hook or crook. It tells them to "go up" and "be successful" in society, even while it completely ignores the political and socio-cultural factors that make this impossible.

The aim of Hindu Brahminical ideology is to increase the profits accumulated and controlled by the Upper Castes, to maintain their status quo relationship of domination of the masses of Indian people: Hindus, Dalit, and other minorities alike. In the Brahminical society, universities and colleges reinforce the status quo by turning the youth of the society into miseducated defenders of its reactionary ideology, into unwitting tools of the exploiters of the masses of the people.

Therefore education will bring no relief to India. The problem of caste and untouchability is very aggravated today mainly because of these "educated" people. The problem of caste exists in the mind. It is a kind of Hindu mental disease. Ambedkar called it a mental twist, saying: "Every Hindu believes that to observe caste and untouchability is his dharma – meaning his religious duty. But Hinduism is more than a religious system. It is also an economic system. In slavery, the master at any rate had the responsibility to feed, cloth and house the slave and keep him in good condition lest the market value of the slave should decrease. But in the system of untouchability, the Hindu takes no responsibility for the maintenance of the Untouchable. As an economic system, it permits exploitation without obligation."

Untouchability is observed even by university professors. Election to university student unions is conducted on a caste basis. Untouchables have hardly any admission to the well-guarded precincts of the teaching professions. Therefore untouchability cannot be removed by education alone. Neither can it be abolished by inter-caste marriages nor interdining. Caste is a state of mind.

DALIT OUTSIDE INDIA

Dr. Ambedkar, the most revolutionary figure of modern India, has the following to say: "The Romans had their slaves, the Spartans their helots, the British their villains, the Americans their Negroes and the Germans their Jews. So the Hindus have their Untouchables. But none of these can be said to have been called upon to face a fate which is worse than the fate of the Untouchables. Slavery, serfdom, villeinage have all vanished. But untouchability still exists and bids fair to last as long as Hinduism. The Untouchable is worse off than a Jew. The sufferings of the Jew are his own creation. Not so are the sufferings of the Dalit. They are the result of a cold, calculating Hinduism which is not less sure in its effect of producing misery than brute force is. The Jew is despised but is not denied opportunities to grow. The Untouchable is not merely despised but is denied all opportunities to rise. Yet nobody seems to take any notice of the Untouchables — much less espouse their cause."

This observation of Ambedkar was made as long ago as 1943. Since then, Israel has been formed in an attempt to solve the problem of the Jews. The American Negro has passed from his non-violent manifestations of 1963 through the crescendo of violent insurrections of 1967. American Black Power has managed to put fear into the heart of the Whites. Besides, the high technology American society will have to search for talent wherever it exists in its eternal pursuit of wealth. Therefore it is compelled to encourage talent and merit, even if it be in the Black. It is not in the interest of a capitalist society in search of peaks of excellence to neglect anybody who helps secure high profit.

In this mad race for dollars, it cannot afford to discriminate against the Dalit if the Dalit help to multiply the dollars, but not so in India. Here talent is crushed. Merit is murdered. Many a flower blushes unseen. Caste is the index and merit is seen only among the high-born. In such a feudal society, merit becomes the worst casualty. Similarly, the Dalit of South Africa have abandoned the path of non-violence and taken to armed struggle after the Sharpeville massacre. The African National Congress has managed to focus world attention on the struggle of the Dalit. Apartheid today is discussed the world over.

The Palestinians, too, have been shaking the entire world, and have attracted international attention to their problems. Though defeated and driven out of Lebanon (1982), they gained world sympathy.

The World Council of Churches sent a team to investigate the plight of the aborigines of Australia. Christians are also fighting on behalf of Maoris, Burakus, Koreans and Sri Lanka Tamils, but have hardly bothered about India's Dalit. They had reservations about our invitation to send a team to India. They said they could visit only on the invitation of the Indian church authorities. But the Indian Christian Church itself is divided into castes, and black untouchable converts are segregated.

Nobody bothers about the Indian Dalit. In sheer number, they exceed the population of the American Negroes, or for that matter, any other struggling, persecuted racial or religious minority group. What can this huge population hope for? Their voice is not only not heard outside India — even inside India, theirs is a cry in the wilderness.

Why does nobody talk about the problems of India's Dalit? The UN General Assembly has had debates on the problem of South African Dalit, Palestinians and other groups who have been denied human rights. But the UNO has not so far cared to spare a thought for the world's gravest problem: the problem of India's Dalit. The point is, nobody has so far complained to the world organization — not the Human Rights Commission, the World Council of Churches nor Amnesty International, not even a representative of the victims. Mother Teresa, the Nobel laureate who operates in India, does not bother about them. There is an all-round conspiracy of silence when it comes to the question of Untouchables.

POSITION OF DALIT IN INDIA

What is the actual position of the Indian Dalit who are not only Untouchables but unapproachables, unseeables and unthinkables — the truly invisible men:

"The Untouchables had different names in different parts of the country. They were called outcastes, Untouchables, *Pariahs, Pancharmas, Ati-Shudras, Avarnas, Antyajas* and *Namashudras*. Their social disabilities were specific and severe and numerous. Their touch, shadow and even voice were deemed by the caste Hindus to be polluting. So they had to step aside at the approach of a caste Hindu. They were forbidden to keep certain domestic animals, to use certain metals for ornament, were obliged to wear a particular type of dress, to eat a particular type of food, to use a particular type of footwear, and were forced to occupy the dirty, dingy and unhygienic outskirts of villages and towns where for habitation they lived in dark, unsanitary and miserable smoky shanties or cottages. The dress of the males consisted of a turban, a staff in the hand, a rough blanket over the shoulder and a piece of loin cloth. The women wore bodices and rough sarees barely reaching the knees.

"These Untouchable Hindus were denied the use of public wells and were condemned to drink any filthy water they could find. Their children were not admitted to schools attended by the caste Hindu children. Though they worshipped the gods of Hindus and observed the same festivals, the Hindu temples were closed to them. Barbers and washermen refused to render them service. Caste Hindus, who fondly threw sugar to ants and reared dogs and other pets and welcome persons of other religions to their houses, refused to give a drop of water to the Untouchables or to show them one iota of sympathy. These Untouchable Hindus were treated by the caste Hindus as sub-humans, less than men, worse than beasts. This picture is still true in villages and small towns. Cities have mostly overcome this state.

"Their miseries did not end at this. As they were illiterate, ill-treated and untouchable, for ages all public services including the police and military forces were closed to them. Naturally they followed hereditary occupations. Some of them plied trades of a lower and degrading order such as street-sweeping, scavenging and shoemaking. Some skinned carcasses and ate carrion, tanned hides and skins, worked in bamboo and cane, and mowed grass. Others who were more fortunate tilled the land as tenants or worked as labourers in the fields; a great number of them subsisted on food or grain given to them as village servants. Thus deprived of social, religious and civil rights, they had no chance of bettering their conditions and so these untouchable 'Hindus' live the life of a bygone and dead age, dragging on their miserable existence in insufficient accommodation, unsanitary surroundings and social segregation. In short, they were born in debt and perished in debt. They were born Untouchables, they lived as Untouchables and they died as Untouchables." Even their shadow brings pollution.

AFTER INDEPENDENCE

After India became independent (in 1947), the successive Governments implemented many plans to better the conditions of the Dalit. The most important of them are the "Reservations" or the "Quota System" (also called "Roaster System"), where many privileges of the Government were to be provided only for Dalit; privileges such as job quotas, admissions to universities, political appointments, political representation, and even promotions within the Government.

This affirmative-action type of policy has led to a lot of controversy and social turmoil in India due to the following reasons:

- Abuse of the system — The rampantly corrupt system of India has been used by non-Dalit to enjoy the benefits meant for Dalit.
- Repeat Beneficiaries — The few Dalit who benefited from the reservations, keep reaping the benefits again and again, thus denying the opportunity to first time beneficiaries.
- Reverse Discrimination — Selecting candidates based on caste, rather than their merit or qualifications has caused a lot of anger and resentment.
- Conflicts with Scheduled Tribes — The reservations for Dalits are often combined with reservations meant for aboriginals and other backward classes of India.

RELIGIOUS CONVERSIONS AND CONFLICTS

Many Dalit who came in contact with Christian missionaries chose to abandon their Hindu roots and adopted the Christian faith. This religious conversion has given rise to two folded turmoil in India. First, due to conversion, the Dalit lost the privileges meant for Scheduled Castes — Christianity is believed to be void of the caste discrimination, and the quotas were meant for people who otherwise were socially backward. Many laws were passed so that people thus converted could continue to enjoy the special quotas, after agitations and counter-agitations. Secondly, the Dalits are torn between retaining their cultural identity and adopting a new one.

Many Dalits are also converting to Buddhism, following the footsteps of Bhimrao Ramji Ambedkar, a great Dalit leader.

CURRENT STATUS OF DALITS

While a lot of progress has been made to improve the status of Dalit, the reform has not transformed the Indian orthodoxy. The Indian newspapers often report incidents when Dalit women are abused; Dalit kids are expelled from schools and the like.

A new generation of Dalit leadership has emerged in India. However, due to other problems of India, their agenda gets twisted, misinterpreted, and even ridiculed. Many Dalits do not wish to be identified as Dalit for obvious reasons, and the Dalit community is losing valuable leaders to *neo-brahmanism*.

A new form of literature has emerged in India, consisting of prose and poetry written by Dalit writers. They document the stories of India, hitherto untold.

Dalits are getting caught in the crossfire between the religious fervor of Christian missionaries and Hindu fundamentalists who are bent on opposing conversions in India.

ONE PROBABLE SOLUTION

It was the British who for the first time united the warring Indians under one government, and the moment they left in 1947, the Indian population was divided into India and Pakistan. The Naga tribes got a separate state. Many more separatist demands are growing. The Sikhs are demanding a separate nation of Khalistan. India will be divided and subdivided again, for the Hindu religion divides and does not unite the Indians. There is no Indian in India. His loyalty is first to his caste if not sub-caste, rather than to the nation. Any visitor to India can make this out in no time. Even Hindus in the USA observe caste rules, untouchability and segregation. The Hindu carries his caste wherever he goes.

Upon the departure of the British in 1947, when the Muslims were accorded Pakistan and the Hindus India, a special system of "reservations" (or affirmative action quotas assuring those jobs within the civil service) was instituted to be of benefit to Dalit. During the negotiations, Dr. Ambedkar, the leader of the Dalit, pressed for a "separate electorate" for Dalit. However, the Hindu ruling classes responded with Mahatma Gandhi's "last unto death", and threatened a wholesale massacre of Dalit if he did not withdraw his demand. Faced with such a threat, Dr. Ambedkar was forced to withdraw the demand for a separate electorate, or separate state, and agreed to what appeared to be an improvement in conditions for Dalit: the Hindu "gift" of quotas.

Quotas or no, the solution to the Dalit quest for equality does not lie in their final absorption into Hinduism. Therefore the Dalit of India are fighting for a homeland, *Dalitastan*. The need for a separate homeland or state for Dalit is clear. They were forced to come out with this demand when inhuman tortures and the burning of Untouchables reached a climax in the State of Maharashtra in the middle of 1978. The government itself had admitted that the atrocities against Untouchables had been mounting year after year. The killings of Untouchables that enveloped almost the whole State of Maharashtra were caused by the simple issue of renaming a university after Dr. Ambedkar. The Hindus, who form the majority in every village, were waiting for an opportunity to pounce on the Untouchables, and Hindu prejudice poured out in full fury as never before. They pounced on the Untouchables like mad dogs. The "Marathwada massacre", both in intensity and total damage, will exceed all other previous atrocities against Untouchables. Never before has the country witnessed such a wholesale war on the Untouchables. The real cause, therefore, was not the renaming of a university, but the constitutional safeguards or affirmative action rights given to the Untouchables. Even these little crumbs of bread, bones and skin thrown at those waiting outside the grand feast in the Upper Caste household led to great heart-burning and jealousy.

The "Marathwada massacre" has confirmed the fears of Dr. Ambedkar that majority rule (democracy) in India means the rule of the majority (dominant) community, which in turn means Brahmin rule. The Marathwada caste war was followed by the "Gujarat caste war" on Untouchables. And such wars have become a daily feature in the life of Untouchables. The Hindus who are so very concerned about cow slaughter are not bothered about the slaughter of human beings.

The Upper Caste control the government, the policy, the judiciary, press and all else, including the military. Whenever there is any violence against Untouchables, the whole world comes down on them. The Marathwada massacre of Untouchables and the Gujarat caste war have proved this once again. As described by the press, it is organized violence against a friendless, helpless social leper. Untouchables are neither allowed to live or to die as human beings. Because if they are killed wholesale, the Upper Caste will be deprived of free servants, slaves. So the Untouchables hover between life and death. They are a having dead.The Dalit of India must reject the whole cultural system of Hinduism. Their willingness to do so is illustrated by mass conversions of Dalit to the religion of Islam. As A. Antony Doss Gupta notes: "The Untouchables know perfectly well that they will lose privileges, concessions, grants and subsidies on their conversion to Islam. Yet they are willing to embrace Islam. What is the motive?

1. *Social inequality:* Social inequality is the primary reason for the Untouchables losing faith in Hinduism. Even after 40 years of India's "independence", they are not permitted to walk on public roads with their chappals on, to drink tea in village tea shops in common tumblers, to ride their own cycles or sit on their own cart when passing through Hindu areas.The Untouchables feel totally insecure in spite of all the assurances written in the Constitution of India.

2. *Sexual abuse:* The upper castes hate the Untouchables from the bottom of their hearts, but not their young daughters, wives and widows. Dishonouring Dalit women is not uncommon, and the majority of clashes are on this account. Dalit know for certain that it they embrace Islam, the lives of their family members, their property and the honour of their women will be well protected. Untouchable women want exactly this. They hope to get this protection only by embracing Islam, rather than the Christianity which in India is nothing but a modified Hinduism, as it still observes the caste system."

What, then, is Hindu in India offering the Dalit when it offers them quotas, if in order to get quotas, the Dalit must accept to become a part of a civilization which by its very structure and philosophy views them as lowest of the low? Does the integration of Dalit in India means the acceptance of crumbs and token concessions and protections on paper in exchange for belonging in the fold of a culture which despises you?

That is why millions of Dalit, disgusted with Hinduism, have become Muslims and Christians. The 1981 mass conversion of Untouchables to Islam in South India is an historic event that unnerved the orthodox Hindus.

The Dalit of India should therefore see no advantage in trying to advance their interests within the context of such a society. Dr. Ambedkar declared that *he would never die a Hindu*. Listen to what the Dalit poets proclaim "I reject your culture. I reject your [Hindu] tradition." For them, the call for a Dalit culture entails a rejection of the whole Hindu cultural system. This is symbolic of change and revolution.

The right of Dalit to quota jobs should not be tied to their declaring themselves to be Hindus. Dalit should have the freedom to create a new cultural system which can promote and sustain their struggle for justice and human dignity. While preserving the right to quotas, they should have the cultural freedom to transform their society, to create and live in a society where the notions of Black untouchability and caste discrimination are non-existent. The present arrangement of tying their economic rights to their participation in the old cultural system is a cruel denial of their full range of human rights.

In this way, the Dalit have been let down not only by the ruling class and the government, but even by the Left parties. The Constitution of India has abolished untouchability – on paper. Nonetheless, in the ensuing more than 60 years, untouchability has continued with full fury. That is because the Constitution abolished only untouchability, not the caste system itself. As long as the caste system as a whole is not abolished, untouchability alone cannot be removed. The ruling class knows it and that is why it has no plans to abolish the caste system.

India's ruling class does not want to abolish untouchability because it provides a lot of socio-economic benefits, and more than anything else, the bulk votes of the Untouchables to the ruling class. They are its "vote bank", which gives interest-free loans.

The Dalit may be large in number, but they are poor, weak, unorganized, and terror-stricken. Caste and sub-castes have divided them also. They have neither political, economic nor social status, and are almost 100 per cent illiterate. They are desperate. There are three types of strength: (1) manpower, (2) financial power, and (3) mental power. Financially, they have no power. With regard to mental strength, the situation is deplorable. How can a set of people accustomed to daily insults get mental strength? As for manpower, their sheer number may make some conclude they have this strength. But they are divided into hundreds of castes and sub-castes and torn into different languages. Political parties have further divided them. So theirs is a pathetic story. Darkness stares at their faces. They are in all-round gloom. In such a powerless state, how can they organize any opposition against a heartless society?

3

Social System Giving Birth to Dalits

Religion plays an important role in the life and growth of people. It has been one of the tools people have used as an agent of bondage or liberation. For centuries, India has been a cradle of religions. Many religions found the Indian soil fertile and flourished here. Some like Hinduism, Christianity, Islam came from outside and others like Buddhism, Jainism, Sikhism, Lingayatism were born here.

Dalit joined religions that preached equality. The conversion of Dalit, in large numbers, to Buddhism, Christianity, Islam and Sikhism, besides being change of religion, was also a search for equality and human dignity. For instance Dr. Ambedkar believed that neither bourgeois nationalism nor republicanism nor traditional Marxism provided any satisfactory solution to the problem of caste. Hence he turned to Buddhism.

His long and arduous search for religious emancipation is enshrined in his *magnum opus: The Buddha and His Dharma.* He rejected Christianity and Islam because, though formally egalitarian religions, they did not face in their origin the task of fighting the caste system. The only Indian religion, for Ambedkar, which arose and grew out of the struggle against the caste system and never succumbed to it, was Buddhism. Ambedkar was the first to characterise it as a revolutionary and the most egalitarian religion of India. Ambedkar noted that the Buddha created his *Sangha* as a model of casteless society and the laity was to emulate the *bhikkhus* in order to bring about such a society into existence.

As Rev. Kappan, an Indian theologian says, it was the Vedic religion, which provoked the first crisis of culture and religion in India. By Vedic religion he means that stage of religious consciousness represented by the *Samhitas*, the *Brahmanas* and the *Upanishads*, spanning a period of over 1500 years ending with the rise of Buddhism. The *Rig-veda* is the earliest written literary source of the ancient history of India (1500-1000 BC). A large part of the text addressed to Lord Indra, narrates a fierce war-encounter between different groups:

One for example is between the deva worshipping *Aryas* and the deva-less and the riteless Dasyus. Number of hymns describes how under the command of Lord Indra, the Aryas defeated, destroyed and looted the Dasyus, the indigenous people who were different from the Aryas, both culturally and racially. Indra is glorified for his capacity for war against his and the Aryas' enemy, Dasyus. The gods were to sanction not only wars but also oppressive social institutions: for example the four *varnas.*

During the Vedic period, the low caste people were denied the right to education and even the right to live. The caste system placed the Dalit people at the bottom of society with least wealth or power. They were the most exploited and oppressed lot, condemned to labour freely or for little remuneration.

ANTI-CASTE MOVEMENTS

Both Vedic ritualism and gnosis [supremacy of Brahmans] were bound to be called in question by the common people. The popular discontent found expression in dissident sects like Jainism (540-468 B.C.) and Buddhism (563-483 B.C.). There is no doubt that Jainism and Buddhism were the first attacks or revolts in general against the caste system.

Lord Buddha initiated a radical critique of contemporary religion and society. He was forthright in repudiating the caste system and the notion of ritual purity associated with it. One of his famous sayings runs like this:

"No Brahmin is such by birth,
No outcaste is such by birth.
An outcaste is such by his deeds,
A Brahmin is such by his deeds."

From out of the struggle between Vedic religion and heterodox movements like Jainism and Buddhism was born what is today called Hinduism, which reached its golden age in the Gupta period (300-700 A.D.). Many factors were responsible for this new development. Brahminism succeeded in integrating within itself popular religions. Popular deities were absorbed into the Vedic pantheon through a process of identification or subordination. Even Buddha was given the status of a vishnuite incarnation.

After the exit of the Buddhist religion from India, there were other religious and anti-caste movements that arose and functioned within the *jati* system and hence they were assimilated by it sooner or later. For examples the Lingayat religion led by Jangam intellectuals, the Sikh by Khatri intellectuals and the medieval Bhakti movement.

The Bhakti movement, a socio-religious expression of the revolt of the masses originated in Tamil Nadu but soon spread to Karnataka and Maharashtra, and eventually swept through the whole of north India. It is undeniable that the Bhaktas represented the aspirations of the downtrodden masses as against the interests of the twice born.

The *Bhagavata Purana,* the main scriptural authority of the movement, comes out with the startling idea of a God who is partial to the poor: "Hari, fond of those persons destitute of wealth and whose sole wealth is himself, and knowing their affection, does not accept the worship of evil-minded persons who by their conceit about their Vedic learning, wealth, family, and deeds bestow harm on good people who are poor."

Saints of the Bhakti movement came from all castes and, the movement had a large mass support. Unfortunately it could not maintain its initial thrust and was domesticated by

Hindu orthodoxy. As Dumont observes, "A sect cannot survive on Indian soil if it denies caste."

In the context of traditional Hindu society, Dalit status has often been historically associated with occupations regarded as ritually impure, such as any occupation involving killing, handling of animal cadavers or night soil (human feces). One million Dalit work as manual scavengers, cleaning latrines and sewers by hand and clearing away dead animals. Engaging in these activities was considered to be polluting to the individual who performed them, and this pollution was considered to be 'contagious'. As a result, Dalits were commonly banned and segregated from full participation in Hindu social life (they could not enter the premises of a temple), while elabourate precautions were sometimes observed to prevent incidental contact between Dalit and other Hindus.

An estimated 40 million people in India, most of them Dalit, are bonded workers, many working in slave-like conditions to pay off debts that were incurred generations ago. The majority of Dalit live in segregation and experience violence, murder, rape and atrocities to the scale of 110,000 registered cases a year according to 2005 statistics. No one believes these numbers are anywhere close to the reality of crimes committed against Dalit. Most crimes go unreported, and few registered cases ever get to trial.

Historically, there may not have been clear demarcation between Dalit castes and the *Shudra* castes. Dalits are not a single identifiable race or caste. Instead, like the rest of the Hindu society, they are divided into various subcastes known as 'jâtis.

One study found some association between caste status and Y-chromosomal genetic markers seeming to indicate a more European lineage of the higher castes. However, there have been other studies done to indicate no racial and genetic differences between upper and lower castes. Many sociologists, anthropologists and historians have rejected the racial origins and racial emphasis of caste and consider the idea to be one that has political undertones. Sociologist, Andre Béteille, who writes that treating caste as a form of racism is "politically mischievous" and worse, "scientifically nonsense" since there is no discernible difference in the racial characteristics between Brahmins and Scheduled Castes such as the jatav. He writes that "Every social group cannot be regarded as a race simply because we want to protect it against prejudice and discrimination".

Dalit diversity may be due to newly outcast individuals or communities over the years. It is noteworthy that regional tribes that are considered Dalit are sometimes seen by Indians as ethnically distinct. In both northern and southern India it is different. For example, in North India, in places such as Rajasthan they are usually lighter because Rajstahan was invaded several times by light-skinned tribes. In addition they also have different colour of eyes and sometimes hair.

Many Dalits who have converted to other religions in the past few centuries continue to retain their Dalit heritage.

Discrimination against Dalit is not limited to the Hindu community. This situation is exacerbated by the fact that non-Hindu Dalit groups have traditionally not been recognized as Scheduled Castes under hiring quota laws. The Dalit Muslims or "Arzal", as well as Dalit Christians form an integral part of the caste system in South Asia among Muslims and Christians. Many Dalit Muslims are discriminated against by the upper-caste "Ashraf" Muslims, and Dalit Christians discriminated against by upper caste Christian priests and nuns.

Some Dalits have successfully integrated into urban Indian society, where caste origins are less obvious and less important in public life. In rural India, caste origins are more readily apparent and Dalit remains excluded from local religious life, though this exclusion in its severity is in fact fast diminishing due to changing social norms of acceptable behaviour.

Dalit and similar groups are also found in Nepal, Pakistan and Bangladesh. In addition, the Burakumin of Japan is also compared to Dalit, as are the Baekjeong of Korea.

Dalit does not mean low caste. Dalit does not mean any religion. Dalit refers to some unique people with distinct culture and traditions.

A Dalit is not only forbidden to enter the home of a Brahmin but he must also not draw water from the same well, not eat from the same pot or place. He must not glance at or allow his shadow to fall on the Brahmin. All these acts will pollute the "pure Brahmin."

CASTE AND THEIR ORIGIN

India, a country with a lot of traditions, culture and beauty, has an unwanted, ugly and inhuman structure called 'caste system.' One cannot but feel ashamed of the caste system in India. The caste system discriminates the human persons and stratifies them into different groups. According to Manu Samhita, the Hindu religious code of conduct, divides human persons into four *Varnas* (Varna means colour, the Caste).

In Hindu society, caste is still the most powerful factor in determining a person's dignity. The caste system is the result of the Hindu belief in 'reincarnation and karma'. The four castes eventually developed into a social mosaic of 3000 sub-castes, with the Untouchables at the bottom of the list and actually outside the list. Such a rigid caste system is not found anywhere in the world outside India. A person is born into a caste. Once born in that caste, his status is predetermined and immutable. Birth decides one's status and this cannot be altered by any talent the person may develop or wealth the person may accumulate. Similarly, the caste in which a person is born predetermines what vocation the person will pursue. One has no choice. Birth decides the occupation of the person in question. Here are the four major castes:

1. BRAHMINS (the Priestly Class)
2. KSHATRIYAS (the Warrior Class)
3. VAISYAS (the Trading Class)
4. SHUDRAS (the Servants)

1. *The Brahmins:* The priestly class came from the head of the God Brahma. They are eligible for learning and teaching and perform sacrifices. The others cannot teach and perform sacrifice.

2. The *Kshatrias:* The warrior class came from the shoulder of the God Brahma. They are eligible for learning. Their work is to protect the people by waging war against the enemies.
3. *The Vaishyas:* The trading class came from the thigh of the God. Their work is to trade and feed the above two classes.
4. *The Shudras:* The servants came from the feet of the God and their work is to do all menial works to the above three classes. They are not entitled to learn anything.

Other sub-castes are more than 3000 in number, with the "Untouchables" or "Dalit" at the bottom and outside. They are the slaves of the above groups and they are absolutely forbidden to learn and teach.

BRIEF HISTORY OF THE INDIAN CASTE SYSTEM

The history of the Indian caste system dates back to the Vedic period.The origin of the caste system as it is today is still obscure.

A 2001 genetic study, led by Michael Bamshad of the University of Utah, found that the affinity of Indians to Europeans is proportionate to caste rank, the upper castes being most similar to Europeans, whereas lower castes are more like Asians. The researchers believe that the Indo-European speakers entered India from the Northwest, admixing with or displacing the proto-Dravidian speakers. Subsequently they may have established a caste system and placed themselves primarily in higher castes. The study concludes that the Indian castes "are most likely to be of proto-Asian origin with West Eurasian admixture resulting in rank-related and sex-specific differences in the genetic affinities of castes to Asians and Europeans." Because the Indian samples for this study were taken from a single geographical area, it remains to be investigated whether its findings can be safely generalized.

An earlier 1995 study by Joanna L. Mountain et al. of Stanford University had concluded that there was "no clear separation into three genetically distinct groups along caste lines", although "an inferred tree revealed some clustering according to caste affiliation".

A 2002-03 study by T. Kivisild et al. concluded that the "Indian tribal and caste populations derive largely from the same genetic heritage of Pleistocene southern and western Asians and have received limited gene flow from external regions since the Holocene." A 2006 genetic study by the National Institute of Biologicals in India, testing a sample of men from 32 tribal and 45 caste groups, concluded that the Indians have acquired very few genes from Indo-European speakers.

According to a 2006 study by a group of prominent academicians "the vast majority (>98%) of the Indian maternal gene pool, consisting of Indio-European and Dravidian speakers, is genetically more or less uniform", while the inavsions after the late Pleistocene settlement might have been mostly male-mediated. The study concluded that the "lower caste groups might have originated with the hierarchical divisions that arose within the tribal groups with the spread of Neolithic agriculturalists, much earlier than the arrival of Aryan speakers", and "the Indo-Europeans established themselves as upper castes among this already developed caste-like class structure within the tribes." The study indicated that the Indian caste system may have its roots much before the arrival of the Indo-Aryan immigrants; a rudimentary version of the caste system may have emerged with the shift towards cultivation and settlements, and the divisions may have become more well-defined and intensified with the arrival of Indo-Aryans.

SCRIPTURES OF HINDUISM AND THE CASTE SYSTEM

Although the Hindu scriptures contain some passages that can be interpreted to sanction the caste system, they also contain indications that the caste system is not an essential part of the Hindu religion, and both sides in the debate are able to find sections in scriptures that support their views.

The most ancient scriptures—the *Shruti* texts, or Vedas, place very little importance on the caste system, mentioning caste only rarely and in a cursory manner. A hymn from the Rig Veda seems to indicate that one's caste is not necessarily determined by that of one's family:

In the Vedic period, there also seems to no discrimination against the *Shudras* (which later became an ensemble of the so-called low-castes) on the issue of hearing the sacred words of the Vedas and fully participating in all religious rights, something which became totally banned in the later times.

Later scriptures such as *Bhagavad Gita* and *Manusmriti* state that the four *varnas* are created by God. However, at the same time, the *Gita* says that one's *varna* is to be understood from one's personal qualities and one's *karma* (work), not one's birth. Some scholars believe that, in its initial period, the caste system was flexible and it was merit and job based. One could migrate from one caste to other caste by changing one's profession. This view is supported by records of sages who became Brahmins. For example, the sage Vishwamitra belonged to a *Kshatriya* caste, and only later became recognized as a great Brahmin sage, indicating that his caste was not determined by birth. Similarly, Valmiki, once a low-caste robber, became a great sage. Veda Vyasa, another sage, was the son of a fisherwoman. Vasishtha was a *Shudra* and he became sage later.

Manusmriti, dated between 200 B.C.E. and 100 A.D., contains some laws that codified the caste system. *Varna* is mentioned as caste equivalent in *Manusmriti*. *Manusmriti* and some other *shastras* mention four *varnas*: The *Brahmins* (teachers, scholars and priests), the *Kshatriyas* (kings and warriors), the *Vaishyas* (traders, landowners and some artisan groups), and *Shudras* (agriculturists, service providers, and some artisan groups). Another group of untouchables excluded from the main society was called *Parjanya* or *Antyaja*. A *varna* can be viewed as a group of castes or a social division that consists of various sub-castes called *jâtis*.

Passages in *Manusmriti* and other scriptures suggest that the Indian caste system was originally non-hereditary.

The various *smritis*, like the *Yagnavalkyasmriti* and the *Manusmriti* strongly disapprove of marrying outside one's caste. The *smritis* also argue that new, despicable castes are formed out of such cases. According to these *smritis*, the *chamars* were born out of the union of a *vaideha* and a *nishada*, the *chandals* were born out of the sexual relations between a Brahmin and a *Shudra*.

HOW THE CASTE STRUCTURES EVOLVE

Megasthenes, the Greek ambassador to Chandragupta Maurya's court in India classified people of India into seven classes: philosophers, peasants, herdsmen, craftsmen and traders, soldiers, government officials and councilors.

In its later stages, the caste system is said to have become rigid, and caste began to be inherited rather than acquired by merit. In the past, members of different castes would not partake in various activities, such as dining and religious gatherings, together. In addition, the performance of religious rites and rituals were restricted to Brahmins, who were the designated priesthood. In recent years, more egalitarian reforms have enabled lower castes and even outcastes such as the Dalit to become religious clerics. The "Pandaram" priests are an example of an order of Dalit priests, based in Nepal and South India. The Pandaram maintain the same tradition as the Brahmin priests, including the use of the Sanskrit language (traditionally reserved for the Brahmins) for the rituals. While they are not generally as well trained as the Brahmin priests, they are highly respected within their community and are addressed with reverence.

According to the *Manusmriti*, every caste belongs to one of the four *varnas* (*Brahmin, Kshtriya, Vaishya,* and *Shudra*). However, there have been many disputes about the *varna* of many castes, such as castes being considered *Kshatriya* by some scholars, while described as *Shudra* by others. While texts such as the *Manusmriti* attempted to rationalize ambiguous castes by placing them in *varna-sankaras* (i.e. mixed varna), the fact remains that Indian society was, and is, composed of numerous geographically diversified but endogamous groups.

With many occupational groups practicing endogamy within a particular region, as well as numerous sub-divisions within the four main castes, a more complex system of subcastes and *jâtis* is evident. The *jatis* have broken up into clans like Agarwal, Iyer, etc.

The view of the caste system as "static and unchanging" has been disputed by many scholars. For instance, sociolgists such as Bernard Buber and Marriott McKim describe how the perception of the caste system as a static and textual stratification has given way to the perception of the caste system as a more processual, empirical and contextual stratification. Other sociologists such as Y.B Damle have applied theoretical models to explain mobility and flexibility in the caste system in India. According to these scholars, groups of lower-caste individuals could seek to elevate the status of their caste by attempting to emulate the practices of higher castes.

Flexibility in caste laws permitted very low-caste religious clerics such as Valmiki to compose the Ramayana, which became a central work of Hindu scripture.

According to some psychologists, mobility across broad caste lines may have been "minimal", though sub-castes (*jatis*) may change their social status over the generations by fission, re-location, and adoption of new rituals.

Sociologist M. N. Srinivas has also debated the question of rigidity in Caste. In an ethnographic study of the Coorgs of Karnataka, he observed considerable flexibility and mobility in their caste hierarchies. He asserts that the caste system is far from a rigid system in which the position of each component caste is fixed for all time. Movement has always been possible, and especially in the middle regions of the hierarchy. It was always possible for groups born into a lower caste to "rise to a higher position by adopting vegetarianism and teetotalism" i.e adopt the customs of the higher castes. While theoretically "forbidden", the process was not uncommon in practice. The concept of sanskritization, or the adoption of upper-caste norms by the lower castes, addressed the actual complexity and fluidity of caste relations.

Historical examples of mobility in the Indian Caste System among Hindus have been researched. There is also precedent of certain *Shudra* families within the temples of the Shrivaishava sect in South India elevating their caste.

FOREIGN RULE IN INDIA AND CASTE SYSTEM

The caste system was first exposed to the modern Western world during the Portuguese occupation and rule of sections of India. The word 'caste' in this context is derived from the Portuguese, 'casta'. Later, other European empires, including the British, occupied parts of the subcontinent.

The earliest use of caste as a basis for interpreting social and demographic data arose from British officials' concern to stamp out female infanticide. Later, the use of caste to classify the population formed a basis for British attempts at social engineering. According to certain British laws (such as the Criminal Tribes Act of 1871), many castes and tribes were described as habitually criminal and adult male members of such groups forced to report weekly to the local police. The caste-based classification (moneylending, agricultural or martial) was also used for other purposes such as legislation controlling land transfers, the grant of proprietary rights, the regulation of rents, recruitment to the armed forces etc. British anthropologist Herbert Risley's *The Tribes and Castes of Bengal*, published in 1892, was one of the first works on the caste system in India written by a Western scholar.

The earliest forms of classification in the British censuses of India (1865, 1872 and 1881) were based on the varna system, with the population being divided into Brahmins, *Kshatriyas*, *Vaishyas* and *Shudras*. Denzil Ibbetson, in his introduction to the 1881 census of the Punjab, argued that the Indian caste system was more of a social than a religious institution, and that conversion from Hinduism to Islam had not necessarily the slightest effect upon caste. He stated that the *varnas* had "no present significance". The 1891 census was based primarily on castes as occupational guilds instead of the *varnas*.

Some scholars state that the caste system was broken up greatly during British Raj in India. However, some other historians suggest that the impact of British reforms has been greatly exaggerated.

Initially, the British strengthened the caste system. They gave the Brahmins back special privileges the Muslim rulers had taken away. During the initial days of British East India Company's rules, caste privileges and customs were encouraged in the Bengal Army. But, British law courts disagreed with the discrimination against the lower castes. Many believe that the lack of British respect for sepoys' caste traditions was one of the reasons behind the Indian Rebellion of 1857.

During British rule, the reservation of seats for the "Depressed Classes" was incorporated into the Government of India Act 1935, which went into force in 1937. The Act brought the term "Scheduled castes" into use, which was later clarified in The Government of India (Scheduled Castes) Order, 1936 which contained a list of scheduled castes.

British Census Officers determined caste hierarchy based on the principle, e.g. someone who accepts food and water from another person but the other person does not reciprocate the same way, then the other person is superior to the former. It was contested at many places (a notable example is that the Koris of UP who said they won't accept water from Brahmins, and so should be placed higher than them). Because it was met with rampant controversies, arbitration was very common during those days. The most notable arbitration stories are:

1. Caste status of Bhumihar
2. Caste status of Kayastha
3. Caste status of Kurmi
4. Caste status of Yadav

It raised more questions than it answered and subsequent census records varied radically, making it free for all, after some time.

PROMINENT GROUPS OF CASTE

According to the 1891 census data, the major caste groups in India were following (listed in the order of population):

Caste-group	Example	Population %
Cultivators	Kurmi, Mali, Lodha	20%
Village Menials	Chamar, Dosadh, Dom	13%
Military	Jat,Rajput, Maratha	12%
Artisans	Lohar, Sunar, Julaha	12%
Pastoral	Ahir, Gadaria, Dhangar	7%
Forest tribes	Santhal, Gond, Bhil	7%
Professionals	Nambudri, Bhat, Kayasth	6%
Services	Nai, Dhobi, Kandoi	6%
Merchants	Agrawal, Khatri, Balija, Barnwal	5%
Labourers	Musahar, Bagdi, Bawari	3%
Fishers	Kahar, Mallah	3%
Other professionals	Vaidya, Mirasi, Bhand	2%
Vagrants	Waddar, Nat, Beldar	1%

Indians have not been able to unravel the mystery that is Hinduism. It stands like a colossus, ageless and deathless, not only withstanding every onslaught, but getting fresh props as years pass. The most important and durable institution created by Hinduism — the third largest religion in the world — is the caste system: a four-fold division of Hindu society founded on ethnicity and arranged on the basis of ascending order of reverence and descending degree of contempt.

This hierarchical caste system — a primitive but ingenious Aryan invention — is a fantastic institution if taken seriously as anything other than a technique of oppression.

Rewarded or punished by rebirth in a caste level that fits its deeds and misdeeds in a previous life, the individual soul supposedly endeavors to progress in holiness up the stairs of the caste ladder toward the godhead. The Brahmin, belonging to the ritually purest and highest caste group, stands at the apex of this pyramid of spiritual ascent. The castes are listed below in descending degrees of contempt:

The Brahmin:	5% of the Hindu population
Kshatriya:	4% of the Hindu population
Vaishya:	2% of the Hindu population
Shudra:	45% of the Hindu population

This is the Hindu Pyramid. The fact that the vast majority of the population is at the bottom is a sure sign that it serves to legitimize the rule of the few over the many.

A Hindu's caste is decided on the basis of his birth. Each caste group is divided on the basis of its profession — fixed and permanent -reserving the intellectual pursuits to the Brahmin. Though forming just about five per cent of the total Indian population, Brahmins are the most powerful caste group in India, without whom the country cannot think or act. Brahmins control everything not only as "intellectual" leaders but also as political and Government leaders.

The ruling class of India consists principally of the Brahmins, described as the "*bhoodesatvas*" (Gods of the earth). Dr. Ambedkar says:

"That the Brahmins are a governing class is hardly open to question. There are two tests one could apply. First is the sentiment of the people, and second is the control of the administration. I am sure there cannot be a better and more decisive test than these two. As to the first, there cannot be any doubt. Taking the attitude of the people, the person of the Brahmin is sacred.

Today's India of exploitation and misery cannot think without the Brahmin, it cannot live without the Brahmin. They have a stranglehold on the life of this country. The entire "sacred scriptures", the *Vedas*, the *Upanishads*, the two *Puranas*, the *Bhagavad Gita*, the *Manu Smirti*, are mostly their creations. As the priestly class manning the millions of temples that dot the length and breadth of India, they are the custodians of God. No, its very creators. Therefore, Hindus consider the Brahmin as superior to God.

While the Brahmin stands at the apex of this caste pyramid, the *Kshatriya* (warrior), Vaishya (trader) — together forming a negligible percentage of the Indian population — also control enormous wealth. These three top caste groups are called *dwijas* (twice-born), and to distinguish them from the *Shudras* (once-born), they have the sacred thread. But it is the fourth group, the "*Shudras*", who form the bulk (about 45%) of the Indian population, divided into hundreds of castes and sub-castes. Being a heterogeneous group, it embraces the most powerful land-owning community at the top and other service castes — each alloted a particular duty: barbers, fishermen, shepherds, carpenters and scores of such professions that are necessary to run a village. As India is essentially a land of villages, these caste and subcaste groups are faithfully following their predestined caste profession. There may be occasional rumblings but because of the powerful Hindu religion which has mesmerized the whole country, for the most part, everybody does his duty without a murmur. The high caste Hindus who own the property and retain most privileges are able to get the work done by the low castes with hardly any violence such as occurs from time to time in South Africa and elsewhere. They do this by replacing violence by an ideology, which is the other word for Hinduism. If Fascists, racists, capitalists, and dictators have to use violence to subjugate the ruled, Hindus use the magic mantra of Hinduism with stunning effect. Hinduism is such a primitive and powerful ideology that it has made the slaves enjoy their slavery.

So far we have only touched the Hindus coming under the four-fold division. But the Untouchables do not come under this four-tier caste system and therefore they are said to be outside the caste-fold.

At the time of its devising, the Aryans did not admit the original black inhabitants of India into their caste system, or, in other words, into Hinduism. Unlike the Christians, the Aryans did not want these people to enter their religion. Equally, the original peoples refused to join the Hindu caste system, though at one point offered entry to the *Shudras* caste by the Hindus in an attempt to end the 3,000 year hostility between the invading and dominated groups.

Hindu scriptures condemned the original inhabitants of India to be Untouchables (meaning, among other things, enemies), to be kept outside of their system and maintained as slaves. No matter how poorly the upper castes may treat their own *Shudras*, the bottom layer of their caste system, it is important to remember that the Black Untouchables are neither *Shudras* nor Hindus as defined by Hindu scripture.

It was the English who invented the suffix "caste", mistakenly applying it to all populations in India, Untouchables included. By so doing, they and the orientalist scholars mistakenly categorized all Indian peoples (other than the religious minorities) as Hindus, (a term invented in fact by the Muslims in the period in which they ruled India.) In reality, the Hindus, consisting of the four castes, comprise a small minority of the population, while the religious minorities and those populations regarded as outside the caste system — the Scheduled Castes (Dalit), Scheduled Tribes (tribals) and Backward Castes — are very large in number.

The error of the English, whether it was or wasn't an intentional tactic to exert control over the whole of India through giving dominance to a minority population, proved advantageous to the Hindus. In order to try to maintain their benefits as a dominant population after the British departed, the Hindus, despite the prohibition of their own scriptures, launched a massive drive to try to "Hinduize" the Untouchables and other out-castes, referring to the Untouchables as *Shudras*, ie. as within the fourth tier of the Hindus caste system, and therefore, Hindus.

The advantages to the Hindus of winning the numbers game and appearing to be the majority population are clear as a majority in a democracy, their preponderance in the various institutions of power is unquestioned; they can reserve unwarranted power over the minorities and frighten them into acquiescence. By convincing the Black Untouchables that they are Shudras, ie. Hindus, they count on them as a "vote bank". Furthermore, they use them as a social counterforce to subjugate the Muslims, Christians, Sikhs and Buddhists. Today it is the Backward Castes and Scheduled Castes who are used to attack and kill the Muslims. These SCs and BCs are quite unaware that their attacks on Muslims and Sikhs only strengthen the Upper Castes, who have to keep the flame of communalism alive and divert the minds of SCs and BCs from fighting for their own rights and dignities. It is in the interest of the Upper Castes to encourage these "communal riots"; it is the only way to keep their monopoly power over the state and society.

The effort to Hinduize the Black Untouchables has the additional intention of seeing that they do not turn to Islam or Christianity, as they have in fact been doing in large numbers, arguing: "Why should a *Harijan* remains a Hindu and suffer all kinds of humiliation if he can easily get respect and recognition by embracing Islam or some other religion?" A Christian or a Muslim can draw water from a well, but if an Untouchable does the same he is either hounded out or lynched. A massive defection of Untouchables from the Hindu ideology into the shelter of Islam as in Tamil Nadu threatens the Hindu power structure.

The assimilation of Untouchables into the bottom tiers of the Hindu caste system has yet another asset for the Brahminical and higher castes: the Hindu religion provides an effective ideology for the suppression of resistance to injustice, having as a central tenet of its propaganda the idea that those in the lower castes are poor and suffering because of their misdeeds in the previous birth. And accordingly, as their sufferings are of their own making, and in fact reflect the working out of some inexorable justice, the higher castes are absolved of any responsibility for their condition, and need do nothing to help them even though these ruling castes control the power and resources of the country.

How has this Hindu propaganda affected the Untouchables? Like any victims of a concentrated and pervasive propaganda, they are influenced to believe they are *Shudras*, to desire to be *Shudras*, even though the Hindu scriptures tell them that they are outside the caste system. The incentive to "reclassify" themselves as *Shudras* is great, given their persecution as Untouchables. Those without a name, fame, identity and religion of their own become an easy prey for disintegration and "assimilation" — meaning enslavement under the label of absorption or "integration". They seek a recognized name to cover their "shame".

For the most part, their position remains ambiguous. Whether seeing themselves as Untouchables or as *Shudras*, they are under the spell of Hinduism. But as Untouchables, they cannot worship Hindu Gods and cannot touch Hindu scriptures. Even in matters of words they are not allowed free choice. They should not use decent, cultured language. They cannot keep decent names for themselves. They are persecuted daily — killed, kicked, burnt, and raped because they are not Hindus. Yet, though they are outside the caste system and outside Hindu religion, they form the foundation of the Hindu human pyramid. They carry the weight of the entire Hindu population. The ideology of Hinduism saps their resistance, whether including them as *shudras* or excluding yet defining and dominating them as a *varnas*, ie. those outside of the caste system.

Such a hierarchical caste pyramid is something unique, unparalleled in the whole world. Muslims may be divided into Shias and Sunnis, Christians into Catholics and Protestants and other sects, but one sect does not claim superiority over the other. But in Hindu India, it is a graded inequality. The Untouchable is servile, heinous, lowest of the low, condemned to the meanest professions such as scavenging, garbage cleaning, sweeping, and removing dead cattle, shoe-making and generally landless agricultural labour. The Hindu religion prohibits an Untouchable from owning land. Christianity, Islam or other religions have only "classes", which are mobile. A rich person can become poor and vice versa. But in Hindu India, a Brahmin cannot become a *Shudra* and a *Shudra* cannot become an Brahmin. There is neither a promotion nor demotion under Hinduism. If under Christianity and Islam, society is mobile, under Hinduism, society is static, fixed. Caste is decided on the basis of birth, not merit, scholarship or bank balance.

DALITS AND THEIR ORIGIN

The last two hundred years have seen the emergence of a new consciousness and a new identity among the 200 million people who have been considered "outcaste" or "untouchables". Today they call themselves *Dalit,* a new name they have coined for themselves, and demand aggressively their share in the shaping of the destiny of the nation. It is not a mere name or title, in fact it has become an expression of hope and identity.

The term *Dalit* in Sanskrit is derived from the root *dal* which means to split, break, crack and so on. When used as an adjective, it means split, broken, burst, destroyed, crushed. It is said that Jyotiba Phule(1827-1890), the founder of the Satyashodhak Samaj, a non Brahmin movement in Maharashtra, a social reformer and revolutionary, used this term to describe the outcastes and untouchables as the oppressed and broken victims of the Indian caste-ridden society.

The Dalits of today were known as "untouchables" and "outcaste" for centuries. These degrading terms were changed by the British administration into "Depressed Classes" in 1919. Gandhiji called them Harijans (people of God), his favourite term to be used in the place of Untouchable. Ambedkar did not accept Gandhi's term. He demanded a separate electorate for the "Depressed Classes", and proposed the term "Protestant Hindus". In 1935, the British government defined them as the "Scheduled Castes." It was during the 1970s that the followers of the Dalit Panther Movement of Maharashtra gave currency to the term *Dalit*. Today the term is used frequently and has become popular among the Dalit people of various religions and protest movements.

The origin of the Dalit goes back to 1500 BC. Studies about their origin tell us that they were a people without a name and without a place in the social organisation of the time. They were not only ostracised from the mainstream society and relegated to the status of "untouchables" but were also subjected to various forms of exploitation and oppression which have always been supported by religion directly or indirectly.

According to an Indian historian, S.K. Chatterjee, the original Indians were the *Shudras* (the serving caste people) today's Dalit. These were the pre-Aryan people who lived for thousands of years on the Indian soil. The Aryans are said to have come into India around 1500 BC and made the local people their servants and slaves. The Dalits are the descendants of the earliest settlers of India. Because of the long history of oppression, they have lost their self-identity as full human beings.

There is also other category of people who don't come under any of these above caste groups, since they are not considered as human beings. They are called the "the Outcaste or the "Untouchables," or the Unseeables. There are hundreds of codes of conduct written for them. Now these people call themselves as ' Dalit.' The word ' Dalit' means 'broken, torn, scattered and crushed.' M.Gandhi called them as ' Harijans' which means God's Children. But the word ' Harijans' does not describe their condition adequately. Therefore, the Outcaste preferred to call themselves as ' Dalit.' The word ' Dalit' is an expression of hope to recover their self-identity.

As we have already seen, Dalit means 'broken, scattered and oppressed'. So the Dalits are the broken and scattered people, the oppressed masses. This implies that they were of one community before they were broken; they were together before they were scattered; they were free people before they were oppressed. It also implies that there must have been an agent and an instrument by whom and by which this free people were subjugated and oppressed. So the starting point of Dalit history is the moment when this 'breaking', 'scattering' and 'oppression' of the Dalit began, when exactly the Dalit began to be treated as degraded human beings and when exactly the Dalit lost their identity. To understand the Dalit as an indigenous people, we need to go to their historical roots.

ARCHAEOLOGICAL AND LITERARY EVIDENCES

ARCHAEOLOGICAL EVIDENCE

Prehistoric India was inhabited first by the Negritos. The second group that migrated in was the Australoids. The Santals and Bhils belong to the Australoids. The third group that inhabited India was the Mongoloid family. To the present time the Mongoloids have maintained their distinct cultural, racial and religious identities.

The fourth and largest group that inhabited ancient India was the Dravidian. Most scholars agree that the Dravidians came into India from the Eastern Mediterranean in the third millennium B.C. By 1400 B.C., the Dravidian civilization in India extended across the entire land.

Munshi says: "The Early Dravidians, who arrived in India prior to 2000 B.C., possessed a highly developed material culture as would appear from their early speech forms and the findings in Mohenjodaro, Harappa and Lothal". Goetz speaks of the Indus Valley Civilization as ranging from Lothal to Mohenjodaro and from 3000 to 1400 B.C., and having cultural connections with Sumer, the earliest known cradle of human civilisation.

The Indo-Aryans in the 2nd millennium B.C. migrated from their homeland of Eranvej (the present Russian Turkestan) via Afghanistan into India. Thus the Aryans moved eastwards, fighting the indigenous Dravidians whom they exterminated or enslaved. They overran the open country, stormed the fortified towns (pur) of the Indus Valley and slowly migrated eastwards, conquering the whole of Northern India around 1400-1000 B.C.

Mishra, the archaeologist endorses this view. This coincides with the records of Wheeler, the original authority on the Indus Valley civilisation. These conquests are described in numerous verses of the Rig Veda.

In the Rig Veda, the natives are described as dark-skinned, snub-nosed enemies of alien language and religion. Marshall and Cunningham who did the original archaeological excavation on Indus civilisation, Yuria Knorozov who did the deciphering of the Indus pictographic writings and authorities such as Madho Sarup Vats, Dikshit, N.C. Majumdar, Rapson, Wheeler, R.D. Banerjee, B.B. Lal point to the fact that the native black Dravidians were largely exterminated by the light-coloured Aryan invaders, their 'Puram' (meaning fort or town) civilisation was destroyed and those who were not killed were made slaves.

When the Aryans began to spread eastward and southward from Punjab, they spread too thin. Therefore the policy of total annihilation of the Dasyus was found unnecessary as well as impossible. Instead the Dravidians were made domestic and village slaves. In earlier civilisations, slavery or extermination were the only two methods used by most of the conquering races.

Therefore the Dasyus (slaves, now known to us as the Scheduled caste) of the Rig Veda were the Dravidians living north of the Vindhya Satpura range and now enslaved by the invading Aryans. The distinguished indologist Basham says: "In the reduction to bondage of the many dasas captured in the battle, we find the origin of Indian slavery."

LITERARY EVIDENCE

Here are a few of the earliest literary sources available to us. In all these sources, we find the Dalit, Das, Chandala, Avarna, Panchama were reduced by their oppressors to a non-human level, with no identity or dignity.

1. *Rig Veda:* (1500-1000 B.C.) The earliest available literary source is the Rig veda. Its Purusa sukta hymn talks about the origin of the four *Varnas*, Brahmanas, Kshatriyas, Vaishyas and Shudras. The Dalits find no place in it under this name: they are referred as Avarna, Dasa and Dasyus. (6th and 10th Mandala)
2. *Upanishads:* (800 - 600 B.C) By the time the Upanishad texts came into existence, the problem of the Dalit was becoming deeper and clearer. For example, the famous Chandogys Upanishad not only refers to the first three upper castes, but also compares Chandala (Outcaste) with a dog and a swine. (Ref. Chandogya Upanishad. Khanda 10, verse 7)
3. *Ramayana:* In the time of Lord Rama's rule, only the upper three castes were allowed to do 'tapasya' (penance and meditation). Now it so happen that one of low caste, a Shudra, undertook penance in order to attain divinity (dignity). As soon as Lord Rama heard this, he killed the Shudra for such presumption. If this happened to a Shudra, we can imagine what would have happend to a Dalit, so much lower in status.
4. *Mahabharata:* It describes the degraded state of the Dalit. It is the story of Ekalabya, an indigenous boy, who has to lose the thumb of his right hand because he has learnt archery and has come to be no less skilled than Arjuna in this art.

The Dalits today were addressed by different names:

Late 19th century to 1930s - 'Outcastes' - 'Depressed Castes' - 'Exterior Castes'

- *1917:* 'Adi-Dravida/Adi-Karnataka/Adi-Andhra' originally used by Untouchables to identify themselves.
- *1933:* 'Harijan' 'Harijan', literally mean people of God, used by Gandhi ji to identify Untouchables.
- *1936:* Scheduled Castes by the Britishers.
- *1970s:* 'Dalit' used by Dalit to identify themselves.

Government of India identified and located 450 Scheduled Castes and 45 unlisted sub-groups in 1963-64.

4

Religious Aspects of Dalits

Hinduism is not the religion of the Dalit. To understand the religion of the Dalit, we must understand the religion of Mohenjodaro. They had and have to this day the strong concept of a personal transcendent creator God. However their popular religion gradually degenerated to the worship of malevolent spirits and demigods. They also worshipped the spirits and Mother-goddess. They believed in sorcery. The Aryans worshipped the impersonal phenomena of nature, viz., Prithvi, Varuna, Indra and the Sun. Hermann Goetz states that the Dravidian Shiva and Parvati link up with the cult of the moon god and the 'Lady of the Mountain' at Ur. K.M.Munshi says that Shiva, the Dravidian father god with his bull, was known to Harappan civilization as the lord of creation and Ma, the mother of goddess of the Mediterranean people with lion as her mount, was worshipped in many parts of Asia, though unknown to Vedic Aryans. The Sumerian moon god, Nannar, is the Sivan of the Dravidians and the multi-armed Ishtar of Ur with her lion is the Kali of the Dravidians. Scholars are now finding that the Sivan of the Dravidians is none other than Adam of the first man.

The trantric forms of worship, human sacrifice, walking on fire, are of Dravidian origin. Besides the above, the Dasyus worshipped demi-gods, demons, trees, animals, etc. The Chamars of northern India, to this day worship as gods, Saliya, Purbi, and as demons Vetal, Baital, Churail, Gayal,

Paret, Pisach, Masau, Dund etc. The Untouchables of South Bihar have as their gods Surjahi, Barachi Vir, Basumit, Masana and Kunwar. Dr. Vidhyarti, the famous anthropologist studying the religion of untouchables, says they follow their own native festivals of Karam puja, Sohrai, Phagua Kadleta, Nawan, Jitaya, Chhat, etc. It must be noted that all these are etymologically Dravidi gods and Dravidi words.

According to the Smritis, the Untouchable is prohibited from hearing any Sanskrit scriptures, much less reading or writing them. Molten lead must be poured into his ears if he does - decreed Manu. Basham, the great historian, records, "It was with the conscious motive of preserving ritual and religious purity that all contact with the untouchables was avoided." That is why, the Dalits were not allowed into any temple in India for the last 3000 years. The reason was clear racial and religious distinctives. The recent opening of some Hindu temples for the Scheduled Castes (Dalit) is purely a political action to get the votes of the Dalit. Such move was vehemently opposed by honest Hindu saints like Puri Shankaracharya who are bold enough to tell the truth.

The Vedic Aryans and the Dasyu slaves had distinct religions of their own. There was no chance of mixing the two faiths, at any time of history, because of the most stringent rules of untouchability and isolation. To put it more exactly, it was out of the greatest concern to keep the two faiths separate, that untouchability and isolation were stringently maintained. Therefore, to call a person as Hindu Scheduled Caste is absurd and irrelevant.

LIBERATION IN CONTEMPORARY INDIA

Siddhartha, when under the pipal tree in Gaya became Buddha, he started profound upheavals in India with his new faith. Buddhhism attracted many untouchables because it practised no caste and no untouchability. The Buddhists rejected the authority of the Vedas and condemned blood sacrifice. The egalitarian outlook was viewed with great alarm by the Brahminical writings of the time - Yuga Purana, Mahabharata, Patanjali Bhasya, Bana, Manu and others. In spite of the

Brahminic elimination of the Buddhism from India, the aspiration of the Scheduled Castes for an egalitarian faith did not end. The Neo Buddhist movement of today, when started from Nagpur in 1956 with Dr.Ambedkar and five lakhs of his followers becoming Buddhist must be understood in the light of this background. The quest continues equally into other egalitarian faiths like Kabir Panth, Nanak Panth, etc. Kabir made a great impact on the religious pursuit of the untouchables.

Kabir, while powerfully appealing to the untouchables, equally influenced Sur Das, Tulsi Das and Guru Nanak. The untouchables as a result joined the Kabir Panth and Nanak Panth in great numbers. Another significant impact of the monotheistic bhakti movement among the untouchables was initiated by Jagjivan Das of Lucknow, who was himself initiated by a Fakir. The movement, Satnami, as it was later called, euphorised monotheism with the abolition of all symbolism and castes, though later symbols and castes made partial re-entry. The above monotheistic pietistic egalitarian faiths in a personal God and brotherhood of classless believers are close to the Christian faith.

Thus the untouchable slaves in India, who are non-Aryan by race and religion have in the past 2500 years, voluntarily chosen several egalitarian faiths, that gave them religious and social satisfaction.

The 'Untouchables' of India, consisting of several hundred caste groups, taken together form some 15 per cent of the total Indian population. Victims of 'upper'-caste Hindu persecution in a centuries-old system that has sought to legitimize their oppression by granting it religious sanction, the 'Untouchables' are today growing increasingly assertive, demanding their rights and articulating their protest against 'upper'-caste Hindu hegemony through different channels. Because the subordination of the 'Untouchables', reducing them to the status of non-humans or even worse, has been given religious sanction in the Hindu scriptures, one of the most important means that the 'Untouchables' themselves have historically resorted to in protest against the Brahminical system in their quest for equality and self-respect has been conversion to other religions.

In post-1947 India, conversion of 'Untouchable' people to various religions carried on a pace, as a new generation of educated 'Untouchables' grew increasingly resentful of the subordiantion that they were subjected to. No longer willing to be treated as untouchable, as passive victims of Hinduism, they sought to be articulate a new identity for themselves. Thus emerged the consciousness of being 'Dalit', or 'oppressed', a term that was sought to be given a militant import, inspired by the example of the Black Panthers in the United States. Leading the militant and resoultely anti-Brahminical Dalit struggle till his death in 1956 was the charismatic barrister and brilliant scholar, Dr Bhimrao Ramji Ambedkar, known to his followers as Babasaheb. Ambedkar insisted that the Dalit, being considered outcastes and hence outside the caste system, were not Hindus. Rather, they were a seperate people whom the Brahimins had sought to Hindunise in order to incomposate them into the caste system as slaves. The Hindu religion, he argued, was based, at root, on the caste system, legitimising the cruel oppression of the Dalit. Hence, if the Dalit were to free themselves from the shackles of caste oppression, there was no way out for them but to convert to a non-Hindu religion.

Ambedkar's firm conviction of the need for Dalit conversion developed gradually. At first, he pinned his hopes on the efforts of 'upper'-caste. Hindu reformers, believing that this might open new spaces to the Dalit which traditional Hinduism had denied them. Soon, however, he seems to have been disillusioned by the reformists, going so far as to accuse M.K. Gandhi of being 'the greatest enemy of the Untouchables'. In 1935, at a public meeting, he declared, 'I was born a Hindu, although this was not in my power. But I can certainly choose not to die a Hindu'. From then on, Ambedkar devoted himself to the study of various religions, including Islam, Christianity Sikhism and Buddhism, finally converting to Buddhism along with 300,000 of his followers in a mass conversion ceremony at Nagpur in 1956. One month later he died under mysterious circumstances, but the Buddhist conversion movement that he inaugurated still continues in India, with considerable numbers of Dalit having embraced the faith in various parts of the country in recent years, following their master's footsteps in a search for social liberation and a new identity.

HINDU DALITS

The large majority of the Dalit are Hindus, although some in Maharashtra have converted to Neo-Buddhism. In Pakistan, a predominantly Muslim nation, more than 60% of the 1.4 million Hindu minorities are Dalit.

Forming almost a fifth of the Indian population, the Scheduled Castes or the Dalit, a conglomeration of numerous caste groups considered as ritually 'polluting', and therefore 'untouchable', by caste Hindus, are victims of the most sternly hierarchical social order that human beings have ever devised. Buttressed by religious sanction, the caste system consigned the Dalit to subhuman status, relegating them to the bottom of the social order as slaves or worse. Since the social and economic oppression of the Dalit has been so closely intertwined with the Hindu religion, over the centuries many Dalits have sought to escape from the shackles of the caste system by converting to other religions, particularly to Islam, Buddhism, Christianity and Sikhism.

Recent decades have witnessed a remarkable upsurge in radical Dalit assertiveness. The Dalit struggle has been waged simultaneously on various fronts. Large numbers of Dalit have converted to Buddhism in the last half century, following in the footsteps of undoubtedly the most charismatic modern-day Dalit leader, Dr Bhimrao Ramji Ambedkar, who, along with 300,000 of his followers, abandoned Hinduism for Buddhism at a mass conversion ceremony held at the town of Nagpur in 1956. On the economic front a new generation of Dalit has emerged, beneficiaries of the spread of modern education and jobs reserved specially for them in various government undertakings and departments. On the political front, from being treated as a passive vote-bank of the Congress Party the Dalit are today experimenting with political parties of their own. Alongside this is a growing interest in developing alternative Dalit-centred literature and culture that champion what are seen as the traditional Dalit values of harmony and egalitarianism, placed in sharp opposition to the hierarchy and inequality that are so central to Brahminism.

This resurgence of Dalit awareness and consciousness is an all-Indian phenomenon, albeit marked by regional and caste-specific differences. Its influence has not been limited to those defined according to the law as Scheduled Castes, though. Rather, the Dalit struggle for human rights has had a profound impact on other communities as well, most particularly the large category of castes known collectively as the Other Backward Classes (OBCs), who form over half the Indian population, as well as the Christians and Muslims, most of whom share, in terms of social and economic background, much in common with the Dalit.

THE DALIT MUSLIMS

Many Indian Muslims are descendants of 'untouchable', 'low'-caste converts and of indigenous peoples whose ancestors were not considered part of the Hindu fourfold social order, with only a small minority tracing their origins to Arab, Iranian and Central Asian settlers and invaders. Although the Qur'an is fiercely egalitarian in its social ethics, insisting on a radical equality of all believers, Indian Muslim society is characterized by numerous caste-like features, consisting of several caste-like groups *(Jatis, biraderis)*. Muslims who claim foreign descent, such as the Sayyeds, Shaikhs, Mughals and Pathans, claim a superior status for themselves as *ashraf* or 'noble'. Descendants of indigenous converts are, on the other hand, commonly referred to contemptuously as *ajlaf,* or 'base' or 'lowly'. In the centuries of Muslim rule in India, the *ashraf* played a key role in the state administration, as advisors, ministers, governors, army officials and estate managers, as well as Sufis and *'ulama*. On the other hand, despite their conversion to Islam, the social and economic conditions of the mass of the *ajlaf* Muslims hardly changed, and they remained largely tied to their traditional occupations as artisans, peasants and labourers.

As among the Hindus, the various *Jatis* among the *ajlaf* Muslims maintain a strong sense of *Jati* identity. The emergence of democratic politics is, however, bringing about a radical change in the manner in which this sense of identity is articulated. Aware of the importance of numbers in acquiring political power and the economic benefits that accrue from it, the Dalit movement has sought to establish a wider sense of Dalit identity that transcends inter-caste and inter-religious divisions and differences among the 'lower'-caste majority. This wider Dalit identity does not seek to deny individual *Jati* identities. Rather, it takes them into account but seeks to subsume them within the wider collective Dalit identity based on a common history of suffering as well as common racial origins as indigenous people. This seems to have been a crucial factor in the emergence of a specific 'Dalit Muslim' identity.

The issue of linking religious affiliation to Scheduled-Caste status is a long and complex one, in which issues of power and communal politics seem to be inextricably involved. Special facilities for the benefit of the Dalit owe their origin to the 1935 Government of India Act, according to which a list or schedule was drawn up containing the names of castes considered to be low in the social hierarchy for whom special facilities were extended in order to partially compensate them for centuries of deprivation and to enable them to advance economically and educationally Many of these castes had members who claimed different religious affiliations, not all of them being Hindu. Several Scheduled Castes, such as the Banjaras, Dhobis, Nats, Lalbegis, Halalkhors, Jogis, Pasis, Mochis, Kahtiks, Julahas, Darzis and the Rangrezes, consisted of both Hindus and Muslims. However, in 1950 a Presidential Order was passed amending Article 341 of the Indian Constitution, which enables the President of India to notify a particular caste as Scheduled Caste. According to the amended law only those Dalit who claimed to be Hindus could be considered members of a Scheduled Caste and hence eligible for the special benefits that such castes enjoy. Furthermore, a non-Hindu Dalit would be considered for such benefits only if he or she converted to Hinduism or declared himself or herself to be a Hindu, this itself being a violation of Article 25(1) of the Indian Constitution, which lays down the right to the free practice of religion. With one stroke of the pen, millions of Muslim, Christian, Sikh and Buddhist Dalit were struck off the Scheduled-Caste list. Increasing Hindu numbers and preventing Dalit conversions to non-Hindu religions seem to be among the probable reasons behind the amendment. Owing to massive struggles launched by Dalit Sikhs and Dalit Buddhists, the law was later amended to allow for Scheduled-Caste status to be extended to Dalit professing Sikhism (in 1956) and, later, Buddhism (in 1990). The two other major Dalit groups, the 'Dalit Muslims' and the 'Dalit Christians', are still denied the rights available to other Dalit. While various Christian groups have been prominent in protesting against this discrimination, it is only recently that the 'Dalit Muslims' have also begun to mobilize to fight for what they see as the rights that have been denied to them by law, branding this as a gross violation of the secular character of the Indian Constitution.

Besides being considered 'anti-secular', the law as it stands today is condemned as a gross violation of human rights. Furthermore, it is seen as a ploy to keep the more than 100 million 'Dalit Muslims' in perpetual thraldom, a conspiracy in which both the Hindu and the Muslim 'upper'-caste elite are seen as being involved. Extending Scheduled-Caste status to 'Dalit Muslims' is an urgent necessity and not simply to bring the law in line with the spirit and explicit commands of the Indian Constitution. Because they have been denied Scheduled-Caste status and the benefits that accrue from such status, the 'Dalit Muslims' are said to lag far behind the Hindu Dalit, who have been able to make considerable progress in all fields because of the special facilities that the state has provided for them.

Muslim society in India can also be separated into several caste-like groups. Descendants of indigenous lower-caste converts are discriminated against by "noble" or "ashraf" Muslims who can trace their descent to Arab, Iranian, or Central-Asian ancestors. There are several groups in India working to emancipate them from upper-caste Muslim discrimination. The Dalit Muslims are referred to by the Ashraf and Ajlaf Muslims as *Arzal* or "ritually degraded". They were first recorded in the 1901 census as those "with whom no other Mohammedan would associate, and who are forbidden to enter the mosque or to use the public burial ground. They are relegated to "menial" professions such as scavenging and carrying night soil. Babasaheb Ambedkar, a renowned Dalit activist and the framer of the Constitution of India, wrote about the Dalit Muslims and was extremely critical of their mistreatment by upper-caste Muslims quoting that "Within these groups there are castes with social precedence of exactly the same nature as one finds among the Hindus".

In Pakistan, there are estimated to be 6.8 million Mayazurs (bonded labourers) in Punjab and another 7.5 million in Sindh. Although the Pakistani Supreme Court has ruled bonded labour unconstitutional and the National Assembly has passed laws prohibiting it, these laws remain largely unenforced due to the influence of large landlords. Furthermore, the AIBMM is striving to achieve the SC status for India's Dalit Muslims. The lowest of among the Muslim communities is a "Muhajir". They are mainly assigned the position of a labourer and looked down upon by the ashraf.

THE CHANGING DISCOURSE OF COMMUNITY IDENTITY

Deconstructing the notion of Muslims as a homogenous bloc, it brings to the fore the existence of caste distinctions among the Indian Muslims, which it sees as one of the primary and defining features of Indian Muslim society in articulating a separate 'Dalit Muslim' identity it finds itself at odds with the traditional, largely 'high'-caste, Muslim leadership, which, in seeking to speak for all Muslims.

Islam as having historically played a key role in the emancipation of the Dalit, a role which was gradually watered down over time. Islam spread in India principally through the agency of the Sufis whose teachings of love, brotherhood and social equality attracted many Dalit to the new faith, shackled as they were by the chains of the caste system and the Brahminical religion. Seeing the early Muslims eating from the same dish and praying together in the same mosque, the Dalit entered the Muslim fold in droves.

It was not by the sword, but through the love and compassion that the Sufis exhibited in their behaviour towards the poor, principally the Dalit, that large numbers of Hindus converted to Islam. With the establishment of Muslim political power in various parts of India, however, this radical egalitarianism of the early Sufis gave way to hierarchical forms of religious expression. 'High'-caste Hindus, in order to save their property or to secure high positions in Muslim-ruled territories, converted to Islam, bringing with them notions of caste superiority that are foreign to pristine Islam. Doctrines were developed that sought to legitimize caste inequalities by seeking Qur'anic sanction for them. Gradually the 'spirit of Islam' was replaced by the 'rituals of Islam'.

One of the crucial tasks before the 'Dalit Muslims' is to rescue Islam from the clutches of those who claim to speak in its name, the 'high'-caste Muslim leadership. Thus, he calls for a revival of 'the true spirit of Islam', which fiercely condemns all caste and racial divisions. This would entail a radical questioning of widely prevalent norms and customs and a total transformation of attitudes. The practice of untouchability which Islam roundly condemns is still observed to varying degrees by 'upper'caste Muslims, who look down upon 'lower'-caste Muslims as inherently inferior. While Islam calls for Muslims to share in the plight of their fellow believers and to work for their social emancipation, the Muslim 'upper caste feudal lords' are said to be 'deaf, dumb and blind to the suffering of backward caste Muslims'.

The ruling class among the Muslims displayed no concern for the plight of the 'Dalit Muslims', who remained tied to their traditional occupations, mired in poverty and ignorance. The only concern of the ruling-class Muslims was to perpetuate their own rule, and for this they entered into alliances with 'upper'-caste Hindus, keeping the Dalit, Hindus as well as Muslims, cruelly suppressed under their firm control. 'While they built large palaces for themselves' 'they did not establish even one primary school for the poor'. This disdain for the

Dalit was carried down right through the period of Muslim and then British rule, and continues to this day. The present-day Muslim 'high'-caste leadership is playing the 'minority card' and practising the politics of 'minority-ism' in order to garner power for themselves while claiming to speak on behalf of all Muslims, the vast majority of whom are Dalit.

They refuse to recognize the acute problem of caste within the community because 'they do not want to lose their *jagirdari* (power and privileges)'. Yet they cling to their caste titles, such as 'Sayyed', 'Shaikh' and 'Khan', simply to 'produce an impression of supremacy and to demoralize the backward caste Muslims'. In their attitudes towards the latter they are said to be acting hardly differently from how the Hindu 'upper' castes treat their own Dalit, having never shown any genuine concern for their social and economic advancement. He talks of the 'vice-like grip' that the Sayyeds, those who claim descent from the Prophet Muhammad, are said to hold the 'Dalit Muslims' in, adding that 'the Islamic concepts of equality non-discrimination and fraternity [are] a hoax in the Indian context.

The Indian Muslim community as a whole as having 'all the ingredients of the Brahminical order'. The 'upper'-caste Muslim leadership demands special privileges, such as reservations in government services, for the entire Muslim community as a whole, but this is 'harmful to the backward caste Muslims', for not only are such benefits for an entire religious community unconstitutional, they would also, if granted, benefit only the elite. The 'upper'-caste Muslim leadership thrives on championing such 'communal' 'non-issues' as the protection of the Muslim Personal Law or the Babri mosque, which have only helped militant Hindu 'upper'-caste forces, resulting in terrible violence unleashed against Muslims and communal riots in which the major victims are the Dalit, both Hindu and Muslim. By playing on such 'non-issues' they have also been able to garner vast amounts of money from Muslim countries for themselves. 'The time has now come' for the 'upper'-caste Muslims to 'stop thinking of the entire Muslim community as they have been clearly reduced to their [own] caste leadership, which they were doing from the very beginning under the pseudo-umbrella of Muslim unity'.

Given the stress that Islam places on radical social equality on the one hand, and the failure of the traditional Muslim leadership in championing the rights and interests of the Backward-Caste Muslims, on the other, call for a 'power shift' from the 'Arab-origin *ashraf* to the 'oppressed Muslims'. A new, 'Dalit Muslim' leadership is called for, for it alone is seen as able to champion the rights of the oppressed among the Muslims. Hitherto, all Muslim movements in India, having been led by 'elite' Muslims, have brought no gains to the really oppressed, in whose name these struggles were waged. Rather, they have all been undertaken with the hidden motive of advancing the interests of the elites. The Prophet Muhammad's early followers were largely poor and dispossessed people, and because he spoke out on their behalf he was fiercely opposed by the rich Qur'aish of Mecca. Islam insists on a passionate commitment to the poor. By denying the existence of caste within the Muslim community the traditional Muslim leadership is only helping to perpetuate it.

Nothing less than a *jihad,* in the form of a non-violent struggle, needs to be waged to fight to extend Scheduled-Caste status to 'Dalit Muslims', but this *jihad* is to be fought by the 'Dalit Muslims' along with non-Muslim secular and progressive forces, to which stiff opposition is expected from many 'upper'-caste Muslims as well as 'upper'-caste Hindus. The struggle would need the help of non-Muslim Dalit as well, for if the 'Dalit Muslims' gain Scheduled-Caste status they could join hands with Dalit from other religions and become one strong force, almost half the Indian population. They could, together, even capture political power, bring their interests and demands to the centre of the Indian political agenda and put an end to atrocities against them. The other Dalit need to be convinced that the inclusion of the religious clause in Article 341 is a 'powerful plot to destroy the strength of the indigenous Dalit', creating division among them on the basis of religion. It is, moreover, a clever ploy to drive a wedge between Hindus and Muslims. Hence, removal of the religion clause is seen as a necessary step both to cement a broader inter-religious Dalit unity and to bridge the divide between Muslims and Hindus.

The new Muslim leadership that envisages as being drawn primarily from among the Backward-Caste Muslims who form the vast majority of the Muslim population in India, for they alone can truly speak for their people. The 'upper'-caste leadership are left to represent their own people. Since the primary concerns of the Backward-Caste Muslims are sheer physical survival, jobs, wages and the like, this new leadership would seek to bring about a 'revolution of priorities'. Instead of taking up 'communal' issues that would further exacerbate Hindu-Muslim differences by playing into the hands of fiercely anti-Muslim Hindu zealots, which only works to further the interests of the Hindu and Muslim elites, this new leadership would focus on issues such as employment, food, housing and elementary education, issues which affect the daily lives of all poor people irrespective of religion. In this way, Hindu-Muslim antagonisms would fade away, the Dalit of all religions, the primary victims of the politics of communal hatred, would unite, and the conditions of the poor would improve.

Since the 'Dalit Muslims' share similar concerns of sheer survival with Dalit of other religions, the new Muslim leadership would seek to build bridges between the Muslim Dalit and those of other faiths. This entails a crucial redefinition of what it means to be a Muslim in India today. As caste is probably of greater significance in defining community identities than religion. All Dalit, irrespective of religion, belong to the same 'nation' *(qaum)*, he says. Mere change of religion cannot wipe away the common blood that runs in their veins. The Dalit 'nation', representing the indigenous inhabitants of India who today follow various different religions, has been fractured into various antagonistic groups, but they must be united. The first step in this direction is to remove the religious clause attached to Article 341 that seeks to divide the Dalit on the basis of religion and to prevent them from coming together on a common plank. The 'divided Dalit nation' will be united once again when all Dalit, irrespective of religion, are granted the same status as

Scheduled Castes. Hence, in order to reunify the Dalit 'nation' so that the Dalit emerge as a powerful collective force all Dalit must unite to support the demand for Scheduled Caste status for the 'Dalit Muslims' (as well, interestingly for the 'Dalit Christians', who are also denied such status).

By joining hands with Dalit of other faiths and jointly struggling to improve their living conditions the 'Dalit Muslims' would be able to join the 'national mainstream' of Indian society The 'elite' Muslims have all along had a 'vested interest' in 'maintaining exclusivism' among the Muslims, preventing them from establishing ties with others, so that they could pursue their own interests in the guise of promoting the cause of the community as a whole. It was this exclusivist mindset, he says, that led to the creation of Pakistan, which actually benefited only the Muslim elite and only further exacerbated the problems of the 'Dalit Muslims'. With a new Muslim leadership drawn from the 'Dalit Muslims' coming to the fore, the community would turn its back on the communal antagonisms of the past rooted in a tradition of exclusivism and separatism. The 'Dalit Muslims' would begin to collaborate with other Dalit, with whom they have 'a great commonality of interests', pursuing the same occupations and facing the same economic and social problems. In this way a joint struggle for social justice and inter-communal harmony can be launched for all Dalit, irrespective of religion.

A new leadership, consisting of 'Dalit Muslims' themselves, is being promoted, one that seeks to bring about a radical shift in the priorities of the community-away from what it sees as the 'symbolic' 'non-issues' that have only further exacerbated Hindu-Muslim antagonisms and served the interests of both the Hindu and Muslim elites, and towards issues that affect most intimately the sheer survival and life chances of the poorest of the poor. Demanding Scheduled-Caste status for the 'Dalit Muslims' may in itself, not be a very radical step, given the present climate of privatization in the country, where the numbers of government jobs are being sharply curtailed and public expenditure and subsidies drastically reduced. However, its wider implications are certainly more momentous in their probable consequences.

CONVERSION OF DALITS INTO ISLAM

Ambedkar's conversion marked the rebirth of Buddhism in the land of its birth, it having earlier been driven out or appropriated by an increasingly aggressive and assertive Brahminical revivalism from the fifth century CE onwards, culminating in the complete extirpation of Buddhism from India save in the remote mountainous borderlands with Tibet and Burma.

In the centuries following this, conversion to Islam seems to have been a particularly attractive option for many Dalit, and scores of them did resort to this, with numerous cases being reported right into the twentieth century, till 1947. The Partition of India in 1947, accompanied as it was by fierce Hindu-Muslim rioting, reduced the Muslims of India into a relatively powerless and insecure minority. This, coupled with growing anti-Muslim prejudice, manifesting itself most strikingly in the form of bloody anti-Muslim pogroms on an increasingly menacing scale, meant that for the Dalit conversion to Islam for social emancipation no longer remained a practical, feasible choice. Thus, accessions to Islam in post-1947 India witnessed a dramatic decline. Indeed, scores of nominally Muslim 'lower' castes in northern India actually consciously renounced their Muslim identity for fear of 'upper'-caste persecution, claiming to be Hindus instead.

Although isolated cases of Dalit conversion to Islam continued to be reported from time to time, this did not take the form of a mass movement, as in the case of conversions to Buddhism.

Further, the Indian state, which prided itself on its 'secular' foundations, itself made Dalit conversion to Islam an unviable choice by denying the special benefits that Dalit enjoyed in government services and programmes to Dalit converts to Islam. While this has put a brake on Dalit conversions to Islam, it has not had any significant impact on Dalit-Muslim unity efforts, which are increasingly emerging as an important agenda for the Dalit movement in India today. With the growing political consciousness of the

Dalit that emerges from increasing education and participation in social movements, many Dalit ideologues are now advocating Dalit-Muslim unity as an indispensable means of the overall liberation of all oppressed groups in India. Such unity does not rule out Dalit conversion to Islam, but conversion, is not indispensable to the unity project.

Conversion to a non-Hindu religion is advocated not simply for the sake of the presumed superiority of its doctrines over Hinduism, which is assumed, but, more importantly, as a means of Dalit empowerment, arming the Dalit with the power to counter their oppression by the 'upper'-caste Hindus. Conversion, therefore, is explicitly recognized as an indispensable means to a worldly purpose-the liberation of the oppressed.

SIKH DALIT

Sikhism appears to have exercised a significant liberating influence on the *Dalit* in the Punjab. The teachings of the Sikh Gurus, the religious institutions of 'sangat' and 'langar', the absence of a caste-based priesthood, and the respect for manual labour, all these were together aimed at creating a caste-free Khalsa Brotherhood. When the Singh Sabha leadership chose to assert a separate and distinct identity to underline their boundary demarcation from the Hindus – '*Hum Hindu Nahin*' – at the beginning of the 20th century, the key differentiating factor they referred to, was rejection of '*varnashram*' and purity-pollution syndrome which were central to Hinduism. The people of the untouchable castes in the region converted to Sikh religion in large numbers with a view to improve their status. Their gain was not small. However, there was a wide gap between the doctrinal principles and social practice.

The evolution of the Sikh community proceeded through a complex dynamics of interaction between religious principles, tribal cultural patterns of the dominant caste of Jats and their power interests. This resulted in the evolution of a Sikh caste hierarchy, distinct from and parallel to that of the Hindu caste system. It is important to understand the form in which casteism has continued to survive in the Sikh community and the reasons thereof. Two episodes may be of particular relevance in this context. Babasaheb Ambedkar had in 1936 seriously considered en masse conversion of the 'Depressed Classes' to Sikhism with a view to liberate them from the shackles of 'Manuvadi' caste system. It remains to be adequately probed how and why the project came to be dropped and never pursued thereafter; persuading Ambedkar to lead his people to convert to Buddhism instead, after a period of 20 years. The other relates to Sikh political struggle for constitutional recognition of the Sikh scheduled castes after the independence of India. This amounted to seeking the grant of the same constitutional status and special safeguards for the Sikh scheduled castes as were provided for the Hindu scheduled castes.

After the annexation of the Punjab in 1849, when the British administrators and anthropologists started looking closely at the social hierarchy in the province they discovered that the Punjab represented 'a notable exception' to the caste system in India. It appeared that the continual influx of foreign people of diverse stocks made the people of this region extraordinarily mixed. Buddha Prakash depicted, in a way, the special quality of the region, when he described it as "The socio-cultural panmixia of Punjab". He also noticed that this region was 'practically abandoned' by the orthodoxy (brahmins), most of whom had quite early shifted to the Indo-Gangetic region. The British administrators noticed, during the 19th century that, by religion, Punjab 'is more Mohammedan than Hindu', and that 'Islam in the Punjab is as a rule, free from fanaticism'.

In the western part of Punjab where there was a larger concentration of Muslims and the society was organized on tribal basis, it was found that 'caste hardly exists'. Part of the reason for such a characteristic of Muslim social life in the region was the Sufi influence which was brought from Persia by 'the early Sultans of Ghor'. Historians noticed a significant mobilization among the artisan castes/classes during the period of Turkish rule. The teachings of the Bhakti poets, particularly the ridicule of the brahmin by Kabir and Ravidas, were perhaps as much an evidence of a challenge to the structure of social difference, as a reflection of a shifting structure of social hierarchy. However, in central Punjab, broadly the area of present Punjab, it was the emergence of Sikh Panth which was believed to have made a definitive influence with respect to caste. Arnold Toynbee took note of evidence that the Hindu society had, by the time of the Turkish invasions, started to break down under 'the morbid social growth' of caste system, resulting in revolts of the proletariat led by Kabir and Nanak. According to J S Grewal, "Toynbee sees the rise of Sikhism, thus, as an act of secession on the part of the internal proletariat of the Hindu society in its disintegrating stage".

The rejection of the caste system by Guru Nanak, the first Guru of the Sikhs, appeared categorical. One of the widely quoted of his 'sabads is': Fakar Jati phakar nau, Sabhana jia ika chau (Worthless is caste and worthless an exalted name; For all mankind there is but single refuge). Another composition is reproduced below:

> Neechan andar neechJati, Neechi hun ati neech
> Nanak tin ke sang sath, Vadian siyon kya rees
> Jithe neech sanmalian, Tithe nadr teri bakhshish
> (I am the lowest of the low castes; low, absolutely low; I am with the lowest in companionship, not with the so-called high. Blessing of god is where the lowly are cared for.)

Guru Nanak's primary quest is for salvation; union with god. In front of god; caste is irrelevant. God bestows greatness irrespective of caste. One's association with one's caste or pride of caste is a positive hurdle. "There is no caste in next world". Apparently Guru Nanak's rejection of caste, as also his conception of equality, is in terms of religious criterion. As Grewal explained "Guru Nanak does not conceive of equality in social and economic terms". However, its social implications were evident. "Just as every human being was equal before God so every individual who accepted the path of Guru Nanak was equal before the Guru and all his followers were equal before one another".

A major impact was made through the institutions of 'sangat' and 'langar', equality in religious gatherings, and eating of food together. Another innovation was the practice of offering 'karah prasad' by any one including from the low castes, which is then deposited in a single dish, and out of which thereafter, a portion of the holy 'prasad' is distributed to each one in the gathering. This custom was observed as early as the time of the fifth Guru. "This ensures that high castes consume food received in effect from the hands of the lower castes or even outcastes and that they do so from a common dish". Further, when Guru Gobind Singh established the institution of Khalsa brotherhood in 1699, a distinct ceremony of baptism ridiculed caste distinctions. All the first five initiates came from the lower castes (though none from the outcastes). It was required that all the candidates drink from a common bowl of 'amrit' (sweetened sacred water). All these rituals gave a striking blow to the notion of ritual purity, in contrast to the ritual rigidity in the Hindu religious places. Violations were not ruled out. But the holy injunctions and intentions were clear. There was neither a religious support for caste distinctions, nor for caste/birth based priesthood. As for wearing of arms, caste made no difference.

After the 10th Guru, as per his command, there was to be no living guru. Hereafter the holy book containing the word of the *Gurus – Guru Granth Sahib* – was to be followed as the Guru: "ye whose hearts are pure, seek Him in the Word". The Granth also included the compositions of a number of saints such as Sheikh Farid and the Bhagats, such as Kabir, a julaha (weaver) and Ravidas, a chamar (leather worker); both considered to be from the outcastes. Their compositions in fact appeared to be more radical in condemnation and rejection of caste. Their sayings as part of the holy scripture of the Sikh Panth appeared to have given to even outcastes a welcome feeling of affinity with and honour in belonging to the new religion.

More fundamental, however, was the question of survival of caste and of what treatment members of lower castes or outcastes entering the Sikh Panth received at the hands of the dominant section of the people composing the panth. All the 10 Gurus came from khatri families and in the early years it was largely the khatris who were the followers and who exercised influence in the panth. One who entered the panth, entered with his caste intact. He was neither required nor expected to discard caste-belonging. All the Gurus married their sons and daughters in khatri families. The followers were not expected to not follow the customary practice of endogamy. They were considered equal in several respects and yet were separate in kinship. There is no evidence, however that the outcastes in general ceased to be outcastes after joining the panth.

The large-scale entry of the Jats from the time of the sixth Guru, tended to alter the caste equation in the panth. The Jats constituted the rural elite who dominated rural Punjab. By the 18th century the Jat constituency was preponderant among constituent groups in the panth. The precise proportion became clear only when the British conducted the 1881 Census, which took stock of the caste variable. At that time it was found that among 1,706,909 persons who returned themselves as Sikh, about 63 per cent were Jats. The proportion has, more or less remained in the range of 60-66 per cent.

The Jats were sturdy owners and cultivators of land. Their pride in manual labour – *dabb ke vaah, te rajj ke khah* (till the land deep and eat to your fill) – tended to erase the distinction between non-manual and manual labour which was a significant marker of the high-pure and the polluting-low in the Hindu caste system. In the varna order, the Jats (cultivator Jati) were classed as *Shudra*. Guru Nanak, after his settlement at Kartarpur, following his Udasis (travels), is known to have taken to cultivation of land. In his teachings, God came to be conceptualized as *Sacha Wud kirsan* (The True Great Cultivator). Guru Angad is believed to have earned his living by making ropes through twisting dry grass. *Kirat Karo* (do labour) was a part of the three fold holy injunction: *Kirat Karo, Vand Chhako, Naam Japo* (do labour, eat by sharing and recite god's name).

The Jats were known for their indifference to brahminical social stratification and the Gurus "willingly raised Jats to positions of high authority in the new panth". "The inevitable result was development along lines dictated by the influence of Jat cultural patterns". Whereas the Hindu varna order was altered, it did not end caste distinction. More significantly, the change did not seem to affect the attitude and treatment towards the outcastes. The burden of tradition appeared to have been heavy among the rising number of the followers of Sikh faith. The Sikh Misals (militias) were organized along caste lines. We do not know the number of the outcastes who entered the panth at that stage. It is clear, however, that their number was small until large-scale conversion to Sikhism which began towards the end of the 19th century.

Ideologically the doctrine of Guru-Panth had given place to that of Guru-Granth, in recognition of the prevalent social inequality. "Every Sikh was equal in the presence of the Granth Sahib, in the sangat and the langar, but in the life outside, social differences were legitimized".

Consolidation of Caste Power

When the Singh Sabha movement – the most powerful movement for reform in the Sikh community – was launched during the 1880s, one of the 'classic' expositions was made by Bhai Kahn Singh in his *'Hum Hindu Nahin'* (we (Sikhs) are not Hindus).

However, it was the political logic of *Hum Hindu Nahin,* which swayed the minds of the Sikh political class. Judge points to the dialectics of Sikhism becoming a key factor in elevation of Jats to a higher caste status and the social and political domination of the Jats in Sikh community contributing to the consolidation and expansion of Sikhism. "Each reinforced the other. It is this dialectics of social change that significantly contributed to the emergence of communalism in Punjab".

The social universe of the Sikhs at that time was defined by, what was described as 'Sanatan Sikh tradition' – primarily a priestly religion. Giani Pratap Singh, later the head priest at the Golden Temple, noted that the mazhabis were forbidden to enter the Golden Temple for worship; their offering of karah prasad was not accepted and the Sikhs denied them access to public wells and other utilities.

Khalsa Dharam Sastrar of 1914 – which laid down that the members of the untouchable groups (like the Mazhabi, Rahtia and Ramdasia Sikhs) did not have the right to go beyond the fourth step in the Golden Temple and the members of the fourfold *varnas* including Nai, chippe (sic), jhivar, (shudra sub-castes) were instructed not to mix with persons belonging to the untouchable castes. Those who were guilty of breaking caste rules were classified as 'patit' and shunned by civil society. The organization of Khalsa Brotherhood was very active in converting the untouchable castes to Sikhism through ritual baptism.

However, it did not seem to bring any noticeable change. Overall the Singh Sabha Movement devoted more attention to bringing more and more numbers of the low castes into the Khalsa Sikh fold and opening of schools and colleges. "Though removal of untouchability was also a part of this movement, but the (same) amount of attention which was paid to the opening of schools and colleges, was not given to this aspect". Thereafter, engagements relating to the Akali struggle for liberation of Gurdwaras 1920-25, "did not leave the time for removal of untouchability". It was not surprising. For the Jats, who composed 70 per cent of the Akalis, and other high castes, caste equality or removal of untouchability was contrary to their disposition for social domination and hierarchy.

The growth of communal competition and politics in Punjab since the beginning of 20th century made removal of untouchability, and conversion or reconversion ('Shuddhi') politically significant to the political classes of each religious community. It facilitated a phenomenal and fast rise in the population of the Sikh community and assertion of distinct identity. However, this became, in fact a masked struggle for protecting and strengthening the special rights and domination of the high castes, both within the community and in the domain of political power in the province.

A PARALLEL CASTE HIERARCHY

Sikhism did not lead to the creation of an egalitarian community or end of caste hierarchy and discrimination. But the caste pattern had undergone a change. Scholars have pointed to the construction of a Sikh caste hierarchy, parallel to that of the Hindu caste hierarchy. Prominent among these are W H McLeod (*The Evolution of Sikh Community* 1976), Ethne K Marenco (*The Transformation of Sikhism* 1976), and Inder Paul Singh ('Caste in a Sikh Village' 1977). The emergent comparative picture may be described as under:

1. In the Hindu caste system, the hierarchy of the actually functioning *Jatis* is ordered with reference to the *varna*shram – the traditional four *varnas* order – and attributable to scriptural sanction. As Ambedkar underlined in one of his exchanges with Gandhi, in Hinduism it was not the practice you disapproved of, but the ideals. In Sikhism, there is no scriptural sanction for caste distinctions. The emphasis has been on the brotherhood of all under one god – equality among all human beings. The problem is with the practice, not the ideals.
2. Brahmins are at the top in Hindu caste hierarchy. Among the Sikhs, on the other hand, Jats who had graduated to the position of a ruling class under Maharaja Ranjit Singh, remained on top of the hierarchy. Generally speaking, khatris, aroras and lobanas came after them, followed by the artisan castes among which ramgarhias (Sikh carpenter caste) enjoy higher status than Ahluwalias (kalals). The menial or untouchable castes are at the bottom, just as among the Hindus. However, the perceptions regarding which caste is placed second, third and fourth varied both by the village and the caste one belonged to.
3. The structure of caste discrimination in the Sikh community was considerably liberated from the purity-pollution frame of relations, as against the Hindu community in which that consideration is relatively more prominent.
4. Sikhism altered the principle that knowledge is acquired and produced only by priestly class (such

as brahmins). There is no permanent class of priests or producers of religious knowledge in Sikhism. Even the initial advantage enjoyed by the Bedis and Sodhis on that score was obliterated after the Gurdwara Reform Movement. Priests and ragis and sewadars (as employees) now largely come from the lower castes, including a noticeable number from the scheduled castes; and, it may be surprising, very few from the Jat caste. Jat Sikhs would rather control the SGPC.

5. Castes are endogamous both in the Hindu and Sikh caste systems. But going by the field studies, (mentioned below) the endogamy was a little weaker, and hypergamy a little stronger among Sikhs than Hindus.

AMBEDKAR'S MOVE FOR EN MASSE CONVERSION OF DEPRESSED CLASSES TO SIKHISM

There has been a lack of clarity about why Ambedkar's resolution for conversion of India's scheduled castes to Sikhism in 1936 was quietly dropped. Sikhism was considered to be the best available option for moving out of the oppressive stranglehold of Hinduism. Understanding the reasons for rejection of this option and his conversion to Buddhism instead, 20 years later, is important to help make sense of the position of lower caste people in the Sikh community. A part of the suggestive explanation comes from Ambedkar's biographer Dhananjay Keer, M S Gore and L R Bally. Perhaps another significant part of the explanation lies in a disclosure made by Sardar Kapur Singh in his *Saachi Sakhi.*

On October 13, 1935 Ambedkar made a solemn statement at the Yeola conference of depressed classes that whereas unfortunately he was born a Hindu untouchable, "I solemnly assure you that I will not die a Hindu". This rightly came as 'a thunderbolt', for it rocked political parties and social institutions in India. It was not simply a question of Ambedkar's personal choice because of spiritual or religious reasons. He exhorted his followers to change their religion en masse: "you have nothing to lose except your chains, and everything to gain by changing your religion". This made it a political question. The leading figures from all other religions approached Ambedkar separately, inviting him to convert to their religion, promising different rewards.

After serious thinking and consultations with a large number of people, Ambedkar had decided by June 1936 to embrace Sikhism along with his followers. This had the approval of the leaders of the Hindu Mahasabha and of Shankracharya Kurtakoti. Conversion to Sikhism was, as Ambedkar argued, the best choice from the standpoint of the Hindus. After participating in the Sikh Missionary conference at Amritsar in April Ambedkar sent his son, Yashwant Rao, and nephew to the Golden Temple in May, where they stayed for one month and a half, to observe the situation and meet with leaders of the community. On September 18 a group of 13 followers was deputed to visit Amritsar to meet the 'Sikh Mission'. There was already an understanding that the Sikh Mission was going to start a college in Bombay in the interest of those Depressed Classes who would convert to Sikhism.

One of the reasons for the change in Ambedkar's programme may have related to his anxiety about the 'chinks in the untouchable unity'. According to M S Gore "Ambedkar had always been conscious of the Mang community's coolness towards his movement. Ambedkar responded by leaving the final decision on conversion to the future". Keer tends to suggest that the reason for postponing the idea of conversions related to his anxiety about the fate of the Depressed Classes' share in political power after conversion to Sikhism. Bally, who has been a leading Ambedkarite activist, writer and editor of Bhim Patrika, provided another explanation. According to him, the untouchables of Punjab had conveyed to Ambedkar the atrocities they suffered at the hands of the dominant community of Jat Sikhs and appealed to him to ensure that the untouchables never become Sikhs.

However, a part of the reason why they failed to hit it off may well be related to a rethinking and opposition to the move among the Sikh political class. The logic of power and personal political interest of leaders may more often be a more decisive factor than ideology.

LEGAL RECOGNITION OF SIKH DALITS

After independence, one of the major demands put forward unanimously by all the 22 Sikh members of the East Punjab legislative assembly in 1948 related to securing for the former untouchable castes converted to Sikhism the same recognition and rights as would have been available to them if they had not become Sikhs. In the memorandum given to the advisory committee on fundamental rights, minorities, etc, of the constituent assembly of India it was pleaded that the lower castes in the Sikh community – namely, mazhabis, ramdasias, kabirpanthis, baurias, sareras and sikligars – who suffered the same disabilities as the members of the (Hindu) scheduled castes, should be included in the list of the scheduled castes.

In 1953, after the demand for Punjabi Suba had been raised, Master Tara Singh and Shiromani Akali Dal asked for inclusion of all the 'untouchable castes' converted to Sikhism in the list of scheduled castes. That only four major castes (covering 85 per cent of all Sikh untouchable/backward classes) were included in the list was condemned as highly discriminatory – "a conspiracy to crush our religion". Master Tara Singh threatened to go on a fast unto death if all the "*Acchuts* who had become Sikhs were not given the same rights as were given to Hindu Achhuts'. He led a march of 25 Sikhs to Delhi on October 1, 1953. The government conceded the demand and Master Tara Singh hailed the victory.

PRESENT STATUS OF DALITS IN SIKH COMMUNITY

The green revolution added to the economic and political clout of the Jat landowning class in general, while further widening social inequalities. Things could have improved had land reforms been allowed. The political clout of the richer landowning Jat Sikhs ensured that the policy was squarely defeated. The Jat control of leadership in Shiromani Akali Dal since 1962 added to fear and apprehension among the lower caste Sikhs. While a lot of change under the impact of Dalit political assertion, social welfare measures and spread of education is visible, it has also led to more tension and conflict. The sexual exploitation of Dalit women, which was considered more or less common until ten years ago, is more often challenged.

Most of the Sikh values are Jat values and the Jats assert that they occupy the highest position among the Sikhs castes. Ownership of land was the chief criterion for determining the status of various people in Indian villages and "it becomes more important in Sikh villages as most of its adherents are agriculturalists". This gets reflected at the village level in various ways. A chamar respondent gave a very simple explanation for lack of support for the communists among the low castes: "They (the communists) are our class enemies". The Communist Party was regarded as a party of the Jat Sikhs. One of the most frequently encountered expression among Dalit is "When some one says 'I am a Jat', his chest expands. But when we say 'chamar', we contract to nothing".

Markedly different from the practice in Hindu religious temples, there is a noticeable number of mazhabi and ramdasi granthies (priests or professional readers of the holy scripture) among the Sikhs. Such a transformation started quite early, as Giani Pratap Singh referred to in 1933. There is no overt restriction on the entry of the lowest caste people to the gurdwaras. However, whereas 80 to 90 per cent of the Sikhs, in general, believed that there was no discrimination, at least 30-35 per cent of the scheduled caste Sikhs felt a sense of humiliation, that the upper caste Sikhs did not like their presence in their gurdwaras. Respondents among the latter cited instances of contempt or ridicule, instructions to sit at the end of the rows, to come for the langar at the end; to keep out of the service of cooking or serving food at the langar and occasionally not allowed to carry the Granth Sahib from the Jat gurdwara to a Dalit home for akhand path, etc.

A more significant marker of the resistance against a sense of discrimination among the scheduled caste Sikhs is the large scale construction of separate gurdwaras by the mazhabis, Kavidasis, Kabirpanthis and other caste groups, parallel to the ones controlled by the Jats. Villages had separate gurdwaras of the Dalit and there were separate cremation grounds for Dalit.

The construction of separate gurdwaras was so normal a practice that such constructions have never been met with resistance either from the dominant castes in the village or from the religious establishment of the Sikh community. The contention may, however, be qualified. A number of cases of resistance and conflict have been reported from Punjab's villages during the last few years. Such construction of a separate gurdwara was invariably symbolic of the assertion of the Dalit communities, which became a cause for resentment among Jat zamindars and the SGPC.

Ravi Dasi temples in some cases, had pictures of 'Guru Ravi Das' and occasionally also of Babasaheb Ambedkar installed within the precincts. The presence of an idol of Guru Ravidas, close to the Guru Granth Sahib (which is considered improper according to Sikh tenets) became, for example, a cause for Jat-Dalit tension in basti Jodhewal of Ludhiana.

Another significant dimension of Dalit search for alternative cultural spaces to overcome the experience of indignity and humiliation is reflected in large scale movement of Sikh Dalit towards a large number of deras and sects such as Radhasoami, Sacha Sauda, Dera Wadbhag Singh, Piara Singh Bhaniarawala, etc, or their turning to various other Sants, and dargahs of Muslim Pirs. This was highly resented by the SGPC and other Sikh organizations. The rise of a Dalit holy man, Baba Bhaniara, as the head of a dera and the alleged publication of his own separate holy book for worship, which led to violent clashes reflected the urge to reject the conventional religious spaces. Observers attribute this rebellion of the weak, to the arrogant and crude behaviour of the Jats with the lower caste people.

The rising incidence of atrocities on the Dalit in Sikh villages is another dimension of the caste divide within the community. A survey of the press reports of atrocities on Dalit in the Punjab during the last five years brought up over a dozen cases of rape, gang rape, stripping naked, stripping and walking Dalit women by Jat zamindars in the villages, invariably with covert support from policemen, in order to punish the Dalit for non-payment of loans taken by male members and to avenge felt insults. The underlying purpose, stated or unstated, remains one of 'teaching a lesson to the Dalit'. Social boycott of the Dalit in the village is another method which has, of late, been reported more frequently than earlier, leading inevitably to intervention by district administration for '*razinama*' (compromise).

An understanding of the distinctive pattern of caste hierarchy in Sikhism which points to a new pattern of competing hierarchies, parallel to that of the Hindus, calls for deeper insight into the dynamics of political power and economic relations both at the local and regional levels. Not looking closely at the ground level social reality may leave the impression that overall the Sikh community represents homogeneity of castes rather than division.

In the explanations rooted in the primacy of ideology or culture, on the other hand, the survival of casteism ("it is very clear and open truth that the Sikh society is as casteist and racist as the Hindu society"), is sometimes regarded as a consequence of incomplete liberation of Sikhism from the stranglehold of brahminism, emphasizing greater distancing of Sikhs from the Hindus. Interactions with the Dalit in Punjab, however, reveal a pervasive tendency to view the interests of economic and political domination as the force behind caste-based humiliation, rather than ideology as the primary reality. Yet it did not mean proximity to Marxian framework of class conflict. Their solidarity and resistance against social oppression is rooted in a discreet caste category.

DALITS IN CHRISTIANITY

The term Dalit Christian (sometimes Christian Dalit) is used to describe those Christians who have converted to Christianity from Hinduism and are categorized as Dalit in Hindu, Christian and Islamic societies in India and Pakistan.

In the Indian state of Goa, mass conversions were conducted by Portuguese missionaries from the 16th century onwards. Despite Christian egalitarianism formerly Hindu converts often retained their caste prejudices. The continued maintenance of caste prejudices among Christians in Goa is attributed to the effectively involuntary nature of mass conversions, sometimes of entire villages. Without conscientious understanding of Christian belief existing social stratification was often left unaffected.

The Portuguese colonists, despite their violent anti-Hindu iconoclasm, were unable to destroy all aspects of the indigenous culture. Thus, the Dalit who converted to Christianity were still referred to as "Maharas" and "Chambars" (an apellation of the anti-Dalit ethnic slur "Chamaar"). Several ethnic groups who did not convert to Christianity and remained Hindus (such as Marathas) were nevertheless incorporated into the predominately Christian group "Chaddho".

Attempts by Christian Missionaries to convert Dalit to Christianity continue. The Constitution of India guarantees religious freedom and the right to choose one's religion. However, controversies related to mass-conversions have led to laws being passed against such events in some Indian states. Occasionally Christian converts return to Hinduism after financial rewards some missionaries may have promised as a benefits of Christian life are not forthcoming, although there are allegations that some of those conversions are coerced under threats as well.

Through this traditional practice of untouchability, the Dalit Christians suffer social, educational and economic disabilities on a par with Dalit of other religions. The change of religion does not change the social, educational and economical status.

Statistics show that more than 70% of the Christians in India are Dalit. When Christian missionaries began their work in India in the decades before Independence, their promise of equal treatment and opportunity for all castes became the prime reason for Dalit - who find themselves at the socio-economic lowest rung of Hinduism's hierarchy - to embrace the missionary message. But as is now well documented, conversion offered no escape from caste prejudices. Now the population may worship Maria instead of Maariamma (a manifestation of goddess Kaali) but the discrimination continued. Conversion to Christianity did not automatically bring equal treatment "In villages still not allowed into some areas where the upper caste population lives. We are offered menial labour, and most of the time not paid for it. At tea shops there are separate utensils for us just like for [Hindu] Dalit."

The success of the faith in India may itself be part of the problem. As Christianity spread, upper caste members too embraced the new religion. And with them came the caste prejudices of old. Post independence, the administration of churches was taken over by these upper caste members. This meant that Dalit Christians faced discrimination at churches too.

When the Vatican appointed India's first Dalit archbishop in Andhra Pradesh, there was a furore from the majority of the upper caste church goers. The outgoing archbishop made a public statement that the Vatican was ignoring "ground realities" by appointing the new archbishop.

Although the Church never openly acknowledged the presence of casteism within the church, it set up a Commission for Scheduled Castes/Tribes and Backward Classes of the Catholic Bishop's Conference of India (CBCI) to study and address the problems of backward communities within the Church. The biennial report submitted by this commission at the CBCI Annual General Body meeting in 2000 at Chennai, says "Dalit Christians, forming the majority in the Christian community, suffer humiliation, discrimination and socio-educational disabilities even after conversion due to the traditional practice of untouchability in the Church and in society."

The Commission had earlier submitted a memorandum to the Vajpayee Government demanding "restoration of rights to the Dalit Christians." However Dalit Christian leaders say the commission has not been proactive due to pressures from the upper caste Christians.

DALIT AND NEO-BUDDHISM

In Maharashtra, Uttar Pradesh and a few other regions, Dalit have come under the influence of the neo-Buddhist movement initiated by Ambedkar. Some of them have come under the influence of the Neo-Buddhist and Christian Missionaries and have converted away from Hinduism into religions such as Christianity and Buddhism in what they have been told is an "attempt to eliminate the prejudice they face". Activists such as Udit Raj have claimed that such conversion will solve all discrimination problems faced by Dalit. Such claims have been criticised as "fragile at best". The conversion attempts have also been criticised by Hindu advocacy groups as "unhelpful" as Casteism is a complex dynamic that extends across all religions in India.

However, several Dalit have understood the neo-Buddhist movement to only be a movement which criticises the Brahmins and does not accomplish anything for the upliftment of the Dalit.

In the State of Nepal, Dalit and other popuiations are turning to Buddhism from Vedic Hinduism. Reasons cited are to embrace non-violence and as a response to the caste system, which has led to a substantial increase in Buddhists in the population while those professing Hindusim have decreased from 88% in 1961 to 80% and declining at present.

The Dalit Buddhist movement in India began with support of Sri Lankan Buddhist monks. It received an impetus with B. R. Ambedkar's call for conversion of Dalit to Buddhism.

Buddhism was once dominant through much of India; it had however begun to decline by the 12th century. The Buddhist revival began in India in 1891, when the Sri Lankan Buddhist leader Anagarika Dharmapala founded the Maha Bodhi Society. The Maha Bodhi Society mainly attracted upper-caste people.

In 1890, Pandit C. Ayodhya Dasa (1845-1914), better known as Iyothee Thass founded the Sakya Buddhist Society (also known as Indian Buddhist Association).

Thass, a Tamil Siddha physician, was the pioneer of the Tamil Dalit movement. He argued that Tamil Dalit were originally Buddhists. He led a delegation of prominent Dalit to Henry Steel Olcott and asked for his help in the reestablishment of "Tamil Buddhism." Olcott helped Thass to visit Sri Lanka, where he received *diksha* from Bhikkhu Sumangala Nayake. After returning to India, Thass established the *Sakya Buddhist Society* in Madras with branches in many places including Karnataka.

Thass established a weekly magazine called *Oru Paisa Tamizhan* ("One Paisa Tamilian") in Chennai in 1907, which served as a newsletter linking all the new branches of the Sakya Buddhist Society. The magazine discussed traditions and practices of Tamil Buddhism, new developments in the Buddhist world, and the Indian subcontinent's history from the Buddhist point of view.

In the early 20th century, the Barua Buddhists of Bengal under the leadership of Kripasaran Mahasthavir (1865-1926), founder of the Bengal Buddhist Association, Calcutta (1892) established viharas in cities such as Lucknow, Hyderabad, Shillong and Jamshedpur.

In Lucknow, Bodhanand Mahastavir (1874-1952) advocated Buddhism for Dalit. He was initially attracted to Christianity, but became a Buddhist after a meeting with Buddhists monks from Ceylon at a Theosophical Conference in Benares. He later lived in Lucknow where he came in contact with Barua Buddhists, many of whom were employed as cooks by the British.

Acharya Ishvardatt Medharthi (1900-1971) of Kanpur also supported the cause of the Dalit. He had studied Pali at Gurukul Kangri and Buddhist scripture was well known to him. He was initiated into Buddhism by Gyan Keto and the Lokanatha in 1937. Gyan Keto (1906-1984), born Peter Schoenfeldt was a German who arrived to Ceylon in 1936 and became a Buddhist. Although Medharthi heavily criticized the Indian caste system, he didn't criticize Hinduism. He claimed that the Dalit ("Adi Hindus") were the ancient rulers of India and had been trapped into slavery by the Aryan invaders. He also claimed that the sanatana dharma was the religion of "Adi Hindus", and tried to reconcile Buddhism with the Sant Mat.His follower, Bhoj Dev Mudit, converted to Buddhism in 1968 and set up a school of his own.

Rajendranath Aherwar appeared as an important Dalit leader in Kanpur. He joined the Republican Party of India and converted to Buddhism along with his whole family in 1961. In 1967, he founded the Kanpur branch of "Bharatiya Buddh Mahasabha". He held regular meetings where he preached Buddhism, officiated at Buddhist weddings and life cycle ceremonies, and organized festivals on Dr. Ambedkar's Jayanti (birth day), Buddha Jayanti, Diksha Divas (the day Ambedkar converted), and Dr Ambedkar Paranirvan Divas (the day Ambedkar died).

The Dalit Buddhist movement in Kanpur gained impetus with the arrival of Dipankar, a Chamar bhikkhu, in 1980. Dipankar had come to Kanpur on a Buddhist mission and his first public appearance was scheduled at a mass conversion drive in 1981. The event was organized by Rahulan Ambawadekar, an RPI Dalit leader. In April 1981, Ambawadekar founded the Dalit Panthers (U.P. Branch) inspired by the Maharashtrian Dalit Panthers.

In 2002, Kanshi Ram, a popular out-caste political leader from a Sikh religious background, announced his intention to convert to Buddhism on October 14, 2006, the fiftieth anniversary of Ambedkar's conversion. He intended for 20,000,000 of his supporters to convert at the same time. Part of the significance of this plan was that Ram's followers include not only Untouchables, but persons from a variety of castes, who could significantly broaden Buddhism's support. However, he passed away October 9, 2006 after a lengthy illness; he was cremated as per Buddhist rituals.

Another popular Dalit leader, Bahujan Samaj Party chief Mayawati, has said that she and her followers will embrace Buddhism after the BSP gains control of the government.

AMBEDKAR'S CONVERSION

At the Yeola conference in 1935, prominent Dalit leader B. R. Ambedkar declared that he would not die a Hindu, saying that it perpetuates caste injustices.

After publishing a series of books and articles arguing that Buddhism was the only way for the Untouchables to gain equality, Ambedkar publicly converted on October 14, 1956 in Nagpur. He took the three refuges and the Five Precepts from a Buddhist monk, Bhadant U. Chandramani, in the traditional manner and then in his turn administered them to the 380,000 of his followers that were present. The conversion ceremony was attended by Medharthi, his main disciple Bhoj Dev Mudit, and Mahastvir Bodhanand's Sri Lankan successor, Bhante Pragyanand. Ambedkar would die less than two months later, just after finishing his definitive work on Buddhism.

Many Dalit employ the term "Ambedkar(ite) Buddhism" to designate the Buddhist movement, which started with Ambedkar's conversion.

VOWS OF AMBEDKAR

After receiving ordination, Ambedkar gave *dhamma diksha* to his followers. The ceremony included 22 vows given to all new converts after Three Jewels and Five Precepts. On 16 October 1956, Ambedkar performed another mass religious conversion ceremony at Chanda. He prescribed 22 vows to his followers:

1. I shall have no faith in Brahma, Vishnu and Maheshwara nor shall I worship them.
2. I shall have no faith in Rama and Krishna who are believed to be incarnation of God nor shall I worship them.
3. I shall have no faith in Gauri, Ganapati and other gods and goddesses of Hindus nor shall I worship them.
4. I do not believe in the incarnation of God.

5. I do not and shall not believe that Lord Buddha was the incarnation of Vishnu. I believe this to be sheer madness and false propaganda.
6. I shall not perform *Shraddha* nor shall I give *pind-dan.*
7. I shall not act in a manner violating the principles and teachings of the Buddha.
8. I shall not allow any ceremonies to be performed by Brahmins.
9. I shall believe in the equality of man.
10. I shall endeavor to establish equality.
11. I shall follow the noble eightfold path of the Buddha.
12. I shall follow the ten *paramitas* prescribed by the Buddha.
13. I shall have compassion and loving kindness for all living beings and protect them.
14. I shall not steal.
15. I shall not tell lies.
16. I shall not commit carnal sins.
17. I shall not take intoxicants like liquor, drugs etc.
18. I shall endeavor to follow the noble eightfold path and practice compassion and loving kindness in every day life.
19. I renounce Hinduism, which is harmful for humanity and impedes the advancement and development of humanity because it is based on inequality, and adopt Buddhism as my religion.
20. I firmly believe the Dhamma of the Buddha is the only true religion.
21. I believe that I am having a re-birth.
22. I solemnly declare and affirm that I shall hereafter lead my life according to the principles and teachings of the Buddha and his Dhamma.

DALIT BUDDHISM MOVEMENT AFTER AMBEDKAR'S DEATH

The Buddhist movement was somewhat hindered by Dr. Ambedkar's death so shortly after his conversion. It did not receive the immediate mass support from the Untouchable population that Ambedkar had hoped for. Division and lack of direction among the leaders of the Ambedkarite movement have been an additional impediment. According to the 2001 census, there are currently 7.95 million Buddhists in India, at least 5.83 million of whom are Buddhists in Maharashtra. This makes Buddhism the fifth-largest religion in India and 6% of the population of Maharashtra, but less than 1% of the overall population of India.

The Buddhist revival remains concentrated in two states: Ambedkar's native Maharashtra, and Uttar Pradesh — the land of Bodhanand Mahastavir, Acharya Medharthi and their associates.

MAHARASHTRA

It must be noted that earlier there wasn't much friction between upper caste Hindus and Dalit in the Marathi society, although sporadic incidents of discrimination have been recorded. Especially, the Marathas, who comprise close to half the Maharashtrian population have had good relations with Marathi-speaking Dalit. Indeed, the person who helped Ambedkar pursue higher studies was Shahu Maharaj, a Maratha prince. However, there has been a history of animosity between lower caste Marathi Hindus like OBCs (which include such castes as Kunbis, Malis and Telis) and Dalit. In fact, the Kherlanji Massacre was wrongly attributed by many to forward caste Maharashtrians, when it was perpetrated by a few members of the OBC Kunbi community.

DISTINCTIVE INTERPRETATION

Most Dalit Indian Buddhists espouse an eclectic version of Buddhism, primarily based on Theravada, but with additional influences from Mahayana and Vajrayana. On many subjects, they give Buddhism a distinctive interpretation. Of particular note is their emphasis on Shakyamuni Buddha as a political and social reformer, rather than merely as a spiritual leader. They point out that the Buddha required his monastic followers to ignore caste distinctions, and that he was critical of the social inequality that existed in his own time. Ambedkar's followers do not believe that a person's unfortunate conditions at birth are the result of previous karma.

They also point out that Ormvedt's idea of an 'Enlightenment version of the dharma' opposed to a traditional 'acceptance by faith' is a misapplication of Western categories, since the Buddha encouraged people to put all teachings - including his own - to critical test and not to accept anything on the basis of tradition.

5

Discriminations Against Dalits

India is a great nation and it will occupy its rightful place as a global leader in the comity of nations. But it will not happen unless the caste system is abolished and along with it the terrible discrimination against Dalit in present-day India.

No nation can achieve its true greatness and potential if a vast majority of its people are discriminated against on the basis of descent and occupation. Caste discrimination and prejudice in the new India continues to banish nearly a quarter of its population to a world of abuse, exploitation, bonded child labour, sex trafficking, landlessness, illiteracy, dehumanisation and disempowerment.

This has been described by Dalit leaders as India's silently sustaining apartheid against its own people based on an evil and sinister grading and classification of society on the basis of birth and the accompanying occupation. This takes away the dignity of human identity and dignity of labour as labour gets classified into that which is 'pure' and 'impure'. Working with the skin of dead animals for example is an 'impure' occupation and consigned to the 'untouchables' or 'Dalit'. You will never see anywhere in India a 'Brahmin' caste person ever working with the skin of dead animals. Nor will you ever see a 'Brahmin' caste person ever cleaning the toilets, even tilling the land because that too is the work of the 'Dalit'.

India's tragedy is that society continues the practice of the caste system even though the practice of untouchability stands abolished by the Constitution. Year after year the statutory ST/ SC Commission tables its reports in Parliament on the atrocities and discrimination against Dalit but there is no action taken.

One element of restorative justice provided in the Constitution was 'reservation' – a quota system – for Dalit. If it was not for this we would have not seen any Dalit leadership and intellectuals emerging from those communities in modern-day India – leadership that today campaigns for the abolishment of caste.

However, in an interesting twist that ended up in blatant discrimination against Dalit Christians, a presidential order of 1950 provided affirmative action only for Dalit who subscribed to Hinduism and keep suffering caste and untouchability. The argument was that since Buddhism, Sikhism, Christianity and Islam did not teach the practice of the caste system, Dalit who had converted to these religions would not receive 'affirmative action'.

At one stroke this presidential ordinance violated the constitutional provision which states the state will not discriminate on the basis of religion. Again the state became guilty of using 'affirmative action' benefits to keep Dalit enchained within the Hindu caste system.

Though Caste discrimination is worse than slavery and Apartheid in many respects, the West has not taken any significant position against Caste. Is it because Caste falls outside the definition of discrimination for reasons of race and ethnicity? Perhaps it is because of a widespread view in the West that Indian notions of life are more religious than their Western equivalents. Yet what have passed as religious views in India are very often mundane theories and rules of social control that have been deemed sacred. On this basis, it is possible to argue that if serfs still existed in Europe believing it their religious duty to remain subservient to aristocrats, Europe too would have been a more religious place than it is now.

Ludicrous as this may seem, it is the way the claim to special religiosity of Asia is made in defence of Caste. Even prominent intellectuals like Ananda Coomaraswamy have written, 'If it be asked what inner riches India brings to aid in the realisation of a civilisation, then from the Indian standing, the answer must be found in her religion and her philosophy and her constant application of abstract theory to practical life.'To make this the 'Indian' paradigm, the views of vast masses of 'low Caste' Indians must be excluded. In fact, discourses on India constantly ignore their perspective.

Folk life is distinguished from organised forms of political life. This is not to say the two are not interrelated, but only asserts that they are distinct. The way discrimination and tolerance are looked at and practised in folk life, and the way they are looked at within the frame-work of the organised political system of a given society need not always be the same; often they are very different.

Experience shows that frequently a particular form of discrimination against a particular group is created in the process of making a particular political system. The political system introduces the problem, leaving a need for solutions by way of changes to the legal system. The solutions may fall far short of the problem and seemingly permanent forms of discrimination may arise as a result. These seemingly permanent forms of conflict are then attributed to the folk life, as inherent conflicts that had always been present among the peoples of a particular locality.

It is also necessary to clarify that folk life does not mean a disorganised way of life. Folk life has its own modes of organisation. At risk of generalising, it may be said that the chief characteristic of folk life is spontaneity of relationships among the folk. The relationships are marked by something more than mere tolerance. Sharing, compassion and basic justice remain the overarching considerations in folk life.

In the Indian Caste system, the following features stand out:

1. Caste was not present in India at all times.
2. Caste is not based on race or ethnicity.
3. A Caste is not a mere social group, like a class or religious group.

4. The essential feature of Caste is its enclosed nature, from the moment of birth.
5. Among the upper Castes, (Brahmins, *Kshatriyas*, Vaishyas,) Brahmins enjoy an incomparably advantageous position over the other two.
6. Every form of social and political power is completely withdrawn from the lowest Castes (Shudras, Dalit).
7. The overwhelming majority of people in India are of lower Castes.
8. Caste discrimination, based on birth, violates all human rights norms on which UN instruments are founded.
9. Rejection of equality prevents the possibility of associated living among the people. It thus blocks development of folk life. Politically, it makes the functioning of democracy impossible.

Caste was not present in India since time immemorial. There were many migrations and conflicts among various groups. Over a long period of time a homogenous culture developed and exogamy was normal. Later, with groups enclosing themselves, Caste and endogamy became the rule. Discrimination on the basis of group began during this time, and religious and judicial notions were developed to justify Caste.

Then come a collapse and revolt against Caste, leading to a virtual ousting of this system. The radicalism of Buddhism at this time was its fundamental rejection of Caste and acceptance of all persons on the basis of equality. The results included more widespread democratic practices, equality and freedom. They were accompanied by abandonment of religious and judicial norms justifying Caste and emergence of new ethical and juridical norms.

After this period of sanity, India fell back into the Caste system again. The re-emergence of forces favouring the Caste system led to a protracted contest for supremacy between the two sides. Finally, the Caste system was re-imposed, but this time practices of discrimination were even worse than before and draconian regulations were developed to ensure Caste segregation. The notion and practice of 'untouchability' was introduced. The period of colonialism and subsequent independence weakened legal aspects of Caste discrimination, but at economic and social levels discrimination has remained much the same.

The theological justification of Caste was found in *Purusha Sukta* of the *Rig Veda,* according to which Brahmins came from the mouth, *Kshatriyas* from the arms, Vaishyas from the thighs and Sudras from the feet of Brahma, the Creator. This fourfold division is called *Chaturvarna,* the literary translation of which is four Castes. The Brahmins were in the modern sense the intellectual class, having a monopoly over knowledge. They were also the priestly class, the most powerful and all dominating of the four. *Kshatriyas* were the soldier class and they alone were allowed to bear arms. Vaishyas were traders. The Sudras performed menial jobs. To this a fifth category of 'untouchables' (Dalit) was added later.

As the Brahmins were both the predominant and priestly class, their arguments took the form of theological positions and were called *Dhramma.* Religious rules imposing various forms and rituals were also developed, and these went into minute details of life. Much later came the Law of Manu, which comprehensively entrenched the rules of Caste enclosure.

Importantly, it was the Brahmins who introduced the idea of *Chaturvarna* to the West, asserting that the four-fold division did not involve any form of discrimination. They maintained it was only a division of labour. Prestigious scholars such as Coomaraswamy, well known to the West, accepted the Caste system merely as a division of labour and part of the *Varnasharema* and Sanatana Dharma. Mahatma Ghandi, who strongly condemned the present day manifestation of the Caste system, describing it as leprosy, likewise defended the conceptual basis for Caste along these lines.

Tracing the origin of Caste to division of labour or similar functions is unsatisfactory in that like divisions exist in all societies but do not give rise to such rigid practices. Comparison of Caste to the European guild system is not useful for the same reason. Many misconceptions of Caste have originated due to writers trying to explain it to a European audience (most of whom may not have had a deep interest in the matter) by comparing it with experiences that their audience may understand. However, such explanations understate the discrimination suffered by those bearing the brunt of the Caste system.

It was left to the first generations of educated people among those who suffered under the Caste system to make a more comprehensive critique. Their analyses reflected those of the anti-Caste Buddhist movement centuries earlier. Dr. Bhim Rao Ambedkar (1881-1956) became the undisputed leader of the Dalit and the pre-eminent exponent of their cause. Ambedkar left an examination of Caste that remains unchallenged even by his worst opponents. Himself a Dalit, Ambedkar knew personally the extremes to which Caste discrimination could touch the most rudimentary aspects of daily life:

I would like to tell you some of the reminiscences of my childhood. One day, I remember, I was very thirsty. I was not allowed to touch the water tap. I told my master that I wanted to drink water. He called the peon and asked him to turn on the tap and I drank water. Whenever the peon was absent I had to go without water. Thirsty, I had to return home and then only I could quench my thirst.

Ambedkar argued that Caste practice might have arisen when one social group enclosed itself from others. Exclusion and enclosure may have entailed advantages for this group. From this he argued that only the more socially powerful group would have both found benefit in such enclosure and also had the ability to isolate itself in this manner. Others followed, either by imitation of the more powerful social class or because they had no choice anyway. This is more plausible than any other theory put forward so far on the origins of Caste. Others have not even attempted to explain the unique nature of Caste and the inherent discrimination involved in the practice of Caste. In fact, the labour-function theory is used to explain Caste as inherently neutral (if not good) and to claim that any discrimination is only a result of abuse within the system.

The Dalit movement has always proceeded from this position that the Caste system was discriminatory by origin. The extent of discrimination far exceeded anything that may occur within an otherwise non-discriminatory system. It follows that:

To the Untouchables, the problem of discrimination in order of seriousness is only next to the problem of recovering their manhood. The discrimination against the Untouchables is practised by the Hindus on a scale, the extent of which it is impossible for an outsider to imagine. There is no field of life in which the Untouchables and the Hindus come into competition and in which the former is not subject to discrimination.

Thus, observed Ambedkar, Caste is a division not of labour but of labourers. The annihilation of Caste, he stated, is an undeniable pre-condition for democracy in India.

Every form of discrimination involves some type of enclosure. In Europe, lower classes were denied access to many social privileges by the aristocracy. Dalit in the United States and South Africa were also disenfranchised. The difference with Caste is that enclosure is complete, to the extent that direct contact between Castes is prohibited, in order to avoid 'pollution'. It means total segregation, whether in temples, at wells, on roads, in schools and most importantly, in marriage.

Thus, while discrimination by Caste bears some similarity to that imposed by slavery and Apartheid, the Caste system is in many respects more dehumanising. The very term 'untouchable' means ones with whom no social contact of any sort should be held, under threat of punishment. It degrades beyond all comparison. Thus Caste was not a mere division of labour but the most extreme division of social and political power. The question of balancing interests between groups did not exist, for the simple reason that each Caste was a world unto itself.

Thus it was that Caste became entrenched practically, theologically, and jurisprudentially. In every respect, Caste rejects the notion of human equality and thus justified enclosure of each Caste within its own boundaries on the basis of graded inequality. In this set-up the idea of common good existed only within each Caste group.

THE FIRST GREAT REVOLT AGAINST CHATURWARNA

That there would have been much opposition to Chaturwarna philosophy and practices is natural, for it imposed barbarous conditions upon many. In fact, literature provides many examples of such resistance. However, one great revolt made history and for quite some time kept Indian society open, defeating forces supporting the enclosed Caste units. This was the social revolution led by Siddhartha Goutama Buddha. Buddha refused to recognise Caste distinction. He attacked the Chaturwarna philosophy both theoretically and practically, by creating a new type of a religious leadership, the Sangha. This movement, with begging bowl in hand, entered into communion with all sectors of society, including the lowest Castes.

Himself a born follower of *Sanatana Dharma*, Buddha tested its every tenet and found it false. In his later teaching he repudiated each of these tenets. He refused to recognise the belief in God or soul as a precondition for leading a good life; he rejected the authority of Vedas; he refused to recognise superiority based on birth; he opposed Vedic sacrifices. He repudiated the Caste system.

Buddha recognised the right of everyone to learn. He admitted persons belonging to any Caste into his following, admonishing all who became his disciples to abandon Caste. He allowed women into the Sangha, whereas the Brahmins forbade women even to read the Vedas, considering them as 'impure as falsehood itself'. His fundamentalist position was an all-round attack on enclosed social units and a call for more open social interactions. From rejection of the Vedas and Vedic sacrifices also grew his position on non-violence.

Rejection of violence against all beings, insects, animals and others naturally implied opposition to the use of violence against human beings. The Caste system rested on the threat of violence by a higher Caste against a lower Caste. Without this threat, Caste enclosures could not last.

While all these positions can be considered radical, in my view Buddha's most fundamental attack on the Caste system was the creation of the Sangha. In it, Buddha created a substitute for the Brahmin. Yet these religious leaders differed from Brahmins in every aspect. The most extreme difference between the two was the begging bowl. It is interesting to note that the begging bowl was called bhiksha patra, which literally meant 'sharing bowl'.

Likewise, the word bhikkhu, meaning 'member of the Sangha', is derived from bhik, of the root bhaj, meaning 'the wish to share'. Thus, one religious leadership sought enclosure, the other acted on a desire to share. To beg for food from anyone, including a Shudra, was indeed the very annihilation of Caste.

Taking a crematory pot as a food bowl, taking a robe off a trash bin; these were marks of renunciation, from the prestigious position of the highest Caste to identify with the lowest, the Shudras.

Like the Lutheran Reformation, Buddha's renaissance spread fast. The sheer frustration people would have had under the *Chaturwarna* system may have been the main reason for its advancement. Human nature inevitably revolts against enclosed systems and folk life makes use of every opportunity to rise again when it appears crushed.

During Mauryan Period, as the Caste system declined, ideas of common humanity, human dignity and responsibilities towards each other flourished in its place. As a result, the Caste situation changed dramatically. The dominant Caste, the Brahmins, became marginalised. During at least 140 years of the Mauryan Empire the Brahmins lost the state patronage they had held. As Ashoka forbade animal sacrifices, Brahmins also lost their main occupation as priests offering the sacrifices.

The Caste system revived with greater harshness than before. Bereft of their Sangha, Buddhists soon preferred to be Muslims rather than live under their age-long oppressors, for Islam also rejected the Caste system. Thus there were many conversions to Islam from Buddhism.

ELIMINATION OF DISCRIMINATION

Rejection of equality via Caste prevents the possibility of associated living among the people. It thus blocks development of Folk Life. Politically, it makes the functioning of democracy impossible.

Caste discrimination violates all human rights norms on which UN instruments are founded. In its application, Caste has led to sub-human treatment of a vast population. To this day, the level of violence against Dalit and other 'lower' Castes is atrocious. Social degradation perpetuated under the Caste system has very few parallels in human history. Such treatment continues to this day.

Discrimination is extended to all aspects of life: whether in employment, education, health, land holding, security, and all aspects of women's rights. The psychological effects on 'inferior' Castes constitute gross human rights abuse and a continuing cruelty.

On 26th of January 1950, the Constitution of India came into force. This Constitution accepted the principles of equality, fraternity and liberty. Jurisprudentially, the Constitution outlawed all enclosed units and philosophies that support such enclosures by implication. M.V. Pylee, a foremost authority on the Indian Constitution, remarked, '[The constitution] represents the political, economic and social ideals and aspirations of vast majority of the Indian people.' However, between this legal position and the reality of India there is a vast gap. The world's largest democracy has thus failed to develop beyond a mere formal democracy.

Caste can exist only within a system of Castes. An enclosed unit called a Caste has no meaning if it does not exist in the midst of other enclosed units. The Caste system is one in which doors and windows to other Castes are closed. To open or to break the doors cannot be a decision of just one Caste. It has to be a decision by consensus. The breaking of Caste boundaries involves an exit as well an entrance. Whilst one Caste may make a decision to exit from its boundaries, entering into boundaries held by others requires their consent. When the most socially and politically powerful Castes want to remain enclosed, lower Castes' decisions to break open can have little effect. When higher Castes rules of internal discipline require strict observance of enclosure, revolts by lower Castes can make very little progress.

Emancipation lies in destroying Caste enclosure. In other words, making it open. Yet in India, after a few thousand years of enclosure practice, breaking open has proved near impossible, despite many gigantic efforts. It is perhaps not difficult to understand the inability of some leaders - those who are reliant on the support of the upper Castes - to take a strong position against Caste.

The emergence of Martin Luther King and his ilk in the United States and Nelson Mandela of South Africa were a necessary part of the process dealing with discrimination in those countries. Ultimately, as understood by Dalit themselves, the annihilation of Caste is likewise a precondition for democracy in India. The solution to Caste discrimination does not lie in toleration among the Castes. It demands nothing less than the elimination of Caste itself, from within Caste itself.

Discrimination causes suffering, often very deep forms of inner suffering. People who are thus made to suffer withdraw. As result, they also refuse to co-operate. In such circumstances, if tolerance is to have any meaning, it must be sufficiently genuine and strong enough to restore co-operation. Thus discrimination and toleration both reflect the quality of compassion, mercy and justice. If there is a perception that these qualities are missing, the legitimacy of the social organisation and the political system as whole will be under challenge.

If such legitimacy is finally lost, deep enmities arise, leading to violence. Violence can reach a point that people become indifferent to cruelty; cruelty they cause and cruelty they suffer. Such indifference kills folk relationships and communication. Ultimately, the test of active tolerance is its ability to genuinely revive the folk life in the face of suffering caused by discrimination.

It is well known that caste discrimination against Dalit is rampant in India. In an overt form, it is both a political reality and social fact. Dalit are subjected to violence, especially in rural areas, their women raped, and their land stolen. Dalit perform the most dangerous and odious forms of labour in Indian society including that of manual scavenging (removing human or animal waste) or performing low-end 'dirty' wage labour in tanneries. Nevertheless, the data reveal that the number of manual scavengers has kept increasing and is likely to be between 50,000 and 60,000 in Gujarat alone. Research indicates that social and economic discrimination against Dalit persists to an alarming degree despite all the laws in the books. For example data indicate that more than 40 per cent of manual scavengers are frequently or always denied access to the marketplace, thus preventing normal economic activity or labour mobility.

Dalit are poorly represented in the professions, business, media, and the higher levels of the government including the police, the army, and the judiciary. Recent studies based on available data indicate, for example, that 47 per cent of the Chief Justices of India have been Brahmins (who constitute 6.4 per cent of the population) as have been 40 per cent of all the other judges. There is also rampant social discrimination against Dalit, including through the caste-ridden system of 'arranged' marriages. There is little social mixing of forward castes with the Dalit through shared festivals or even routine social interaction. Residential areas tend to be segregated along caste lines, especially in rural areas where most people still live. Caste discrimination against Dalit is deep-rooted in society and the economy and quick-fix solutions through the law alone will not help. Measures against discrimination are complicated by the fact that there is increasing evidence of intra-caste differentiation among Dalit, with some sub-castes like manual scavengers suffering significantly more discrimination.

The Indian government delegation that appeared before the U.N. human rights body cited a litany of laws that have been passed to end caste discrimination and atrocities against Dalit. This much is, in fact, true and India should certainly take much pride in the establishment of a formal system of equality through laws. The political gains made by Dalit parties in recent years can also be celebrated as a healthy example of the virtues of Indian democracy in ending social ills. But, in practice, these laws are poorly implemented. The Indian delegation refused to share data on implementation with the U.N. body, which it is legally obligated to do. Instead, the government delegation argued that 'descent-based discrimination' does not constitute racial discrimination under the specific U.N. treaty in question, the Convention on the Elimination of Racial Discrimination.

India should also not forget that its current position goes against much of the history of the last 50 years of human rights law making. The irony is that it was India that suggested the definition in the CERD be expanded for 'descent-based discrimination' to include caste when the treaty was being drafted. India's current position simply disavows its own history.

How to end caste discrimination against Dalit is a profound issue because its roots go to the structural importance of caste for the operation of Indian society and the economy itself. After decades of legislating to end caste discrimination, it is legitimate now to ask: can one end caste discrimination without ending caste itself? If so, what does that imply for policy making and law? Caste discrimination exists because people continue to believe in caste. Indian democracy is, paradoxically, a culprit. By encouraging the formation of democratic participation along the lines of identity, caste is, in fact, reinforced every time India goes to the polls. The recent electoral gains of the Bahujan Samaj Party in Uttar Pradesh must be seen in the context of this double-edged nature of caste. It may be hard to imagine Indian society and state outside of the system of caste. Even Dalit Christians, Sikhs, and Muslims find that caste discrimination continues to exist after they have acquired different religious identities. Yet caste discrimination against Dalit, in all its forms, is a stain on the idea of a modern India, and needs to be eliminated effectively.

While the Indian Constitution outlawed untouchability and caste discrimination, it did not abolish caste itself. This was realised by Dr. B.R. Ambedkar, the father of the Indian Constitution, who called for the 'annihilation of caste' itself. It may be time for the government and society to reorient themselves towards this goal and begin the process of ending India's system of apartheid.

UNTOUCHABILTY AND ITS HISTORICAL BACKGROUND

Racial and occupational theory of Untouchabilty is already discarded and contrary, origin of Untouchabilty is already put forward by Dr. Ambedkar long time back and has not been refuted by anybody for last half a century or so. The following is the gist of it:

Ambedkar's analysis takes us farther into the past of Indian society through clearer paths than the work of any writer, Eastern or Western in this field, Ambedkar demonstrated that the case of untouchables of Indian was not only the case of people living outside the village but was an example of a universal phenomenon which was marked by the following features:

1. In primitive times the village settlement consisted of two parts; one part occupied by the Broken men of different tribes. Broken men means: "fugitives from other territories, men in fact, who had broken the original tribal bond which gave them a place in community and who had to obtain and thus get on as best as they might in a new tribe and new place." These men were thus created at times of the disordering of society.
2. The part of the settlement occupied by the tribal village community was regarded as the village proper. The Brokenmen lived outside the village.

3. The reason why the Brokenmen lived outside the village was because they were aliens and did not belong to the tribal community.

The picture of the primitive tribal community in India is thus clear in its main outlines. It can easily fit into the reconstruction of the situation in any part of peninsular India before the advent of the Brahmins and the beginnings of local Hinduism. It was with the arrival of the Brahmins in the scene that further regrouping was started. The Brahmins could only penetrate into the tribe and exercise their social control through religion. If they had attempted bringing the Brokenmen also within the orbit of their social control that would have created conflicts between themselves and the socially integrated and partially aryanised tribes which did not admit the Brokenmen within its ranks. So then, the Brahmins had no other alternative but to leave the Brokenmen in their original condition and remain consistent in the matter of this treatment.

Later on, when the Brahmins as a religious group reoriented their techniques of social control, this attitude became more stiffer and exclusive, so that the Brokenmen, outside the pale of tribal organization under the full or partial control of Brahmins, came to be considered as untouchables. The attitude became one of downright hostility when the Brokenmen came to be absorbed within the fold of secular religions such as Buddhism and Jainism that came into being as violent reactions to the prevailing Brahmanical ascendancy and monopoly in the matter of religious practices. It is in this context that Ambedkar's main propositions regarding untouchability are worth restating:

1. There is no racial difference between the Hindus and the untouchables.
2. The distinction between Hindus and untouchables in its original from before the advent of untouchability was the distinction between Tribesmen and Brokenmen. It is the Brokenmen who came to be treated as untouchables.
3. Just as untouchability has no racial basis, so also has it no occupational basis.

4. There are two roots from which untouchability has sprung: (a) contempt and hatred of the Brokenmen, (b) continuation of beef-eating by Brokenmen after it had been given up by others.
5. In searching for the origin of untouchability care must be taken to distinguish the untouchable from Impure. All orthodox Hindu writers have identified the Impure with the untouchables. His is an error. Untouchables are distinct from the Impure.
6. While the Impure as a class came into existence at the time of the Dharmasutras, the untouchables came into being much later than 400 A. D.

Dr. Ambedkar believed the period from 500 B.C. to 500 A.D. to be most momentous period in history of India. It was during this period that Buddhism and Jainism were founded and spread rapidly to cause consternation in the minds of Brahmins. Dr. Ambedkar interprets the murder of last Maurya king by Pushyamitra Shunga in 2nd century B.C. as the beginning of Brahmanic counter revolution against Buddhism. Brahmins brought out a change in their strategy. Dr. Ambedkar quoted two causes for untouchability. One was general atmosphere of scorn and contempt for Buddhists, and other was habit of beef eating kept on by the broken men, while the Brahmins gave it up and became staunch vegetarians in order to regain their lost prestige and supremacy.

It must be noted that Manusmruti was not because of a struggle of Brahmins against Dalit but against Buddhists. Untouchabilty came much later than Manu.

The space between Indian haves and have-nots is becoming very fast widening year after year. This makes rich richer and poor poorer. How can India ever become developed country when millions of Indians live under poverty line?

Reservation provided in Indian constitution, although hated by general and upper caste community, does help narrowing down the space between Indian haves and have-nots.

Dalit Sikh and Buddhist Reservation after years of Discrimination in Presidential Order list of SC/ST 1950, only the Dalit Hindu members were listed in SC/ST categories while leaving all other religions different from Hinduism. Dalit Sikh is one of the most organized SC communities in India who with political power fought back to be listed in Presidential Order. After 6 years denial of their birth and constitutional rights, Dalit Sikh got their statutory and beneficiaries of SC when Article 341 Para 3 amended in 1956 by including Dalit Sikh in the Presidential Order.

Dalit Buddhist got their birth and constitutional rights after 40 years of struggle in amendment of Article 341 Para 3 in 1990. Forty years of denial was more than enough to keep Dalit Buddhism socially economically and educationally backward. They will struggle to over come the forty years of damage done to them.

Dalit Christian Need to Learn People Power Dalit origins converted to Christianity are denied from the SC/ST list from colonial period but their struggle to be listed under Presidential Order 1950 has been from the time India got Independent. Commissions after Commissions were setup and almost approved to include all the members of Dalit without any religions and faith.

At last the ball has been thrown at vineyard of Supreme Court of India, which has been postponing, seems like done desperately. Supreme Court's direction to study the socio-economic and educational condition of Dalit Christians to National Commission for Religious and Minority (NCRL) headed by Ranganathan Misra former Chief Justice of Supreme Court of India seems only to get feed back from Saffron brigade's rejection of Dalit Christian demand.

Religious discrimination in the country like India is very true and visible in its history. The demand for birth and constitutional rights of Dalit origins who once were entitled and enjoyed SC/ST Provision has been denied from the movement he/she changed his/her faith other than Hindu, Sikh and Buddhist.

Dalit Christian Reservation is much more than just job and educational reservation. Being and born as a Dalit does not change his/her caste discrimination even after converting to any religion. Dalit in all religions suffer caste discrimination inside and outside of Hinduism. Demanding inclusion of Dalit Christians in SC status is much more than just job and educational reservation. It is demand of SC status and beneficiaries, which includes all constitutional provisions of SC communities.

Dalit other than the members of Hinduism, Sikhism and Buddhism do not have title to enjoy SC/ST Atrocity Prevention Act 1989 (Amendment 1995). Once Dalit Christians are listed in Presidential Order List 1950 by amendment of Article 341 Para 3, SC/ST Atrocities Prevention Act will be applicable to the members of Dalit origins even converted to Christianity.

Dalit suffer caste discrimination and their denial to be listed in Presidential Order SC/ST List 1950 after converting to Christianity is double discrimination. Their demand to entitle SC/ST statutory and Beneficiary is their birth and constitutional rights.

INSTANCES OF DISCRIMINATION AND ATROCITIES

Dalits' isolation from the rest of Hindu society, many Dalit continue to debate whether they are 'Hindu' or 'non-Hindu'. Traditionally, Hindu Dalit or Harijans have been barred from many activities that were seen as central to Vedic religion and Hindu practices of orthodox sects. Among Hindus each community has followed its own variation of Hinduism. The wide variety of practices and beliefs observed in Hinduism makes any clear assessment difficult. Each community, including the Dalit sees their importance in the history of Hinduism. For example, Sant Tirumalisai was a Hindu saint.

Not only have the Harijans been discriminated by other Hindus but by Muslims as well because they were always easily targetable. During the reign of several Islamic regimes in India, the backward-castes would be the servants (or slaves) or the regimes. For example Sant Kanhoputra, a Marathi Dalit saint of Hinduism comitted suicide inside the temple of her God Vittal to avoid being molested by the Islamist Bahamani dynasty. Further Sant Namadeva a Dalit was also arrested by a local Mughal sultan saying "*The Qazis and the Mullah show down to me, but this Hindu has trampled my honour.*" Also, when Dalit Temples were ransacked by Islamists, the Dalit no longer had any temples to go to. For example, many temples in which the Mahari (*great dancers*) or Devdasis (e.g. Kanho) Dalit danced, were wrecked leaving the Dalit without a profession.

The oppression of Dalit has occurred for the past 3,000 years. They are segregated in all spheres of social life: in places of worship, education, housing, land ownership, use of common property resources such as wells and village water taps, roads, buses and other public places. They are the people who are made to do all menial and degrading jobs in our society. They are considered to be untouchable, to be too 'polluted' to touch. In their daily lives, untouchability results in, among other things, the following consequences:

- In many dominant caste (rich) families, the servants are Dalit. After a Dalit servant has cleaned the rooms, pots and pans, one of the family members will sprinkle 'holy water' around the house to purify all that has been touched by the Dalit servant.
- Dalit are not allowed to wear shoes; if they wear shoes, they will be forced to take them off when coming into the presence of a dominant caste person.
- In rural areas, Dalit are not allowed to cycle through the dominant caste area of the village.
- Dalit live mainly in separate communities, outside the actual village.
- In general, Dalit are not allowed to sit at bus stops; they have to stand and wait until dominant caste people have entered onto the buses. Dalit are also not allowed to sit on the bus seats, even if they are vacant.
- Dalit are not allowed to enter many Hindu temples, for fear of their polluting the temples. Dalit have been chased out, abused and beaten up for daring to as much as set foot inside a temple, even though it is a temple for their religion.

- After half a century of Independence, even many educated Dalit continue to face discrimination in renting a house to live in.
- Most Hindus will avoid having a Dalit prepare their food, for fear of becoming polluted.
- Dalit have been systematically attacked or socially boycotted for asserting their basis rights to land, minimum wages, education, housing, food, water, etc.

DALIT DISCRIMINATION IN SIKHISM

A more significant marker of the resistance against a sense of discrimination among the scheduled caste Sikhs is the large scale construction of separate gurdwaras by the mazhabis, Ravidasias Kabirpanthis and other caste groups, parallel to the ones controlled by the Jats. In our survey of 116 villages in one tehsil of Amritsar districts 68 villages (during 2001) had separate gurdwaras of the Dalit and there were separate cremation grounds for Dalit in 72 villages. Dalit had separate gurdwaras in as many as 41 villages and "nearly two-thirds of the villages had separate cremation grounds for upper castes and Dalit". This kind of divide has been sensitively voiced by a famous Dalit Punjabi poet, Lal Singh Dil:

Mainun pyar kardiye, parJat kuriye
Saade sakey, murde vee ik thaan te nahin jalaunde

(O' loving me girl of the other caste, (remember) our
kinsmen don't even cremate their dead at one place)

The construction of separate gurdwaras was so normal a practice that, such constructions have "never been met with resistance either from the dominant castes in the village or from the religious establishment of the Sikh community". The contention may, however, be qualified. A number of cases of resistance and conflict have been reported from Punjab's villages during the last few years. Such construction of a separate gurdwara was invariably symbolic of the assertion of the Dalit communities, which became a cause for resentment among Jat zamindars and the SGPC. The practice of untouchability by the upper caste women against Dalit women was found to be higher in every respect. In this case, it was division of high-low among the Dalit *Jatis*. The inspectors sent by the SGPC to dissuade the mazhabis from constructing their gurdwara failed. Reacting to the resistance by the others and the pressure put by the SGPC, the mazhabis warned that, "if not allowed to construct our own gurdwara, we would convert to Islam". Then the inspectors relented. This was only one of several similar cases. Perhaps an indication of mobility of mazhabis.

Ravi Dasi temples in some cases, had pictures of 'Guru Ravi Das' and occasionally also of Babasaheb Ambedkar installed within the precincts. The presence of an idol of Guru Ravidas, close to the Guru Granth Sahib (which is considered improper according to Sikh tenets) became, for example, a cause for Jat-Dalit tension in basti Jodhewal of Ludhiana.

Another significant dimension of Dalit search for alternative cultural spaces to overcome the experience of indignity and humiliation is reflected in large scale movement of Sikh Dalit towards a large number of deras and sects such as Radhasoami, Sacha Sauda, Dera Wadbhag Singh, Piara Singh Bhaniarawala, etc, or their turning to various other Sants, and dargahs of Muslim Pirs. This was highly resented by the SGPC and other Sikh organizations.

The rise of a Dalit holy man, Baba Bhaniara, as the head of a dera and the alleged publication of his own separate holy book for worship, which led to violent clashes reflected the urge to reject the conventional religious spaces. Observers attribute this rebellion of the weak, to the arrogant and crude behaviour of the Jats with the lower caste people. A radical Dalit Sikh, observed, however, "But all these deras, spread all over Punjab areas are controlled by the Jats and other upper castes. Everywhere these Sikhs (SC/BC followers) are mere worshippers, high and low sewadars. Every religious sphere is managed and manipulated on caste basis". It was described as 'Slow Death of Sikhism'.

The rising incidence of atrocities on the Dalit in Sikh villages is another dimension of the caste divide within the community. A survey of the press reports of atrocities on Dalit in the Punjab during the last five years brought up over a dozen cases of rape, gang rape, stripping naked, stripping and walking Dalit women by Jat zamindars in the villages, invariably with covert support from policemen, in order to punish the Dalit for non-payment of loans taken by male members and to avenge felt insults.

The underlying purpose, stated or unstated, remains one of 'teaching a lesson to the Dalit'. Social boycott of the Dalit in the village is another method which has, of late, been reported more frequently than earlier, leading inevitably to intervention by district administration for '*razinama*' (compromise). Six serious cases of that kind have been reported during the last three years. Despite the very stringent provisions under Scheduled Castes and Scheduled Tribes (Prevention of Atrocities) 1989 Act and directions given to the state governments and police, convictions are rare. The details of the public nature of the caste atrocities are illustrative. One such case of the local power dynamics may well be related.

The lowly Sikhs On January 4, 2000 Jat zamindars of the village Bhail, near Taran Tarn, Amritsar did not allow a mazhbi Sikh Hazara Singh to cremate his 22-year old daughter in the village. The helpless 60-year old father was forced to lug the dead body on a trolley and dump it inside the river three miles away.

The provocation, as reported, was that in Bhail, a 'Jat-ruled village' near the Beas 24 km from Tarn Taran, a 1,000 strong mazhabi Sikh community decided to take mustered Rs 10,000 for the holy purpose. 'This seemed to be an open challenge to the Jat supremacy'.

Retaliation was swift. Armed with sticks, a party of Jat Sikhs encircled the village for three days and prevented the mazhbis from entering their fields even for daily Gurpurb procession in the village against the wishes of the ruling community.

A farmer Kartar Singh declared with contempt, "it is all their mistake. We are superior to them". A Jat Sikh woman adds, "The mazhbis never had enough money to organize such a function. I don't know how they did it this time".

The police intervened to affect a razinama (compromise). No complaint was lodged because the police viewed it as 'paartibazi' (groupism). The mazhbis say they were forced by the police: "We are oppressed by both the police and the zamindars, both are one".

More than a month thereafter, when one mazhbi Sikh woman Pritam Kaur died, her son was prohibited from cremating her at the village cremation ground.

According to the latest report the mazhbis have been asked to create their separate site for cremation. Harinder Singh Khalsa, a member of the National Commission for scheduled castes and scheduled tribes, observed, evidently with some pain, "Punjab has no untouchability, probably because of Sikhism, but I am ashamed to say that in committing atrocities on Dalit, we do not lag behind".

DALIT CHRISTIANS AND SOCIAL DISCRIMINATION

Dalit Sikhs and Dalit Buddhists campaigned long and hard to extend the affirmative action benefits to them. Their argument was potent: Caste is a social stigma and identity that does not vanish when Dalit turn to another religion. Their Dalit stigma goes with them. Their Dalit discrimination still goes with them. Wider society still stigmatises and oppresses and discriminates against them because they are Dalit. Their socio-economic conditions do not change and the long history of exploitation does not come to an end when they adopt a non-casteist faith.

After a long campaign both Dalit Sikhs and Dalit Buddhists had the affirmative action benefits restored to them.But Dalit Christians continued to be oppressed because of the denial of 'affirmative action' to them.

The usual argument posed against the extension of reservation to Dalit Christians is that there is no caste system in Christianity. This is right. Christianity does not preach any caste discrimination. But the situation in India is different. Our society is based on the caste system. From cradle to grave, caste considerations rule the roost. Dalit of all religions live in the same society ruled by caste values. A change of religion does not alter the socio-economic status of Dalit. The social stigma and ostracism in society continue to haunt them wherever they go. A Dalit is considered untouchable, irrespective of the religious faith he or she may profess. As for atrocities, there is no discrimination between a Hindu Dalit and a Christian Dalit."

Furthermore, the presidential order of 1950 violates the letter and spirit of many articles of our Constitution. Article 15 says: "The state shall not discriminate against any citizen only on grounds of religion, race, caste, sex, place of birth, or any of them". But here we see the state itself discriminating on the basis of religion within a given caste group. Article 25 reads: "...all persons are equally entitled to freedom of conscience and the right to freely profess, practice and propagate religion". But the order denies the freedom of religion to Dalit. In fact, it amounts to forced inducement or allurement by the state by offering constitutional protection and privileges to Dalit in order to stay in a religion and by punishing them by withdrawing the same benefits if they dared to profess a religion of their choice."

A number of commissions and even the Supreme Court have vindicated the stand taken by Dalit Christians that the change of religion does not change their status and identity in society – it will afford them a way out from a religion that teaches the caste system as something that has come from the creation order of god. One of the Supreme Court's rulings has the following paragraph in it: "...to deny them [Dalit Christians] the constitutional protection of reservation solely by reason of change of faith or religion is to endanger the very concept of secularism and the raison d'etre of reservations" (Article 271 of the Mandal case judgement, Cfr. Page No. 367, Vol. 6, No. 9, Nov. 30, 1992, *Judgment Today*.)

Now in a recent development due to the filing of a petition in the Supreme Court by a human rights organisation and a Dalit Christian lawyer, which asks for a review of the presidential order of 1950 as it violates the fundamental rights of Dalit Christians, the Supreme Court asked for the government's response to this petition.

The present UPA government once again in a delay tactic asked for more time and announced that it has passed the matter to a commission. On October 18, 2005 this petition comes up for hearing again in the Supreme Court by which time the Government of India has to give its answer. The petitioners are asking for a bill in Parliament which will give the same affirmative action as given to other Dalit.

It is simply amazing that nearly 70 per cent of India's 30 million Christians who are Dalit have been denied basic benefits that rightly should be theirs.

Christian Dalit continue to suffer for their allegiance to the Christian faith. They are discriminated against both within the church and outside of the church. Their rights are trampled upon. Their very existence is one of misery and suffering.

According to the 1991 census, Dalit Christians constitute about 75 per cent of the total Christian population in India. Yet educationally, culturally and economically, Dalit Christians are treated as people who have no rights and they occupy the lowest position in society.

Realising their plight in the church and outside, Dr BR Ambedkar had strongly condemned the suppression and oppression of Dalit Christians. Mahatma Gandhi in his newspaper *Harijan* dated 26.12.1936 supported the cause of Dalit Christians. Even former deputy prime minister, Babu Jagjivan Ram openly voiced his concern over their plight and fought for their rights.

Various state governments and commissions like the Mandal Commission, the Backward Classes Commission of Andhra Pradesh, the Kumara Pillai Commission in Kerala, the Elayaperumal Commission, the Sattanathan Commission, the Chidambaram Commission, the Kaka Kalelkar Commission and Union Minorities Commission reports had recommended to the central and state governments to extend SC reservation privileges to Dalit Christians.

The Supreme Court on a number of occasions had clearly given verdicts to support Dalit Christians. The only legislation directly impinging on caste autonomy was the Caste

Disabilities Removal Act (Act XXI of 1850 also known as the Freedom of Religion Act), which provided forfeiture of civil or property rights 'by reason of renouncing or having been excluded from the communion of any religion or being deprived of caste'.

Although Sikhism and Buddhism do not recognise the caste system, Dalit Sikhs and Buddhists are given SC reservation privileges. In the same manner, tribal Christians are considered as socially backward people and they are treated as tribals. And no religion is referred to while giving privileges to tribal Christians. In the same manner Dalit Christians may be extended Scheduled Caste reservation privileges.

Overwhelmingly, the mistreatment comes from Hindu society - in our village, in our working place, from our landlord, at our village school, the village well, and the village shop. 85% of the Dalit Christians continue to live in the same segregated place, the same colony or slum, even two generations after becoming Christians.

A Dalit works in the same village, for the same wages, for the same masters, enduring the same tyranny and abuse, beatings and killings. His wife and daughter face the same molestation, rape and burning of huts and killing of children. Except for the (wrong) records in the revenue offices, he or she remains a Dalit in every sense of the word - ethnically, linearly, racially, socially, economically, culturally, vocationally, geographically, relationally, contextually and emotionally. When Irulappan becomes Arulappan, his DNA does not change. (Irulappan is a Hindu-sounding name: Arulappan sounds Christian.)

Actually, he encounters more torture and persecution now because he is a Christian. The masters of the Dalit slave do not relish the idea of a Dalit rising into anything that can point to an end of the eternal slavery.

Through this traditional practice of untouchability, the Dalit Christians suffer social, educational and economic disabilities on a par with Dalit of other religions.. The change of religion does not change the social, educational and economical status.

COMMON DISCRIMINATIONS

The following discriminatory practices are found in general against the Dalit:

- Construction of two chapels, one for non-Dalit and the other for the Dalit. In some parishes liturgical services are conducted separately.
- Separate seating arrangements within the same chapel. Dalit are usually seated at the two aisles. Even if there are benches or chairs, Dalit are required only to be seated on the floor.
- The existence of two separate cemeteries and two separate hearses to carry the dead.
- The operation of two separate queues to receive the sacred body of Christ. In some places, Dalit are required to receive communion only after the non-Dalit.
- Dalit boys are not allowed to be altar boys and lectors at the sacred liturgy.
- Non-Dalits restrict the Corpus Christi procession, Palm Sunday procession and other processions to the limits of their streets.
- Dalits are not invited to participate in the washing of feet ceremony on Maundy Thursday.
- For fear of claiming equal participation in the celebration of the feast of the parish patron saint, Parish Councils decide not to collect financial contribution from Dalit.
- The feast of the village patron saint is celebrated separately.

Using various statistical computations, namely, combined frequency technique, ratio technique, average and dispersion technique, Fr Antony Raj has tried to gauge the nature and extent of discrimination. Questions relating to the nature and extent of discrimination as practiced by high caste Hindus, caste Christians, caste nuns and caste priests are: Do they visit your home? Do they drink water in your home when offered? Do they eat in your home when invited? Are you able to have them as your close friends? Do they accept you as colleagues? Do they admit you into their homes? Do they expect submissive forms of address and body postures when you speak to them? Do they address your elders respectfully? Do they speak about your caste mentality? Do they call you by your caste appellation?

It is evident from the statistical data to the first nine questions that the caste Hindus and caste Christians are more discriminating than nuns and priests. However, the difference is only marginal. All four groups exercise a degree of discrimination which is quite substantial. The last two questions offer some startling revelations. Non-Dalit nuns and priests are more discriminating than caste Hindus and caste Christians. In terms of percentage frequency nuns (78 per cent) and priests (79 per cent) speak about caste mentality, which is a discouraging factor. The same applies to the fact that they call Dalit by their caste appellation - nuns (81 per cent) and priests (84 per cent).

"The practices of Christianity as observed through exploratory observation and empirical data (statistical analysis) have their roots in the Hindu social order. Christianity in India is a hinduised idea which has incorporated all socio-cultural caste rites and rules of the Hindu community."

For the Dalit Christians, the first aim must be to obtain from the Indian Government those basic rights that are owed to them under the Constitution. This is the first step to gaining that minimum of economic freedom necessary for survival and reasonable progress in terms of equality in society and in the church. Dalit Christians must be able to earn a decent living in society, and to live in dignity within the church.

One of the State Commissions has pointed out that the Dalit Christians are "twice discriminated against" - in society and in the church. This statement is true as far as it goes, but actually the Dalit Christians face discrimination from multiple sources:

The Upper Caste Lay Christians;
The Upper Caste Hindus;
The Dalit Hindus;
The State and Government;
The Clerical Authorities in the Church.

The caste system has penetrated deep into the Indian psyche. There do exist some honest individuals who do not practise discrimination by caste but there is hardly a section of society that is totally free from this deplorable attitude.

While certain clerical authorities in the church have been remiss in this regard, certain other authorities in the church have from time to time seen their way to raise a voice of appeal and to condemn this denial of rights to Dalit. These appeals, however, have not been pressed with enough vigour and constancy to produce tangible results. In many parts of the country, the Dalit faithful continue to be the victims of this baseless and irrational practice at the hands of their fellow Christians.

Even today Dalits are victims of being untouchable. It is the Indian expression of apartheid. Despite the Constitutional guarantee of abolishing untouchability, Dalit are victims of many violations. Bonded labour, child labour, prostitution and Devadasi (slave to god and men) come largely from Dalit communities. Dalits live in separate colonies, far away from the Caste Hindu localities. They do not have access to public wells to draw water or to public eating-places. Dalit have separate glasses for drinking tea or coffee at the village restaurants. They can not enter Hindu temples. Inter-caste marriages are forbidden both by religion and practice. Atrocities against Dalit, basically arise in the context of 'keeping Dalit' in their place within the social hierarchy, mediated by caste and untouchability.

The untouchability is the basis for atrocities and violence, denial of basic needs, land rights, legal discrimination, infringement of civil liberties, inferior or no people status, de-humanizing living and working conditions, impoverishment, malnourishment, bad health conditions, high levels of illiteracy and continuing social ostracism.

Dalit are poor, deprived and socially backward. Poor means that they do not have access to enough food, health care, housing and/or clothing (which means that their physiological and safety needs are not fulfilled). They also do not have access to education and employment. With deprived we would like to underline the injustice they face in every days life. Officially, everybody in India has the same rights and duties, but the practice is different. Social backwardness, lack of access to food, education and health care keeps them in bondage of the upper castes.

The oppression of Dalit has been going on for over 3000 years. They are segregated in all spheres of social life: places of worship, education, housing, land ownership, use of common wells, roads, busses, etc. They are the people who have to do the menial and degrading jobs. They are considered to be untouchable. In their daily life untouchability results in, among others, the following consequences.

- In a lot of the upper caste (rich) families the servants are Dalit. After the servant has cleaned the rooms, pots and pans, one of the family members will sprinkle 'holy' water to purify all that has been touched by the servant.
- Dalits are not allowed to wear shoes; if they wear them, Dalit will have to take off their shoes at times they meet a higher caste person.
- In the rural areas, Dalit are not allowed to cycle through the village streets in which the higher caste people live.
- The Dalits mainly live in separate communities, outside the actual village.
- In general, Dalits are not allowed to sit at the bus stop; they have to stand and wait till upper caste people have entered the bus. Dalits are also not allowed to sit on the seats, even though they are vacant.
- After half a century of Independence even the educated among the Dalits are not free to get a house for rent of their choice to live in.
- Most Hindus will avoid having a Dalit to prepare

their food, because they fear becoming polluted.

- The government has made reservations for Dalit, so that they can enter into jobs in the public sector, parliamentary State Assemblies and universities. This reservation, however, makes them even more vulnerable in the society.
- Mira Saroj: Daughter of a toddy tapper in Uttar Pradesh, she is enrolled at Delhi University but jumps in with manual labour at home when she is free from studies. 'Sadly, an educated Dalit women is almost a contradiction in terms', says Mira.
- 'We may touch a cat, we may touch a dog, we may touch any other animal, but the touch of these human beings is pollution.'

ECONOMIC DISCRIMINATION

The plight of the Dalit' economic position has been to the issue of landlessness. In an agricultural society like India, land is an important consideration. The landed high caste had deprived the Dalit of owning land or property of any kind. This is intended to ensure the supply of a stream of continuous and permanent labour force. Landless and dependent, the lower castes lead an economical unfree and penurious life.

From the survey, it is culled that 12,086 persons out of 9,000 families sell their labour, and 607 persons have to sell themselves to eke out a living. They are called unfree labourers. Of the 607 unfree labourers, 243 are indebted to the landowners. Out of 9,000 families, 3744 (41.6 per cent) have taken loans and are indebted to various types of creditors. About 71.23 per cent have borrowed to meet their daily consumer needs. Only 599 out of 9,000 households (6.6 per cent) have savings below Rs 3,000. Thus 93 per cent of the Dalit Christians have no saving at all.

While the majority of the Dalit Christians (around 58 per cent) are able to have three meals a day, over 39 per cent are unable to do so. More than 25 per cent of the families have clothes valued at Rs 100 or less for the whole family, and over 65 per cent have clothes worth less than Rs 200. Hence, 65 per cent of the Dalit Christians have clothes worth less valued less than Rs 39 per head.

Over 19 per cent of the Dalit Christians do not own homes. Since nine-tenths of the rural households in the Tamil Nadu have their own homes, 10 per cent of the Dalit Christians have no homes of their own. As of 31/01/1988, 99.4 per cent of the villages in Tamil Nadu have been supplied with electricity. But 67 per cent of the Dalit Christians do not enjoy this facility.

Dalit Christian children are prone to attacks of fever. As much as 17.62 per cent of the Dalit Christian children are killed annually by this sickness for which simple medical remedies could be procured. About 4.97 per cent of the Dalit children become victims of dysentery and diarrhoea. All this underscores the extent of poverty and lack of financial means o obtain these simple facilities by Dalit Christians. Needless to say, the economic situation of Dalit leaves much room for improvement.

EDUCATIONAL DISCRIMINATION

A report of UNICEF says to be illiterate is to be excluded. When a Dalit was asked why she did not send her son to school, she answered: "My son is not going to be a collector, so why brother?" For this Dalit, education is a gateway for status and lucrative employment, which she feels is closed to her kind. The attitude of this woman will reflect the position of the Dalit in general.

A lack of economic resources of Christian Dalit is one of the main reasons for the poor showing as seen from the survey. The attitude of priests and nuns in our Christian schools is not helpful to the cause of the Dalit Christian students. There is also a small percentage of Dalit Christian students who dropped out of school. Maybe education, as they see it, does not promise them a good future either. Even after completing school they are unable to obtain employment. Bribes, even in Christian institution, are also a deterring factor.

POWERLESSNESS

The experience of Dalit Christians is one of felt of powerlessness. Among those who are involved in politics non are given any important position at the national or at state level. There has not been any evidence of Dalit Christian representation either in the central or state cabinet. Even at the party rank and file no Dalit Christian is given any importance. Political reservation of seats in Parliament and state assembly is non-existent. As they have been marginalized in politics, their grievances go unheard, naturally.

More than ever, the state wields extraordinary power through the legislative, executive and the judiciary. There is no Dalit Christian either in the legislature, executive or judiciary. The non-representation in these bodies renders the positions of Dalit Christians weak and impotent. The government does not offer the Dalit Christians any privileges that are enjoyed by the Hindu Dalit.

The press as a powerful agency for social change pays scant or no attention to the problems faced by the Dalit Christians.

The Church has under its control vast land property, medical and educational institutions, and developmental organs like multi-purpose society. These various departments are largely managed by non-Dalit. In fact, the authority of the Church is in the hands of non-Dalit priests. Non-Dalit priests occupy 92.3 per cent of the offices in the five Catholic dioceses. The lack of Dalit representation in the administrative and consultative bodies means lack of opportunity to present their cause at the decision-making level. This is crucial factor. For example, out of the 9,000 respondents, 5,766 (64 per cent) said they were not consulted by their priests on parish activities. Only 305 (9.43 per cent) said that they had been consulted. That too not in any significant way.

Finally, the ennui of powerlessness faced by the Dalit Christians in the Church is a matter of deep concern. Out of despair, frustration and confusion, the powerless Dalit may garner and muster enough strength and conviction to fight back. If they do, the struggle could be violent. When violence is the end product, the outcome will be uncertain.

These facts have been unmistakably established by observations carried out by the various Commissions on the Backward Classes appointed by the Government of India and by judgements rendered in the High Courts and in the Supreme Court.

HISTORIC EVIDENCES OF DISCRIMINATION

At this point, it is necessary to give the lie to a certain lame excuse used by the Indian Government and the Hindu fundamentalists, an excuse for not coming to the aid of the Dalit Christians. Their plea is that Christianity does not believe in casteism, so Dalit Christians cannot be suffering caste discrimination. In point of fact, and unfortunately, as various government commissions have indicated, precisely this form of discrimination has been inflicted on Dalit Christians by Christians within the Christian sphere. For example, even today, inter-caste marriage is difficult if not impossible in the Indian churches.

Papal Document, 1623

The converts from Hinduism to Christianity brought with them their caste practices and symbols even after conversion.

The Bull of Pope Gregory XV, "Bulla Romanae Sedis Antistitis", dated 31 January 1623, accedes to the requests of the missionaries to accommodate themselves to certain caste practices and usages of the new converts. The Pope was granting this permission only as a provisional and conditional measure.

The Bull agreed to tolerate the continuance of certain traditional customs and usages. Taking into account the difficulties encountered by the Brahmin converts if they were obliged to abandon certain external signs (such as sacred thread, sandals, ablutions), and considering that these external rites could be interpreted as meaning signs of nobility and function (nobiliatis et officii) and to show some empathy for human sensibilities, the Bull agreed to tolerate those usages, provided all danger of superstition was avoided and the convert showed charity and respect towards people of obscure condition, this presumably being a reference to Dalit. This document shows the prevalence of the caste mentality among the convert Christians.

Letter of the Propagation of Faith, 1779

With regard to the distinctions of caste in the churches, the congregation for the Propagation of the Faith wrote in 1779:

"The separation in the church and at the entrance of the church, also the distinction of cemetries may actually be tolerated for fear of greater evil."

The Synod of Pondicherry, 1844

This Synod was convoked to foster harmony between the Dalit Christians and the Caste Christians, who wanted to have a partition in church to separate them from the Dalit.

1929: Christian Depressed classes of South India submitted a Memorandum to the Simon Commission.

1985: Court verdict upholding the 80 years old practice of separate graveyards for Dalit Christians of Trichy, Tamil Nadu.

There is an abundance of official church and police records on cases like K.K. Puthur, Thatchoor, Pondicherry, Thondamanthurai. However, at no time of history did the Church in India officially affirm or promote the perpetuation of social discrimination inside the Church.

In all this, the Church itself isn't saying much; efforts to get Church authorities to comment for this article yielded no response. The doctrine forbids casteism, but the actual practice of Christianity in India has not adhered to this moral high ground; Arulappa's guarded reference to 'ground realities' in opposing the appointment of a Dalit archbishop is as close as the authorities are to admitting wide-spread casteism in the faith. This may be one reason that Dalit Christians, just like their fellow Dalit in Hinduism, are taking their protest beyond the religion and into the legal arena, hoping that the State will guard their interests any better - or that, at any rate, they can force the State to do so.

6

Untouchability and the Reform Movements

Traditionally, Dalit (Untouchable Castes) were not allowed to let their shadows fall upon a non-Dalit caste member and they were required to sweep the ground where they walk to remove the 'contamination' of their footfalls.Dalit were forbidden to worship in temples or draw water from the same wells as caste Hindus, and they usually lived in segregated neighbourhoods outside the main village. However, there have been cases of upper caste Hindus warming to the Dalit and Hindu priests, demoted to outcaste ranks, who continued practising the religion.

An example of the latter was Dnyaneshwar, who was excommunicated from society in the 13th century, but continued to compose the Dnyaneshwari, a Dharmic commentary on the Bhagavad Gita. Other excommunicated Brahmins, such as Eknath, fought for the rights of untouchables during the Bhakti period. Historical examples of Dalit priests include Chokhamela in the 14th Century, who was India's first recorded Dalit poet, Ravidas, born into Dalit cobblers, and others.The 15th century saint Ramananda also accepted all castes, including untouchables, into his fold. Most of these saints subscribed to the Bhakti movements in Hinduism during the medieval period that rejected casteism. Nandanar, a low-caste Hindu cleric, also rejected casteism and accepted Dalit.

Many movements in Hinduism have welcomed Dalit into their fold, the earliest being the Bhakti movements of the medieval period. Early Dalit politics involved many Hindu reform movements which arose primarily as a reaction to the advent of Christian Missionaries in India and their attempts to mass-convert Dalit to Christianity under the allure of escaping the caste system (unfortunately, there is a Caste system among Indian Christians which retains practices leftover from Vedic Hinduism, but only among certain sections of Indian Catholics).

In the 19th Century, the Brahma Samaj under Raja Ram Mohan Roy, actively campaigned against untouchability. The Arya Samaj founded by Swami Dayanand also renounced discrimination against Dalit. Sri Ramakrishna Paramahamsa founded the Ramakrishna Mission that participated in the emancipation of Dalit. Upper caste Hindus, such as Mannathu Padmanabhan also participated in movements to abolish Untouchability against Dalit, opening his family temple for Dalit to worship.While there always have been places for Dalit to worship, the first "upper-caste" temple to openly welcome Dalit into their fold was the Laxminarayan Temple in Wardha in the year 1928 (the move was spearheaded by reformer Jamnalal Bajaj). Also, the Satnami movement was founded by Guru Ghasidas a Dalit himself. Other reformers, such as Mahatma Jyotirao Phule also worked for the emancipation of Dalit.

Another example of Dalit emancipation was the Temple Entry Proclamation issued by the last Maharaja of Travancore in the Indian state of Kerala in the year 1936. The Maharaja proclaimed that "outcastes should not be denied the consolations and the solace of the Hindu faith". Even today, the Sri Padmanabhaswamy temple that first welcomed Dalit in the state of Kerala is revered by the Dalit Hindu community. The 1930s saw key struggles between Mahatma Gandhi and B.R. Ambedkar, most notably over whether Dalit would have separate electorates or joint electorates with reserved seats. The Indian National Congress was the only national organisation with a large Dalit following, but Gandhi failed to gain their commitment. Ambedkar, a Dalit himself, developed a deeper analysis of Untouchability, but lacked a workable political strategy: his conversion to Buddhism in 1956, along with millions of followers, highlighted the failure of his political endeavours.India's first Prime Minister, Jawaharlal Nehru, based on his own relationship with Dalit reformer Ambedkar, also spread information about the dire need to eradicate untouchability for the benefit of the Dalit community.

In more contemporary times, India has had an elected Dalit president,K. R. Narayanan, who has stated that he was well-treated in his community of largely upper-caste Hindus (24 July 2002).Another popular Harijan includes Babaji Palwankar Baloo, who joined the Hindu Mahasabha and was both a politician and a cricketer. He was an independence fighter. In addition, other Hindu groups have reached out to the Dalit community in an effort to reconcile with them, with productive results. On August 2006, Dalit activist Namdeo Dhasal engaged in dialogue with the Rashtriya Swayamsevak Sangh in an attempt to "bury the hatchet".

Also, the "Pandaram" are an order of Dalit Hindu priests (a task traditionally reserved for the Brahmins) based largely in Nepal and parts of South India. These Pandaram priests maintain the same tradition as the Brahmin priests, including using Sanskrit for the rituals (a language traditionally reserved for the Brahmins). They perform religious ceremonies from weddings to death rituals. They are not generally as well trained as the Brahmin priests, but are highly respected within their community and are addressed reverentially.Also; Hindu temples are increasingly more receptive to Dalit priests, such as Suryavanshi Das, the Dalit priest of a notable temple in Bihar.

Discrimination against Hindu Dalit is on a slow but steady decline. Many Hindu Dalit have achieved affluence in society, although vast millions still remain poor. Recent episodes of Caste-related violence in India have adversely affected the Dalit community. In urban India, discrimination against Dalit in the public sphere is largely disappeared, but rural Dalit are struggling to elevate themselves. Government organizations and NGO's work to emancipate them from discrimination, and many Hindu organizations have spoken in their favour.

SWAMI VIVEKANANDA AND DALITS

Swami Vivekananda is a "Dalit" – Shudra from Kayasth community. When he became a Sanyasi, some social reformers challenged him as to how a Shudra could become a Sanyasi. He gave them suitable reply with supporting evidences from scriptures proving that Shudras were nothing but Kshatriyas: *"I am not all hurt if they call me a Shudra. It will be a little reparation for the tyranny of my ancestors over the poor. If I am a Paraiah, I will be more glad, for I am the disciple of a man, who – the Bahmn of Brahmins – wanted to cleanse the house of a Paraiah"*[21]. He started Sri Ramakrishna Mission only to liberate oppressed and suppressed: "From the Math will go out men of character who will deluge the world with spirituality. The Shudra caste will exist no longer – their work being done by machinery".

He defines "Shurahood" as the status of people "engaged in serving another for pay". Then, perhaps most of the higher castes are "Shudras" and the real shudras are not, as they work for themselves and not for others to get any pay. He also points out as to how the great rishis Vasistha, Narada, Satyakama, Jabala, Vyasa, Kripa, Drona, Krishna and others were Shudras and raised to the status of Ksatriyas and Brahmins. Kausikas, Jambuga, Mandavya, Gangeya, Chavunaga, Gautama, Agastya, Ganatasalya, XGandha, Sukha, Jambavantha, Aswatthama ansd host of others were Shudras / outcastes / oppressed and suppressed heroes who rose to the highest status. From this, one can understand that those who have given Vedas, compiled Vedas, Itihasas and Puranas were all – Shudras. Therefore, understanding the history, the so called "Dalits" should fight against the present 3000 / 4000 Caste-system and liberate by being Hindus.

MOVEMENT BY DALITS

Dalit are the suppressed people at the lost rung of the cast-based hierarchy. Their inferior occupations and low levels of ascriptive status make them vulnerable for attacks at the hands of upper-caste people. The organizational efforts made by Dalit leadership for uplifting their status are known as

Dalit movement. It is a protest against untouchability,casteism and discrimination faced by the Dalit.Dalit movement indicates some trends of protest ideologies which entail the following - withdrawal and self organization, high varna status and extolling of non-Aryan culture's virtues, abandoning of Hinduism and embracing other religions like Buddhism and Islam. Mahatma Gandhi in 1923 founded the All India Harijan Sevak Sangh to start education and schools for the Dalit.

Another most important Dalit leader Dr.Ambedkar struggled to secure the basic human dignity to the Dalit.The Mahad Satyagarh for the right of water led by him was one of the outstanding movements of the Dalit to win equal social rights. The role of All India Depressed Classes Association and All India Depressed Classes Federation were the principal organizations which initiated a movement to improve the conditions of the Dalit.These organizations aimed at improving their miserable conditions and to spread education among them. They worked to secure rights of admission to school, drawing water from the public wells, entering the temples and to use the roads.

Dalit movement has a rich history of rationalism and humanism. In fact, the historical evolution took place with Buddha's revolt against *Varnashram* dharma. Buddha not only rejected supremacy of Brahmins but also of the Shastras. Sanskrit was the language of the Brahmins and knowledge their sole domain and Buddha not only demolished their knowledge base of Brahmins but also popularized among the masses by sermonizing in Prakrit.

And this tradition of revolt continued at the later stage also. All the indigenous reform movement and religions in India had inherently revolted against the Brahmanical value system, which gave divine sanction to untouchability and caste system. After Buddha, Mahavir Swami rejected the notion of caste and violence in the brahmanical structure. Even the birth of Sikhism is related to the caste prejudices rampant in *varna*shram dharma system. In the 15th century Kabir talked of rejection of caste system and talked of one God. He attacked rituals and Shastras and talked of a society based on equality.

Yet the brahmanical system continued by hook or by crook. The brahmanical literature degraded Dalit and talked very cleverly about the pre-birth theory. They promoted Gita which in return promoted not only violence but also caste system. The Brahmin intellectuals carefully planted their own people among Dalit to justify their position.

One is ashamed that even today we have gurus like Dronacharya who supported Varna Vywvastha and denied Eklavya, a Dalit to become the number one arch of his time. Accordingly, Dalit were not supposed to learn arms and only the *Kshatriyas* had a right to learn military training according to Varna Vyawastha. We could have accepted such norms in the primitive time and forgot about it but in the post independence India, the government followed it and formed not only Arjuna Award for best sports person but Dronacharya award for best coaches, indicating nothing has changed the mindset of our rulers. The result is that we have coaches like Dronacharya today who differentiate between their subjects and the condition is that our sports are in the worst shape.

While Mughal rule in India was a status quoits one, the emergence of British power made a lot of difference for the downtrodden people. They brought a sense of liberty for the marginalized communities. Jyotiba Phule belonged to Mali (fishermen) community of Maharashtra. Pune's Chitpawan Brahmin would not allow any Dalit and backward to join schools. Women and particularly of Dalit community could never dream of going to school. Phule realised that unless the community get educated they would not be able to emancipate themselves. So he started a massive work of education by starting various schools in and around Pune. The Brahmins opposed education movement among Dalit which they had denied for years. Phule exposed the brahamnical literature, wrote plays about the exploitation of the farmers and appreciated Christian missionaries for their noble work in school education.

Taking inspiration from Phule, Baba Saheb Dr Ambedkar also talked the importance of education. But education must be rationalists and reasonable. Education agitates our mind.

It gives us thought about what, is good and what is bad. Hence Education is root of every movement. Agitation on certain thing is a uniting factor. It became the famous word of Ambedkar " Educate, agitate and organise'. Ambedkar was one of the tallest intellectuals of the country, a scholar who understood the crookedness of the Shastras. He was an iconoclast and questioned the very essence of Shastras. In his letters to Gandhi he says that we should amend Shastras because they talk of caste system. Gandhi said that we had to believe in Shastras if we want to call ourselves Hindu because if we challenge the very foundation of Hinduism, which is the Shastras, then we have no business in calling ourselves Hindu. In fact, this led to bitter dual between Ambedkar and Gandhi. Ambedkar not only said clearly that he was born as a Hindu but would not die as a Hindu.

Ambedkar read Gita and Ramayana and questioned the wisdom. He was among very few intellectuals of his time who never considered Rama and Krishna as idol for Indians. How can be a person who maltreat his wife, be considered an ideal man, he opined. Gita, he suggested, openly justify killing and Varnavyavastha. He cites example of Krishna's sermon to Arjuna when the latter refuses to attack his own brotherns and relatives, "Oh Arjuna, you are not killing them. You are just killing their bodies, for soul is immortal, ever present. It cannot be burnt, neither could it be dried." Ambedkar wondered that if a person murder some one, it would be easier for his lawyer to make his presentation in the court saying my client has not killed any one. He just killed his body the soul is immortal. Are these arguments valid?

Ambedkar fought for the dignity of Dalit. The Hindu Varnavyavastha snatched the dignity from Dalit. It degraded labour. The person who works hard to earn his bred was considered lowest while the Brahmins with their narrow minded tainted vision became 'Bhoodevatas', gods on the earth. The bloodsucking Gods had inherently anti Dalit bias. So angry was Ambedkar with the Hindu law book, which he considered as the source of caste system and discrimination against Daltis in India that he launched a movement against it.

On December 25th, 1927, Ambedkar launched a Satygrah in Mahad town of Maharashtra for the water rights of Dalit and against the Manu Smriti. He burnt Manu Smriti terming it a document of discrimination with a number of his supporters. It was an act of great courage to do so in the den of violent Chitpawan Brahmins in Maharashtra.

It is interesting that Ambedkar fought for the rights of Dalit and had a broader vision for his community. Unfortunately, when he started thinking of giving them a vision in 1955, he died. It was time when he embraced Buddhism and gave them an identity. Many people question Ambedkar's motivation to embrace Buddhism. Ambedkar has his own definition of Buddhism. He wanted his people to give an identity so that they get out of Varna System. Whatever we say, as long as we are a part of the Varna Vyawastha, whatever we do reflect our caste identities. Ambedkar, Phule and Periyar, all, wanted their followers to be provocative and proactive. Reject caste system and for that complete break up from the Hindu social order and embrace a better system.

Ambedkar wrote many thing over a period of 30 years. Some time he was living in deep anguish, elsewhere working with the government or framing constition and at the end as a Buddhist. And on each of these occasions he had different moods. There was a time when he became frustrated with the Varnavyavastha and he tore the Shastras. Then a time came when Ambedkar's main concern was to ensure fare participation of Dalit in political life of the country and he succeeded in getting separate electorate for them which he had to withdraw to 'save' the life of Gandhi, in 1932, known as Poona Pact. Then as a constitutionalist when he drafted constitution and later worked very hard to ensure fare deal for women in the Hindu Code Bill. In the last phase of his life when Baba Saheb embraced Buddhism, his main concern was providing a political alternative to Dalit.

It is also interesting to note that Dr Ambedkar was a humanist to the core of his heart. Even when his so-called followers have converted him as a caste man or narrowly interpreted his ideologies and perception, Ambedkar could be termed an international humanist. A person who the persecuted all over the world today look to get inspiration. The narrow minded political fringes in the name of Dalit vision should think that Ambedkar first formed Indian Labour Party and later Republican Party of India and at no point of time he formed vision based on caste. Even on his 'thought on Pakistan' Ambedkar suggested that there should a party representing poor Hindus and poor Muslims, entirely secular, only that could save India. Muslim communalism only feed Hindu communalism.

Very unfortunately Dr Ambedkar's untimely death paralyzed the entire Dalit movement. His followers went to different streams. There are so many Republican Party of India that it is difficult who can we call as original party. The Ambedkarite movement (if it ever was), remained confined to 'Sarkari babu log', who will throng the parliament street in Delhi or Diksha bhoomi in Nagpur on December 6th and April 14th every year. It looked Ambedkar never spoke beyond reservation and varnya vyavastha. His writings of 30s were used more then the writings in the later stage perhaps to gain political leverages but that had hurt the movement.

While there is no denying fact that Ambedkar's popularity among the Dalit is not due to the 'Sarkari Babu Log' but the poor Dalit who consider him his emancipator. But hate campaign in the name of Ambedkar are uncalled for. There are many reasons for the same. Ambedkar is a uniting factor for Dalit. No doubt that he has become an icon from North to South from Hindi heartland to the southern Tamil Nadu. To be frank, Ambedkar's reach to areas beyond his traditional domain is not just spreading of his ideology but using him as point of entry to gain a separate political status by the elite Dalit groups. The worst fact is the Ambedkar is mainly known among the working class Dalit and enlightened and numerically powerful communities like Mahars in Maharastra, Chamars and Jatavs in the North India, *Namshudras* in West Bengal, Malas in Andhra and a few others in Tamil Nadu. While Mahars hold sway in Maharashtra and the Jatavs and Chamars outnumber any other community in the north contributed fairly to Ambedkarisation process, that helped people under the banner of Bahujan Political Party which used it as a vehicle to spread its wing. When Mayawati became the chief minister of Uttar Pradesh, analyists mistook it as a great revolution in the Dalit of Uttar Pradesh. The fact of the matter is while it may be proudly said that a Dalit woman became chief minister of Uttar Pradesh and that every Dalit felt proud of her being there at the chair yet the fact of Mayawati's ascendancy to Lucknow's thrown are different then what we perceive. They have very little to do with Ambedkar's movement and more to do with Mayawati's Chamar caste. The Chamar consolidation behind Mayawati ensured that she has an important role to play in Uttar Pradesh.

This irony of the Dalit movement is that it has not resolved its own contradictions because Ambedkar is used as tool to hit at others and not resolve our own contradictions. Ambedkar's use is condemning brahmanical literature and values is no doubt useful in bringing people together but his positive writing for an alternative vision need to reestablished. It is easier to unite the communities on agitational mode against some one but very difficult to manage it when you get power or share in power. Dalit are facing it now. The elite Dalit groups who enjoyed reservation and power now refuse to accept this reality that those living in villages, living as landless, powerless without participation in political life are to be catered. They have no emotion other then selling Ambedkar's portrait and their own self. Today, this growing chasm between different Dalit group is just not an upper caste ploy but their own contradiction. In politics every opponent is ready to hit you when you are weak. Dalit movement failed to resolved many issues important to it and now face flak from all over.

The politics of identity never helps. The Dalit vision is to fight against hegemonies but in this process of breaking hegemonies, if we create our own hegemonies then the movement will break. In our efforts to break brahmanical hegemonies we created hegemonies in our own self and therefore Valmikis (Swachchkars), Madigas, Kuhmhars, Mangs and hundreds of other communities ask question for their fare representation. And a typical elite answer is that they have been allured by the upper castes. But the fact of the matter is that there is a wide gap between the numerically powerful communities in Dalit and the minorities.

The irony of the entire movement is that rather then working on the collective wisdom, the movement though claim to work for all communities, has by and large remain confined to a few individuals who used their community identity to gain the political clout. The Ambedkarite movement rarely talk of violence and violation of human rights. Their obsession with Manu Smriti and Hindu Gods to joke at took a perverted turn as one of the major problem that the Dalit face is to get acknowledgement from the caste Hindus. That a majority of Dalit despite all the facts, go the temples of the Brahmins and follow the same rituals. But these issues are seldom addressed in true sense. They are used as a rhetoric to lumpen the brahmanical system. The system will not go unless we want to get rid of it. The reason for not raising the issue of violence of Dalit is that many 'intellectual' feel 'uncomfortable' on this issue as they used their identity to get the entry into the media and would talk of 'philosophy'. Today, the same intellectuals have left all the work of the brahmanical system and now target the backward communities. Why has the Dalit movement changed its track from anti brahmanical campaign to anti backward campaign?

And as mentioned earlier, it has nothing to do with social movement which we all need to secularise and democratize our societies. The entire campaign is a power game. In this power game no body want to leave anything for others. In these power games we don't talk of philosophy. No doubt the backwards have become radical Hindutva people and have physically hit the Dalit and there is a need to draw a line. Like a few Dalit powerful communities, there are few backward powerful communities. The fight between a powerful Dalit community and a powerful backward community cannot be allowed to create a permanent rift between two groups. It has to be seen that the categorization of castes into backwards and schedule castes had its own flaws. There are oppressed backward communities which should have been in the Scheduled castes.

The non ambedkarite groups, mainly the NGOs, self-styled civil society people don't talk of philosophy. They bring a bundle of individual cases and weep all the time that Dalits are beaten up. One should remember that no movement can succeed without a philosophy and there would be no takers for a philosophy unless it is popularized in the movements. So issue of a broader secular democratic Dalit movement and atrocities on Dalit needs to be worked at the same level. Narrowing Ambedkar's vision to a limited people and communities will damage the entire Dalit movement. Dalit movement is at the crossroad and need various answers.

For all purposes, Ambedkar is considered one of the tallest intellectual, a human rights defender and a humanist. For all his life he never accepted the finality of the religious text, questioned them and even burnt them. Secondly, he was a truly democrat, not a caste-ist and worked over time to talk about labour and women. Ambedkar has been misquoted by every interest group. The upper castes, the Muslims, the Christians and the Sikhs every one has quoted Ambedkar for their own purposes. He embraced Buddhism on his own interpretations and noton the interpretations of any religious guru. He redefined it and probably would have given it the new meaning had he survived some more years.

Ambedkar wonderfully exposed the religious myths attached to Dalit. He tore apart the fundamentals put forward by the Brahmins in their holy texts. But at the same point of time one need to understand Ambedkar fully when he decided to embrace Buddhism with millions of Dalit. Ambedkar's genuine anti Brahmin or anti varna sentiments got exploited by the religious groups for the purpose of prosiletisation. Embracing any tradition or religion is the fundamental right of an individual but the fact remain that where does it help Dalit as an institution. When we challenge the institutions of holy religious text, question their finality and even burnt them when we feel they go against humanity, is it possible that we have the same elsewhere? Dalit have every reason to believe and tear apart the Hindu verna vyavastha but should they keep quiet when the other faiths also become tormentors? Should they not support those who are victims of their own faiths?

If Rama and his brothers were mocked by Ambedkar about how they were born, similar is the case of Christ. It is no point blaming one and keeping quiet on others. Today's favourite things are blame game. A progressive Dalit movement cannot stand on the selective criticism of a few religious texts and conspicuously keeping quiet on other. A movement cannot be build on superfluous philosophy of negativism. It has to provide its own alternative to the people. Dalit have their own distinct identity and culture and those claiming to provide them an alternative God really misquote Ambedkar and kill their revolutionary spirit as suggested by many Dalit activists.

The high voltage of political power among Dalit in Uttar-Pradesh is due to its politicization process while the religious conversion has made them apolitical. The tribals in India became the victim of this apolitical process by NGOs and religious groups going there and taking over the leadership. The result was the tribals remain isolated and exploited. Dalit on the other side remained politically mobile and hence their leadership took over and negotiated in their own terms and conditions. There is another fact that the number of so-called NGOs among Dalit in South is more then what we imagined in the north but the account of political power in the Dalit in the North is much higher then the South. And this is the process of turning them apolitical and more religious ultimately resulted in their exploitation. In the south the conversion process was higher then the North. The Chamars and Jatavs of Uttar Pradesh rarely converted. They always claimed to be Buddhists. In Maharastra, the Mahars became neo Buddhists and the awareness level among them was superb. Buddhism did not take away their politicization process initiated by Dr Ambedkar but the conversion to other faiths actually made them apolitical resulting in more exploitation.

Ambedkar's legacy is very rich and need to be protected by us all. Dalit movement itself is a revolt against the obnoxious brahmanical values but at the same point of time, should express solidarity with all oppressed masses of the world. The movement should build bridges with likeminded groups, secular and democratic organizations, and avoid becoming another cult group. It should broaden its ideas and perception and reach those masses where it has not reached. It should avoid becoming politically correct. Identity will never work and those who have harped thesis of ' I ' only speak for them and nobody else has a business to speak for or on behalf of Dalit should resist such things. Nobody speaks for others.

We all speak our own perception. We should avoid such hyperbole that I speak for my entire community. I speak for my philosophy and experience. Because if identities are our point of speaking then one should remember Dalit are not a homogeneous community. In fact no community in the world is homogeneous. They are as wide as any body else and hence these identities fits in there also. So if this theory of Dalit speak for Dalit is used, then the why should we accept western whites to speak for the Dalit. What prompts the Christians and Muslims to speak for the Dalit after all they have their own history of exploitation everywhere. Why should a Chamar speak for a Valmiki or Mala speak for Madiga? And above all, why should a Dalit male speak for Dalit female?

Tsunami discrimination against Dalit showed that how things take a dangerous if you make a community apolitical. Our political masters want them to be apolitical. But like them the agenda supported and furnished by the religious groups also end up in nothing. Dalit remained pitiable condition in Tamil Nadu and Pondicherry. Their leaders were complaining outside India to the UN and to the Church while the ground level the higher ups among the backward communities ganging up against them. In fact the fishermen who happened to be Christians also refused to eat along with their fellow Christian Dalit. Why did the issue not become a hot issue accept a few headlines. We should have taken head on the prejudiced system.

A religious community cannot fight a democratic battle. If we want to compare ourselves with the history of strong movements for civil rights by the Dalit in the US, we will have to study the politicization process of the Dalit, their fights for the right and broad spectrum of the movement. Moreover, the reach and ideological perspective of the movement were very clear. They revolve around more on the issues of human rights, civil liberties and attracted a very wide range of activists all over the US while the irony of the Dalit movement is that it remains more on the books, with the elite castes and with the organized sector and very little is done for the people sitting on the margin, in the villages.

These are dangerous and superficial ideas by those who have done little for their work. A movement based on negativism will never work. Identities have served the pocket of political masters and their 'intellectual' chums. They will not help the minorities among the marginalized. They are not based on democracy and participation. They are the collective ego of the powerful elite among them. A movement can respect for individual and without a corrective philosophy would not work. Dalit have their own cultural values and system, a system which need to explored and new values added to them. It is time for us to provide our own democratic secular progressive vision and rather then just work on an agitation mode forever. We need to introspect and bring the last man into our mainstream, otherwise these contradiction are powerful enough to destroy the legacy of a powerful man, named as Ambedkar. If we consider ourselves grateful to his legacy, time has come to redefine the Dalit movement.

Some of the movements in Hinduism have welcomed Dalit into their fold, the earliest being the Bhakti movements of the medieval period. Early Dalit politics involved many Hindu reform movements which arose primarily as a reaction to the advent of Christian Missionaries in India and their attempts to mass-convert Dalit to Christianity under the allure of escaping the caste system.

The 1930s saw key struggles between Mohandas Gandhi and B.R. Ambedkar, most notably over whether Dalit would have separate electorates or joint electorates with reserved seats. The Indian National Congress was the only national organisation with a large Dalit following, but Gandhi failed to gain their commitment. Gandhi however, continued to spread his cause for uplifting the Dalit and began the Harijan Yatra. Similar padyatras borrowing from Gandhi's example were established to uplift the Harijans including Vishwesha Tirtha Swamiji's Padayatras in Bangalore. The Pradeshika Harijan Sevak Sangha was Gandhi's organization aimed at working on uplifting the backward-castes. Ambedkar, a Dalit himself, developed a deeper analysis of Untouchability, but lacked a workable political strategy: his conversion to Buddhism in 1956, along with millions of followers, highlighted the failure of his political endeavours. India's first Prime Minister, Jawaharlal Nehru, based on his own relationship with Dalit reformer Ambedkar, also spread information about the dire need to eradicate untouchability for the benefit of the Dalit community.

Also, the "Pandaram" are an order of Dalit Hindu priests (a task traditionally reserved for the Brahmins) based largely in Nepal and parts of South India. These Pandaram priests maintain the same tradition as the Brahmin priests, including using Sanskrit for the rituals (a language traditionally reserved for the Brahmins). They perform religious ceremonies from weddings to death rituals. They are not generally as well trained as the Brahmin priests, but are highly respected within their community and are addressed reverentially. Also, Hindu temples are increasingly more receptive to Dalit priests, such as Suryavanshi Das, the Dalit priest of a notable temple in Bihar. Discrimination against Hindu Dalit is on a slow but steady decline. Many Hindu Dalit have achieved affluence in society, although vast millions still remain poor. Recent episodes of Caste-related violence in India have adversely affected the Dalit community. In urban India, discrimination against Dalit in the public sphere is largely disappeared, but rural Dalit are struggling to elevate themselves. Government organizations and NGO's work to emancipate them from discrimination, and many Hindu organizations have spoken in their favour.

Brahmins like Subramania Bharati also passed Brahminhood onto a Harijan. There have been several Medieval Dalit Hindu movements and Modern Dalit Hindu movements. For example, in Shivaji's Maratha Empire there were the several Dalit Hindu warriors Mahar Regiment and the Scindia Dalit Kingdom.

BHAKTI MOVEMENT

Hindu religious movements in which the main spiritual practice is the *fostering of loving devotion to God,* called bhakti. They are monotheistic movements generally devoted to worship of Shiva or Vishnu or Shakti.

The Bhakti Movement was essentially founded in South India and later spread to the North during the late medieval period. The notion of 'Bhakti' (loosely translated as devotional love to God) is of antiquity. A nascent consciousness of what 'Bhakti' constitutes is already to be found in the earliest Vedas, especially in relation to deities such as Varuna. A clearer expression of Bhakti began to be formed during the so-called Epic Period and the Puranic periods of Hindu history. Texts such as the Bhagavad Gita and the Bhagavata Purana clearly explore Bhakti Yoga or the Path of Devotion as a means to salvation.

The Bhakti Movement itself is a historical-spiritual phenomenon that crystallized in South India during Late Antiquity. It was spearheaded by devotional mystics (later revered as Hindu saints) who extolled devotion and love to God as the chief means of spiritual perfection. The Bhakti movement in South India was spearheaded by the sixty-three Nayanars (Shaivite devotees) and the twelve Alvars (Vaishnavaite devotees).

It was initially considered unorthodox as it rebelled against caste distinctions and made disregarded Brahmanic rituals which according to Bhakti saints not necessary for salvation. In the course of time however, owing to its immense popularity among the masses (and even royal patronage) it became 'orthodox' and continues to be one of the most important modes of religious expression in modern India.

In the period between the 14-17th centuries, a great bhakti movement swept through Northern India initiated by a loosely associated group of teachers or 'Sants'. Caitanya, Vallabha, Meera Bai, Kabir, Tulsi Das, Tukaram and other mystics spearheaded the Bhakti movement in the North. Their teachings were that people could cast aside the heavy burdens of ritual and caste and the subtle complexities of philosophy and simply express their overwhelming love for God. This period was also characterised by a spate of devotional literature in vernacular prose and poetry in the ethnic languages of the various Indian states or provinces.

As aforementioned whilst many of the Bhakti mystics focused their attention on Krishna or Rama, it did not necessarily mean that the cult of Shiva was marginalised. The growth of the Vira-Shaiva and the older Shaiva Siddhanta schools in this period, which incorporated Bhakti into their teachings are testimony to the growth of the Shaiva faith in this period. In the thirteenth century Basava founded the Vira-Shaiva school or Virashaivism. He rejected the caste system, denied the supremacy of the Brahmins, condemned ritual sacrifice and insisted on bhakti and the worship of the one God, Shiva. His followers were called Vira-Shaivas, meaning "stalwart Shiva-worshippers".

HINDU REFORM MOVEMENTS

Hinduism is going through a phase of regeneration and reform through the vehicle of several contemporary movements, collectively termed as Hindu reform movements. Although these movements are very individual in their exact philosophies they generally stress the spiritual, secular and logical/scientific aspects of the Vedic traditions, creating a form that is egalitarian that does not discriminate based on Jâti (caste or subcaste), gender, or race.

Active Hindu communities are to be found in all parts of the world. In particular, countries of the former Soviet Union and Poland have thriving Hindu communities due to the missionary work of the Hare Krishnas. Most of the Hindu movements, with the exception of the Hare Krishna movement, reflect a more Smarta-like ideology.

There are groups in India that are actively engaged in getting women and those from socially disadvantaged jâtis to become priests of Vedic ritual.

One of the foremost movements in breaking the caste system and educating the downtrodden was the Lingayat movement spearheaded by Basavanna in the 12th century in Anubhava Mantapa in Kalyani of Karnataka. The less accessible Vedas were rejected and parallel Vachanas were compiled.

The new movements look up to Swami Vivekananda; Rabindranath Tagore; Ramana Maharshi; Shri Aurobindo (for his *Integral Yoga*); A.C. Bhaktivedanta Swami Prabhupada (founder of the modern Hare Krishna movement); Swami Sivananda, Swami Ramatirtha; Narayana Guru, Paramhansa Yogananda; Shrii Shrii Anandamurti and for inspiration. More recently, the work of Maharishi Mahesh Yogi, Sathya Sai Baba, Shirdi Sai Baba, Swami Muktananda, Swami Chinmayananda, Dayananda Saraswati, Sri Sri Ravi Shankar, and Mata Amritanandamayi has inspired millions to create new centres of spiritual development. In the intellectual field, the writings of Ananda Coomaraswamy, Ram Swarup, Stephen Knapp, Sita Ram Goel, Subhash Kak and David Frawley have been influential.

In social work, Mahatma Gandhi, Vinoba Bhave, Pandurang Shastri Athavale, Baba Amte and Shrii Shrii Anandamurti have been most important. Sundarlal Bahuguna created the *chipko* movement for the preservation of forestlands according to the Hindu ecological ideas.

BRAHMO SAMAJ

Brahmo Samaj (Bengali *Bramho Shômaj*) is a social movement which culminated in the Brahmo religion. It was conceived as reformation of the prevailing Bengal of the time and began the Bengal Renaissance of the 19th century.

The movement was started on 20th August 1828 by Raja Rammohun Roy and his friends (Brajosundar Mitra and others) when they opened a place for public worship, *Brahma Sabha* (*Bramho Shôbha* "One God Society") on Chitpore Road (now Rabindra Sarani), Kolkata, India. It was publicly inaugurated on 11th Magh or 23rd January 1830. The former date is celebrated as *Bhadrotsab* (*Bhadrotshôb* "Bhadra celebration") and the latter as *Maghotsab* (*Maghotshôb* "Magh celebration"). These are the two main festivals of Brahmo Samaj.

Of Roy's movement the noted physicist, Jayant Narlikar, writes:

> "Roy understood that the emerging knowledge from the West could not be ignored...He was deeply appreciative of the liberal philosophical traditions of India, and he founded the Brahmo Samaj, a religious movement to popularise those enlightened ideas... Since religion played a dominant role in the public life of his times, he went on to reform religion itself... His criticism of the existing religion and its rigid practices and caste barriers was inspired by his desire to make religion consistent with the changing world of his times..."

In all fields of social reform, including abolition of the caste system and of the dowry system, emancipation of women, and improving the educational system, the Brahmo Samaj reflected the ideologies of the Bengal Renaissance.

PROMINENT REFORMERS

JYOTIBA PHULE

Jyotiba Phule (1827-1890), a mali by caste was a leading social reformer, educationist, peasant and Dalit Leader of the 19th century. Being a *Shudra,* he was a victim of Hindu orthodoxy, untouchability and caste barriers, in his youth at Pune. A Pioneer of anti-caste movement, he started the non-Brahmin movement in Maharashtra, which awakened the dehumanized and socially abused classes. He founded the Satya Shodhak Samaj and carried out the movement of social transformation of society. He was the first Dalit who stared a chain of Girls Schools at Pune in 1850 for untouchables education. In 1863 he founded a fondling home to care for the unwanted children of Brahmin widows, a shelter home for neglected widows and orphanage for the poor women.

He also condemned child marriage, sati tradition and favoured widow-remarriage. Phule led the struggle against rigid caste distinctions, age old practice of untouchability and advocated the grievances of the exploited peasants. His educational efforts, movement of social transformation and writings were highly appreciated among the leading social reformers, educationists and social thinkers of the day. He was greatly assisted by his upper caste friends and wife Savitribai Phule. The present study is all about his entire social and educational contribution. He became a legend and pioneer of social transformation and Dalit liberation in his lifetime.

B. R. AMBEDKAR

Upon completing his education abroad, Ambedkar returned to Bombay as a barrister, established a successful legal practice and, in 1924, founded the Bahishkrit Hitkarini Sabha (Association for the Depressed Classes) to promote the spread of education among the socially and politically downtrodden, to improve their economic status, and to provide a voice for their grievances. Between 1927 and 1932, Ambedkar led a series of nonviolent campaigns to assert the right of "Untouchables" to draw water from public tanks & wells and to enter Hindu places of worship. Especially important was the satyagraha (nonviolent civil disobedience) he led in Mahad where tens of thousands of "Untouchables" protested successfully for their right to use water from the public Chowdar Tank, which had been traditionally prohibited to them (though animals were allowed to use the water!).

In a conference in late 1927, Ambedkar public condemned the classic Hindu text, the Manusmrti (Laws of Manu), for ideologically justifying the system of caste discrimination and "untouchability," ceremonially burning copies of the ancient text. Increasingly unpopular with dominant caste Hindus, Ambedkar became even more so due to his insistence on the need for separate electorates for the depressed classes. When the British granted this demand, Gandhi, who felt strongly that this would divide society in future generations and prevent the political and social unity of Hindus, went on a fast until death in protest of the decision. Under massive pressure, in 1932 Ambedkar joined with Gandhi in signing the Pune Pact, in which the demand for separate elections was dropped and replaced with special concessions like reserved seats for "Untouchables" in legislative assemblies.

In the course of the movement for an Independent India, the problem of 'untouchability' and caste discrimination against Dalit became an international issue. It was due to the radical, bold stand that Dr. B.R. Ambedkar, leading Dalit figure of the 20th century and architect of India's Constitution, made on behalf of the ''Depressed Classes' as the British prepared to transfer political power to the dominant castes who influenced the character of the Independence Movement.

He made one of his most brilliant stands on behalf of the "Depressed Classes" in 1930-1931 at the Round Table Conference in London, in which leading representatives of the various communities in Indian Sub-Continent met to discuss and come to an agreement on the main points that must be included in the constitution for a self-governing India. Ambedkar plainly told the Conference that the "Depressed Classes" would not accept any constitution for self-rule that did not guarantee them equal citizenship and fundamental rights and abolish the practice of untouchability.

"The Depressed Classes cannot consent to subject themselves to majority rule in their present state of hereditary bondsmen. Before majority rule is established their emancipation from the system of untouchability must be an accomplished fact. It must not be left to the will of the majority. The Depressed Classes must be made free citizens entitled to all the rights of citizenship in common with other citizens of the State."

Ambedkar's bold, radical stance was strongly resented by many dominant-caste leaders of the Independence Movement, who accused him of dividing the Independence

Movement and playing stooge to the British Raj. They lectured him that the situation of the 'untouchables' was an internal matter and urged him to wait until Independence was achieved and the British were gone to raise their concerns and demands.

Ambedkar, however, saw things quite differently. He knew that the majority dominant caste vision of swaraj had little in common with the Dalit vision of swaraj. Though a few reform movements emerged to address the practice of 'untouchability' and uplift the 'untouchables', they relied too heavily on orthodox dominant-caste leaders and supporters to take any radical action to challenge the caste system and the practice of 'untouchability.' Religious orthodoxy and deep-rooted caste prejudice confined the nationalist movement to largely representing the aspirations of the dominant castes for political and economic power. Ambedkar was keenly aware of this.

'I am sorry to say, Sir, that I have been deluded. I find now that although some of our people would desire me and others to join them in their demand for Dominion Status, they do not join with us in demanding that the Government which will be set up under that Dominion Status shall be responsible to the people of India as a whole. I never thought there would be this division of opinion, and that I should have to stand up to defend the position we take. Now, Sir, speaking on behalf of the Depressed Classes I cannot honestly consent to responsible Government or to Dominion Status unless I can be sure that the people for whom I speak are to have a place in that constitution.

Ambedkar's intervention at the Round Table Conference articulated an authentic democratic vision of Swaraj based on equality, liberty and fraternity, principles alien to a social order based on caste division and hierarchy. It was largely as a result of Ambedkar's interventions at the Round Table Conference that the Indian Constitution guaranteed fundamental rights, established universal suffrage, abolished 'untouchability' and guaranteed reservation in legislature and government services for Dalit, Adi Vasis and minorities.

After Independence, to fulfill the Constitution provisions, the Indian Government has passed various legislations to enforce the abolishment of 'untouchability' and remove the barriers of caste discrimination impeding the socio-economic progress of the Dalit. This included the Protection of Civil Rights (Anti-Untouchability) Act, 1955 and various land reform laws to redistribute land to the landless, a large and disproportionate percentage of whom were and still are Dalit. Later years saw the passage of the Bonded Labour (Abolition) Act, 1976, Employment of Manual Scavengers and Construction of Dry Latrines (Prohibition) Act, 1993, Jogini Act No. 10, and the Scheduled Castes/Scheduled Tribes (Prevention of Atrocities) Act, 1989 & Rules, 1995. The central and state governments also established SC/ST Welfare Departments soon after Independence. In the early 1990s, the Central Government passed legislation establishing the National Commission for SC/ST and the National Human Rights Commission.

There is no doubt that none of these would have been possible without the interventions made by Dr. Ambedkar, to ensure that Independent India would be based on a democratic constitution that guaranteed equality, fundamental rights and dignity to all regardless of caste. Had he succumbed to his contemporary dominant-caste nationalists who pressured him to settle these matters internally, Dalit would be much worse off than they are today.

In recent period, this issue has not only engaged policy makers but has become an important element of political mobilisation. While we shall return to this aspect later, it is necessary to recollect the following warning of Dr. Ambedkar:

> "On 26th January 1950, we are going to enter into a life of contradictions. In politics we will have equality and in social and economic life we will have inequality. In politics, we will be recognising the principle of one man-one vote and one vote- one value. In our social and economic life, we shall by reason of our social and economic structure, continue to deny the principle of one man-one value.

> "How long shall we continue to live this life of contradictions? How long shall we continue to deny equality in our social and economic life?
>
> "If we continue to deny it for long, we will do so only by putting our political democracy in peril. We must remove this contradiction at the earliest possible moment or else those who suffer from inequality will blow up the structure of political democracy which this Assembly has labouriously built up." (From Dr. B.R. Ambedkar's speech in the Constituent Assembly on 25th November, 1949)

On another occasion, speaking of social reform, Dr. Ambedkar had to say:

> "There is nothing fixed, nothing eternal, nothing sanatan; that everything is changing, that change is the law of life for individuals as well as for society....
>
> "Stability is wanted but not at the cost of change when the change is imperative. Adjustment is wanted but not at the sacrifice of social justice....
>
> "The path of social reform like the path to heaven at any rate in India, is strewn with many difficulties... Caste is the monster that crosses your path. You cannot have political reform, you cannot have economic reform, unless you kill this monster."

Yet today, after 60 years of independence, the plight of Dalit and the backward castes, for all practical purposes, has not universally improved. They may be individual cases, but on the whole, the statistical evidence suggests that in achieving the task of converting political independence into real, social and economic independence for the most oppressed sections to our society we still have a long way to go.

In a sense, even after 60 years of independence, it is relevant to recollect a quotation from the poet, P.B. Shelley, which Ambedkar used in one of his writings to describe the plight of the Dalit and the oppressed saying that they are:

> "pale for weariness of climbing heaven, and gazing on earth, wandering companionless

Among the stars that have a different birth"

Addressing himself to the task of eradicating such a plight of the Dalit, Ambedkar had spoken of constitutional safeguards such as reservations. The country had adopted the policy of reservations for the SC and ST initially for a period of 10 years which had to be extended till date. It needs to be extended further as the improvement in their lot has not matched either expectation or requirement.

During the post-emergency period since 1977, rightly the question of proper integration of the Other Backward Classes (OBCs) came to the fore and the Mandal Commission was appointed.

The recommendations of the Mandal Commission, which were finally adopted by the Government, as a policy of reservations in government jobs in 1989, as all of us know, generated a lot of heat and controversy. As the economic crisis in the country was not providing adequate number of jobs or opportunities for education, the upper castes and the privileged sections resisted any measure to share a part of the shrinking cake, so to speak.

While supporting the reservations for the OBCs, recognising the importance of the struggle against social oppression carried on through the caste structure, the CPI(M) had the distinction of being the only political party to speak of combining caste reservations with economic criteria. The reasoning was simple. The benefits of reservations, however limited as we shall see subsequently, must reach those who require them the most. Those economically better off within the OBCs should not corner all the benefits. There was much controversy which finally settled down when the Supreme Court came to our aid through its historic judgement on the creamy-layer.

Despite all such measures, what is the reality today? While constitutional safeguards such as reservations are important, experience has shown that unless the economic status of the oppressed is drastically improved such safeguards by themselves will not radically change the situation. This is a factor that, both Dr. Ambedkar and Shri Mandal in his report, not only accepted but underlined. We shall, however, leave this line of analysis for the moment only to return to it shortly in order to consider the other important aspects of caste mobilisation and review briefly the record of our experiences in the post- independence decades aimed at a proper integration of the Dalit and the backward castes into the social mainstream.

CASTE MOBILISATION IN INDIA

During the recent years, caste mobilisation has become an important factor in shaping Indian politics. Ever since the issue of Mandal commission recommendations for reservations in government jobs for the OBCs came to the national agenda in 1989, it has left an impact on the evolution of national politics. For a Marxist and a communist, it is not only necessary to assess this growing role of caste assertion in Indian political life but also to map out the manner in which the unity of the toilers is strengthened in order to achieve the People's Democratic Revolution. Unless we tackle with clarity this important phenomenon, we will not be able to overcome the potentially disruptive role that caste mobilisation can have on toilers unity. It is for these reasons that this issue needs to be addressed with all seriousness.

At the outset, it is necessary to debunk a common fallacy that attempts to pit caste versus class. Vested interests often advise communists that since they believe in class divisions in society, caste ought not to engage their attention. Such a mechanical distinction between caste and class is not only a vulgar simplification but divorced from the present day Indian reality. The caste stratification of our society is something that has come down to us from centuries. Despite all the refinements and changes within castes and between castes, that have taken place over the years, the basic structure, in so far as the oppression of the Dalit or the backward castes is concerned, remains. It is within this social stratification that the class formation in India is taking place.

Capitalism is still developing in India and the process of the development of society divided into modern capitalist classes, is taking place constantly within the existing caste stratification. The question, therefore, is not one of class versus caste. It is the formation of classes under modern capitalism within the inherited caste structure. To a large extent, the most exploited classes in our society constitute the most socially oppressed castes. And, to that extent, the struggle against class exploitation and the struggle against social oppression complement each other. These sections, as it were, are subject to dual oppression. It is this complementarity that not only needs to be recognised but on the basis of that recognition, it must follow that an important task before the communist movement in our country today is the integration of the struggle against class exploitation with the struggle against social oppression. As we shall see later, it is only through such an integration that the firm unity of the toilers can be forged and strengthened in order to advance towards People's Democracy.

Before we take up the task of trying to understand the nature and characteristics of caste mobilisation in the present day political life, one needs to examine, albeit briefly, as to why caste divisions and social oppression continue to persist even after all the tall claims made by the ruling classes through the post-independence decades to overcome them.

There is a vast amount of literature on the evolution and sustenance of the caste system in India. The large number of such works are only matched by the divergence of their conclusions.

Persistence and Tenacity

This does not mean, even for a moment, that such elimination, through a comprehensive agrarian revolution, however complex and difficult it may be, will automatically eliminate the caste system and the entire range of social consciousness associated with it. As Engels, in a letter to Bloch says, Marx and he had meant that the economic factor is *decisive in the final analysis. Even after a change in the economic base the superstructure and associated social consciousness may persist and would require an intense ideological struggle to eliminate it.* But without the attempt to change the pre-capitalist agrarian order, mere appeals for a change of heart or behaviour cannot and will not eliminate this obnoxious social oppression. There was an opportunity to effect a sweeping agrarian revolution alongwith the anti-colonial freedom struggle. But this was not to be due to the compromising character of the leadership of our national movement.

The main reason for this persistence of social oppression based on caste stratification is the inadequacy of the ruling classes, during the freedom struggle, in addressing themselves to this issue. The overcoming of caste differentiation was sought through proper social behaviour between individuals and castes without going into the social roots of this phenomenon. The sinful heritage of caste oppression was something that the national anti-colonial struggle could not repudiate because the leadership of the freedom struggle was not interested in going to the root of the problem and uprooting it. Even if it had a correct understanding of the social roots of the problem, it did not have the courage to seize it by the roots. By refusing to sweep away the feudal and semi-feudal agrarian relations, which were the bedrock for the continuation and persistence of caste exploitation, the leadership of freedom struggle not only permitted but in later years perpetuated the caste exploitation. Thus, the struggle against caste oppression over the decades of freedom movement and post-independence India was divorced from the anti-colonial struggle earlier and from the struggle for an agrarian revolution later.

Colonial Rule

With the advent of modernisation under the British rule, particularly the railways, many, including Karl Marx, had thought that the old order would crumble, paving the way for a class division of modern society. However, this did not happen as envisaged. This was so because it was not in the interest of the colonial rule to transform Indian society. Its interests lay in exploiting the Indian people and its economy on the basis of their backwardness. This required to keep the rural land relations intact, in class terms, modifying them only to advance the colonial revenue collections without disturbing the economic or social relations. The British also required that a powerful indigenous Indian capitalist class did not arise. The result was an alliance with the feudal landlords for its political survival and the superimposition of minimum modern capitalist relations on the existing feudal land relations which sustained the caste system.

Thus, we find that under the British rule, a contradictory process was set into motion. The effect of modern relations, as Marx had foreseen — railways, communications, growing market, few industries, trade — accentuated the tendency towards destroying the old structure and with it the caste system and replacing it with modern day class divisions. On the other hand, the vital interests of the colonial power lay in seeking political and economic support from the landlords and feudal interests, thus maintaining the old land relations and thereby supporting the caste structure and institutions.

Thus, the process of change of the old society, under the British rule, was slow and painful and never destined to be completed.

TWO TRENDS IN FREEDOM MOVEMENT

Simultaneously, within the freedom movement itself, there were two main trends that contributed to the persistence of the caste institutions. One was the revivalist ideology which gripped a number of leaders of the freedom movement. Coming from upper caste Hindu background, these leaders in the struggle against the British drew sustenance from India's so called past and, in the process, defended the social institutions of that past. Tilak was a classic example of such a tendency. Rajni Palme Dutt in *India Today* summed up this line of thinking most appropriately by the following:

> "So from the existing foul welter and decaying and corrupt metaphysics, from the broken relics of the shattered village system, from the dead remains of court splendours of a vanished civilisation, they sought to fabricate and build up and reconstitute a golden dream of Hindu culture — a `purified' Hindu

culture – which they could hold up as an ideal and a guiding light. Against the overwhelming flood of British bourgeois culture and ideology, which they saw completely conquering the Indian bourgeoisie and intelligentsia, they sought to hold forward a feeble shield of a reconstructed Hindu ideology which had no longer any natural basis for its existence in actual life conditions. All social and scientific development was condemned by the more extreme devotees of this gospel as the conquerors' culture: every form of antiquated tradition, even abuse, privilege and obscurantism, was treated with respect and veneration".

Similar is the attitude of present day communal forces. Precisely because their ideological roots are based on revivalism and obscurantism, they are opposed to a thorough agrarian revolution. Even at the level of the superstructure, despite mouthing radical slogans, they only strengthen the caste hierarchies of the old Hindu order.

The other tendency during the freedom struggle, which prevented the liquidation of the old order, was the vacillation of the Congress towards landlords and feudal interests. At a time when huge mass peasant revolts had started growing against landlords, the Congress in the 1922 Bardoli resolution, calling off the national campaign against the British, stated: *"The Working Committee advises Congress workers and organisations to inform the ryots that withholding of rent payments to zamindar is contrary to the Congress resolutions and injurious to the best interests of the country. The Working Committee assures the zamindars that the Congress movement is in no way interested to attack their legal rights....."* Thus, the Congress's efforts to achieve independence were divorced from the agrarian revolution. In fact, as we shall see later, instead of carrying on a sweeping overthrow of the old feudal order, the Congress compromised with the landlords sharing power with them in post-independent India.

These two tendencies, put together, prevented any meaningful attack against the social oppression of the caste system associated with the feudal and semi-feudal order existing in the country. It was only the Communist Party of India which linked the struggle against British imperialism with a comprehensive agrarian revolution.

Right from the Platform of Action of 1930 to the memorandum submitted to the National Integration Council by the CPI(M) in 1968, the communist movement constantly underlined that caste exploitation and social emancipation could be possible only through sweeping changes in agrarian relations. However, in the absence of a powerful agrarian movement, this task has remained unfulfilled to date. As a result, given the compromising attitude of the bourgeois leadership, the atrocities and caste oppression continue to persist.

SOCIAL REFORM MOVEMENTS

Another current also needs to be properly analysed in order to understand the persistence of the caste stratification to date, i.e, the social reform movement. There have taken place powerful anti-caste movements in the country and they wielded significant political influence at their time. Amongst the giants who stand out in such movements was Jyotiba Phule. Jyotiba was a great secular democrat whose passion for the untouchable and sense of justice was unheard of. He, personally, had absolutely no caste bias and the movement demanding equal treatment was named as the *satyashodhak* — a movement against untruth, injustice and hypocrisy of the Hindu social order dominated by the Brahmins.

Ideologically, Jyotiba's movement was an uncompromising attack on the ancient and feudal superstructure. However, this uncompromising attack did not go beyond to attack the basic agrarian structure based on feudal land relations which was the basis on which this superstructure existed. While this movement contributed immensely to raise the consciousness against caste exploitation, it could not reach the levels of that structure's elimination precisely because it could not mobilise the peasantry for an agrarian revolution.

Similar has been the experience of Ambedkar. This most outstanding and tireless fighter, who on behalf of the Dalit exposed the upper caste hypocrisies and lambasted the Congress and its policies, had to finally ask his followers to embrace Buddhism to escape the injustices of Hindu society. But the grim social reality based on unequal land relations did not change because of conversion to Buddhism. Unfortunately, smashing the present socio-economic system as the decisive step for elimination of caste exploitation was replaced by formal declarations of equality, reservation of seats, jobs, etc. It was once again shown that despite a leader of Ambedkar's stature, and despite the strength of the movement, the objective could not be achieved because it failed to target the basic source of this exploitation, i e, feudal and semi-feudal land relations.

Similar also has been the experience of the Dravidian movement led by Periyar E.V. Ramaswamy Naicker. Periyar did succeed in creating a great feeling against caste oppression and his voice loomed large against untouchability. But yet again, viewing this merely at the level of superstructure without attacking the economic base that nurtured such a monstrous iniquitous caste stratification, the movement could not reach its logical culmination.

Thus, we find that the social reform movement, despite the glorious uncompromising role of its leaders, could not achieve the stated objective as it either ignored or bypassed the tasks of the agrarian revolution.

Thus, we find that at the time of independence, all these currents, put together, had created a situation where the tasks of the democratic revolution — chiefly the agrarian revolution — remained unfulfilled under the bourgeois leadership of the freedom struggle that not only vacillated but compromised with landlordism.

COMPROMISE WITH LANDLORDISM

This process gets manifested in a concrete expression in post- independent India. The Indian bourgeoisie, in its eagerness to capture state power, compromised on the one hand with imperialism and on the other with landlordism and semi-feudal forces. It shared power with the latter in the ruling class alliance. Thus, instead of sweeping away the feudal and semi-feudal land relations in the course of the anti-colonial and anti-imperialist struggle, the ruling classes perpetuated these relations, seeking only to modify them for their interests by attempting to superimpose capitalism. Thus, instead of a sweeping overthrow of the old order from below, what happened over these years of independence was a limited superimposition of capitalist relations in agriculture, that too in limited pockets, without overthrowing the social relations. This only perpetuated the social consciousness associated with the semi-feudal relations — caste and communalism.

Further, the system of parliamentary democracy that was adopted was based on an electoral system which tended to reinforce the caste consciousness. Instead of guaranteeing equality, irrespective of caste, the electoral system, itself, nurtured the perpetuation of caste consciousness in terms of choice of candidates and the appeal to the electorate. The ruling classes have consistently refused to accept the CPI(M)'s suggestion to introduce proportional representation. Apart from its other advantages, as people would have to vote for parties and not individuals, this would have minimised the appeals based on caste, religion, community, etc.

While both these factors tended to reinforce the perpetuation of caste oppression, the Congress leadership continued to mouth concern over caste oppression and continued to appeal to people to change their way of life and outlook rather than attack the economic basis on which this oppression thrived. The inability to proceed with even the limited land reform legislations because of the alliance with the landlords prevented in the past and prevents today the Indian bourgeoisie to complete the tasks of the democratic revolution.

This is reinforced by the attitude of the Congress leaders, even those coming from the Dalit. A case in point is the experiences and opinions of Shri Jagjivan Ram in his book *Caste Challenge in India*. Unlike many other Dalit leaders who stood aloof from the national movement, Shri Jagjivan Ram has a proud distinction of active participation in the freedom struggle, including imprisonment. With justified passion, he recounts the plight of the Dalit and the oppressed castes. Intellectually, he accepts the fact that the struggle against caste oppression can only be successful as an integral part of the struggle of the exploited classes of India. Despite emphasising this consistently in his book, the final solution he offers is characteristic of a bourgeois leader. He abhors class struggle for the emancipation of the poor and urges the people to adopt the Gandhian way, i e, the elimination of such oppression with an exercise of the force of morality. Thus, once again, we find that while understanding the problem correctly, while describing the situation graphically, the modern day leaders of post-independent India also fought shy of mobilising the people for a sweeping agrarian revolution as the basic solution of the problem.

Let us now return to the initial line of analysis concerning the issue of properly integrating the Dalit and backward castes in the social mainstream. The net result of the post-independence decades has been not the building up of a movement for the eradication of social oppression that the caste system represents, but for palliatives offered to redress to some degree the suffering of these sections through the extension of the British concept of concessions such as reservations in educational institutions and jobs. These are projected as an end in themselves. This, despite the plethora of statistical information that this has not substantially altered the conditions of a vast majority of the oppressed. In the absence of any meaningful change in agrarian relations, such concessions must be supported. But no illusions must be entertained that this is the only solution.

In the very nature of things, these palliatives will neither solve the problem of poverty and unemployment nor change the condition of untouchables and other downtrodden castes. They will certainly offer some relief to individuals from these communities, enhance their confidence in their advance, but not change their status. For the ruling classes these concessions play an important role. In the first place, in the general competition for jobs etc, they pit one section of toilers against another. Secondly, they create an impression among some sections that the government is their real friend and they should confine the struggle within the framework of the bourgeois system. It is thus that a challenge to the present socio-economic system from the most downtrodden sections is prevented.

Another phenomenon, which was taking place simultaneously, will also have to be noted. A parallel development that was taking place during the days of the freedom struggle and particularly after the independence was the process of emergence of a modern state in India. The vast multinational character of our country ensured that different sections — caste, religions, ethnic, regional — began to rightfully demand equality of status and opportunity in the new independent polity. But, however, as the economic crisis deepened in the post-independent decades, far from the expectations of these different sections being met, the disparities started growing. This led and continues to lead today to a scramble amongst these different sections for a share of the cake. As the size of the cake shrinks, this scramble takes the form of a conflict between various groups. Hence, the demand for reservations from new sections and the opposition to reservations from other sections becomes a common practice.

CASTE ASSERTIONS

It is, in this background of deepening crisis in our country, that one must understand the nature of the present caste assertion. There are two aspects to this. On the one hand, as a result of whatever limited development has taken place since independence and in the background of the deepening crisis, there is a growing consciousness amongst the oppressed castes to rebel against their conditions of social oppression. This is a positive aspect. Without such a growing consciousness the struggle against oppression and exploitation cannot be carried out decisively. This is a consciousness that needs to be nurtured and strengthened by the communists with an effort to integrate this consciousness with the struggles against the present socio-economic system. It is only through such an integration of the struggle against social oppression and the struggle against modern day class exploitation that the struggle for an agrarian revolution can be strengthened and carried forward to its logical culmination.

There is, however, another aspect to the present day caste assertion. This is the attempt to try and confine this growing consciousness within the parameters of the concerned caste. This is resorted to by the leadership of the present day movements whose outlook is no different from the ones we discussed above. While appealing only to the caste consciousness and ignoring, if not evading, the basic issue of the struggle against the existing agrarian order, these leaders are once again appealing for a change in the superstructure without affecting the base. In doing so, they treat this growing consciousness amongst the Dalit and the backward castes as separate compartments, as vote banks for their political fortunes, rather than addressing themselves for a genuine solution of the problem.

CASTE MOVEMENTS AND THEIR LIMITATIONS

The appeal of such caste leaders to their following is not to strengthen the common struggle to change the present socio- economic system. The appeal is to elect their brethren to power, thus spreading the illusion that coming to power within the same system, that protects the existing socio-economic order, is a solution to their problems. This may serve the lust for power of the leaders but the living conditions of the mass remain as backward as ever. This has been the experience of the governments that have come to power in Bihar and UP. None of them even initiated the implementation of existing land reform legislations that the West Bengal Left Front government has done. By exploiting the growing consciousness amongst the socially oppressed, the leadership is thus perpetuating the very edifice of exploitation of the existing socio-economic system. Instead of sweeping agrarian changes, they seek to preserve the existing order that perpetuates the caste system and its oppression.

Yet, why is it that a significant section of the oppressed castes are carried away, at least momentarily, by their leaders' appeal? Here one must understand the tremendous sense of caste solidarity that exists. In the face of atroci-ties committed by the upper castes, the only source of re-sistance and protection the oppressed have is the strength of their being together. This is particularly so among the Dalit as they are often, and in many cases to date, huddled together and their habitations confined to certain areas. The bonds of kinship forged through common suffering shape a common consciousness of solidarity. Their moving together is not due to lack of education or civility as the upper castes contemptuously tend to describe. It is out of sheer necessity to offer the strongest possible resistance to the oppression heaped on them.

The net result of this is that this dual nature of the present caste assertion presents itself in a manner as though there is a duality of social consciousness amongst the oppressed. The communist movement itself has experienced instances of how the oppressed sections are willing to brave the worst police oppression in their economic struggles under the red flag, but when it comes to electoral preferences and voting, they appear to be guided by their social, kinship and caste affinities. It is this apparent duality of social consciousness that the vested interests of the caste leadership seek to preserve for electoral benefits.

But in the process, they seek to divorce the struggle against social oppression from the struggle against modern day class exploitation. Thus, instead of strengthening the unity of the toilers against the present socio-economic system, they tend to separate the two struggles thereby weakening this unity.

DALIT-BAHUJAN EMANCIPATION MOVEMENT

Another major debate has erupted in Indian political and civil society circles after the October 6, 2005, United States Congressional Sub-Committee hearings in Washington, DC, on the issue of caste discrimination in India. Some questions raised as a result of this hearing are: "Why has it taken so long for the world to hear about the persistent problem of caste discrimination in India ? We thought the caste system was abolished in India ? Why is it that we have not been told about the connection between caste discrimination and the 25 million bonded child labourers, the girl trafficking, the prostitution trade, the illiteracy and poverty, the constant rape and abuse of women, and the plight of the landless labourers?"

Following the hearings in the USA, there was also an extensive debate on the Dalit issue in the British Parliament on November 22, 2005.

The blunt answer to the above questions is that until now the Indian reality has been interpreted and articulated within India and around the world through the worldview of the dominant castes in larger society. For all practical purposes, the dominant castes rule, control and articulate the Indian reality.

The dominant upper castes have been quite content with a "class analysis" of India (focusing attention on the rich, the new middle-class and the poor), knowing very well that it is only a "caste analysis" of India that can uncover the true but hidden reality at the heart of India – the India of the majority masses. One cannot understand India without understanding the complete nature and scope of the caste system in Indian life. Caste considerations dominate people's lives from birth to death. This understanding of the caste system and how it controls and regulates social, economic, political and religious life is absolutely essential to interpreting the Indian reality. Add to this the "corruption factor" in Indian society and the Dalit and other oppressed people who are poor are left in a completely hopeless situation. India is not a homogenous society where there is a level playing field on which everyone can prosper.

Caste continues to dominate Indian society despite the fact that the draftsman of the Constitution, the redoubtable Dalit thinker and lawyer Dr. Bhim Rao Babasaheb Ambedkar, wrote his prophetic work "Annihilation of Caste" to reveal to the world the brutal stranglehold of the caste system. The Indian Constitution, taking the best out of American and British statutes, outlawed untouchability, one of the manifestations of caste discrimination, but stopped well short of abolishing caste.

Dalit-Bahujan leaders across India refer to caste discrimination as " India 's silent apartheid" of 3,000 years against its majority peoples – a full 70% of the population. It is a religiously sanctioned racism that has maimed, dehumanized and destroyed hundreds of millions of people through the ages. The horrendous fact is that we continue to destroy millions of people through this system even today in the 21st century.

Here is what the former President of India, Dr. K.R. Narayanan, recently stated regarding caste: "An empowered India bereft of the respect for women, values of civilized existence and morality will collapse in the face of the disaffection and discontent of those who have suffered for centuries. Day in and day out we take pride in claiming that India has a 5,000-year-old civilization. But the way the Dalit and those suppressed are being treated by the people who wield power and authority speaks volumes for the degradation of our moral structure and civilized standards.

"Dr. B.R. Ambedkar, the principal architect of the Constitution, had said political equality devoid of economic and social equality would bring about contradictions in our democratic set-up which if not rectified will lead to its doom. In the dark cloud of inequality and social injustice the silver lining represented by the assertion of the hitherto suppressed and exploited sections for their rights inspire confidence for their future empowerment. Their struggle for empowerment represents empowerment of India.

> "As the struggle gains momentum and gets accentuated, there is bound to be reluctance and resistance on the part of the high and mighty to accept their upward rise. The killing of Dalit, their exploitation and the brutality they face is a negation of the empowered India."

Increasingly, the Dalit-Bahujan emancipation movement began to gather more strength across the nation. Ambedkar's true contribution to the nation, his work for the depressed castes, was progressively more greatly understood and appreciated. Even the upper caste movements and political leaders began to co-opt Ambedkar's legacy and brand name as their own.

Ambedkar's bitter disagreement with Mahatma Gandhi was no longer locked in archival documents. Suddenly, Ambedkar's opposing sentiment became common knowledge. Ambedkar wanted the abolishment of caste itself, which then would result in abolishing untouchability and the inhuman discrimination against the Dalit. Gandhi's proposal to simply deal with the symptom of untouchability and not touch the issue of the caste system was a major mistake and has marred his otherwise great legacy. Perhaps he was influenced by the orthodox upper caste people who surrounded him, telling him that Hinduism as they knew it would not survive the demise of caste, its foundation, steel frame and bonding force.

Fifty years after Independence, caste prejudice and discrimination continue as a persistent disease. Ambedkar was correct in his thinking that caste must be "annihilated" if untouchability is to be genuinely eliminated.

Ambedkar also concluded that conversion was the ultimate solution if Hinduism was not able to reform itself and annihilate caste. He did not see much hope that this cataclysmic reformation would take place.

Again, fifty years later, nothing of the needed reformation has taken place. If anything, with the emergence of the extremist right-wing Hindu movement, caste discrimination and oppression have increased.

The modern-day increase of caste-based oppression is the reason why the Vice President of the world Hindu federation known as the Vishwa Hindu Parishad (VHP) can say on national television that the life of a cow is more valuable than the lives of five Dalit after five Dalit young people in north India were lynched near New Delhi, when they were found skinning the carcass of a dead cow.

This is why a Shankaracharya (major community leader) said that Dalit should learn to live in the position in which they were born. This leader was more brutal in his statement than was Gandhi who simply said people must be happy and perform to the best of their ability in their given occupation – scavenging, tanning, sweeping, etc.

The movement for emancipation of the depressed classes kept pace with the freedom movement Gandhi led. While Kabir and Phule's folk teachings influenced the masses, Dr. B.R. Ambedkar made a frontal assault on caste, using the brilliance of his legal training and his access to the political negotiating tables in London and New Delhi in the days preceding the transfer of power from Imperial Britain to Independent India.

Ambedkar was an intellectual giant and India's great reformer. Born a Dalit in Maharashtra, he had experienced caste's depravity first-hand. He bitterly disagreed with Mahatma Gandhi's cosmetic solution to the problem of untouchability.

History has proven Ambedkar right. The Indian Constitution should have banned the caste system along with the problem of untouchability. Trying to remove untouchability without removing the caste system was like dealing with mere symptoms rather than combating the root disease.

CASTE UPHEAVAL INFLUENCES INDIAN POLITICS

Caste turmoil and upheaval fully exploded on the national scene when the recommendations of the Mandal Commission were implemented in the mid-1990s. The Mandal Commission indicated that the Backward Castes were no better socio-economically because of the consequences of the caste system. The Supreme Court supported the view of the Commission and granted affirmative action benefits to the Backward Castes. Upper caste mobs resisted the judgment and anarchy prevailed in major cities for many weeks.

Indian politics changed dramatically after the Mandal issue hit the national consciousness. Caste politics became a dominant factor in Indian society, and caste loyalties began to determine elections across the nation. The north Indian states of Uttar Pradesh and Bihar saw dramatic movements of the political empowerment of the Sudras, or Backward Castes. Dalit politics, too, was established with the emergence of the Bahujan Samaj Party as a major player in Uttar Pradesh and the surrounding north Indian States in the so-called "Cow Belt". Consistent with the larger caste assertion by the Backward Castes, the Dalit also began to increasingly assert themselves.

THE DALIT STRUGGLE AGAINST CASTE SYSTEM

It is the process of building a broad-based, pan-Indian alliance of individuals and groups to bring an end to caste discrimination and exploitation. It is a national and global struggle for the human rights of the Dalit and other oppressed sections of our society. The movement seeks to build both a national and global union against the caste system and the ensuing inhuman oppression and discrimination.

The movement works with everyone who is committed to ending the dehumanizing caste system. Caste, creed, nationality and economic standing are no bar in building this alliance for ending India's silent apartheid of 3,000 years. We believe in a better future for all Indians.

Ending Caste Discrimination Around the World

It is the process of building a global alliance to end caste discrimination around the world. Caste discrimination is not limited to India alone. It is rampant in South Asia and extends to wherever the people of the sub-continent live. It is present among Indians living in the United Kingdom, USA, Canada and other places.

The right wing Hindutva movement has now spread across the world with offices in all of the major Western nations including North America, the Caribbean, the UK, and the nations of the European Union. These organizations in the West have financed the violent, caste-based, right-wing Hindu fundamentalist groups in India.

Caste discrimination should be a legitimate item on the UN agenda and on the agenda of global human rights movements and organizations. Without the active collaboration and support of all global entities that believe in the intrinsic dignity of all humans, caste discrimination will not end.

Eliminating and Prosecuting Caste-Based Violence

It is a movement seeking to end caste-based violence against people of depressed castes. The constant rape of Dalit women, the burning of Dalit homes and the blatant physical attacks on Dalit is not acceptable. Year after year physical attacks against Dalit are reported and documented, but fewer than 2% ever reach conviction in a court of law. According to one conservative estimate there are over 50,000 major atrocities committed against Dalit every year. We work towards applying the rule of law to those who perpetrate these crimes.

Eradicating Bonded Child Labour

It is a movement designed to deliver the vast majority of Dalit children who make up the bonded child labour market in India. Bonded child labour is a crime against humanity. Estimates report that at least 15 million bonded Dalit children work in inhuman conditions for a paltry sum. Most bonded labourers in India are from Dalit and other backward communities.

Rejecting Gender-Based Oppression and the Trafficking of Girls

It is a movement seeking to end girl prostitution, trafficking of women in the sex trade, and other violence against women. There is a huge inter-state trafficking of girls in the sex trade. Dalit and other Backward Caste girls from Nepal are bought and sold into the sex trade in the major cities of India.

Sex trade in the sub-continent draws its victims from the Dalit, Tribals and oppressed castes. The targeting of Dalit and Tribal women for these trades is a symptom of the caste system and its view of Dalit/Tribal women in particular and women in general.

The movement is deeply conscious that caste discrimination extends to all women in India and that Dalit women are twice oppressed. We reject this oppression. We are deeply concerned for the hundreds of thousands of minor/teenage Tribal girls who work in affluent homes in the cities and urban areas of India. We are concerned about the abuse they face – sexual and physical.

Caste ideology also places a low value on women. This prejudice and worldview has resulted in the female feticide of tens of millions causing an alarming decline in the female population in many states of India. Unless addressed immediately, Indian society is hurtling towards a major social disaster and increased abuse of women.

Standing Against the Deceit of Cultural/ Extremist Nationalism

It is a movement that rejects the "cultural nationalism" (a direct acquisition from Nazi nationalism) of the extremist Hindu right. The right-wing groups and their silent subscribers have used the idea of "external" enemies like "minorities" to try and cover up caste discrimination and unite the oppressed castes in violence against Muslims and Christians in the name of "nationalism". Muslims, Christians, Sikhs and Buddhists are not the enemies of India, nor are they enemies of the Dalit and other oppressed peoples.

In fact, most Christians, Muslims, Buddhists, and Sikhs were Dalit and Backward Caste people who turned to these religions to escape the tyranny of the caste system. True nationalism is not separating India along false divisions in society, but instead, it should be uniting and integrating the peoples of India. True nationalism must see the larger Dalit-Bahujan population delivered from caste oppression and discrimination. Their children, their girls, their women and their men must be delivered from modern day slavery.

Deploring Religious Exploitation and Encouraging Authentic Spirituality

It is a movement that deplores the religious exploitation of Dalit and other oppressed groups by any religious entity. It is a movement that categorically rejects Pseudo-Spirituality even as it champions religious freedom for the oppressed masses. On the one hand, Dalit have been enslaved by one religious system that denies them any spiritual rights and privileges – such as rights of spiritual equality, access to the temple priesthood, and access to all temples and all religious rites. On the other hand, other religious systems have offered them a place in a "heaven" of the future while continuing to practice caste discrimination within their religious communities.

The Church in India is also guilty in this regard. Large sections of the Church in India have betrayed the legacy of Jesus, the legacy of Wilberforce, and the legacy of William Carey when it comes to dealing with the issue of the caste system and the ensuing inhuman discrimination within society and the Church. At the same time, Dalit leaders acknowledge their debt to those Christian missionaries who reached out to them in love and accepted them as fellow human beings. The present movement seeks an end to this exploitation and Pseudo-Spirituality. It encourages Dalit and other oppressed peoples to seek true and authentic spirituality – spirituality that truly addresses their spiritual, social, emotional and physical needs.

Dalit-Bahujan ideologues speak of this struggle as one of spiritual democracy versus the spiritual fascism of the caste system.

Promoting Full-Life Transformation and Empowerment for the Dalit-Bahujans

The movement is about the economic and social empowerment of the Dalit-Bahujan people through effective economic and educational programmes. It aims to build effective micro-enterprise projects along with macro-enterprises.

It also calls for the review of various foreign governmental aid programmes which do not reach Dalit. We ask for a proportionate disbursement of all aid money and projects. It also calls for a review of funding coming through NGOs into India and the disbursement of the same among the Dalit and other oppressed sections of society.

We acknowledge the heart wrenching poverty that is prevalent among the Dalit majority coupled with the huge problem of overall illiteracy. We believe economic dignity is a critical part of human dignity and that the oppressed must be freed and empowered to take care of their personal economic needs and prosperity.

It aims to provide Dalit-Bahujan children – the future – access to quality English-medium education to allow them to play their leadership role in an increasingly globalized India.

Thus far, Dalit children (and large sections of the Backward Castes) have had no access to such quality education. English-medium education is the preserve of the moneyed upper caste and middle class elite. This movement rejects the hypocrisy of the elitist castes whose children are educated in English, while the children of the oppressed castes are encouraged to study in the "vernacular" in the name of culture and extremist nationalism.

In addition, we are deeply concerned for the lack of medical care and health problems connected with the Dalit-Bahujan people.

We are disturbed that in the battle against AIDS the Dalit and oppressed caste victims of this disease are once again marginalized in the various programmes launched to fight this epidemic. The pattern remains the same whether it is the Dalit victims of the Asian Tsunami of 2004 or the Dalit victims of the Gujarat Earthquake of 2001. Dalit are marginalized even in the midst of catastrophe.

Recognizing the Global Security Threat Caused by Caste Discrimination

It is a movement that recognizes the huge security threat that ongoing caste discrimination against the Dalit people and other oppressed sections poses to India and the rest of the world. Disenchanted, bitter and angry young men and women drive the extremist violent Maoist and Naxalite left-wing movements from Nepal to South India. As India increasingly becomes two nations in one – one for whom India is shining, and the other for whom India is in darkness – these violent movements will only increase and will attack not only local governments but also international institutions they deem as collabourators with the elitist castes who oppress the masses.

The movement also recognizes the threat of the oppressed castes exiting into other faiths, legitimizing violence and attacking the ruling castes and their institutions. All in all, these facts produce a depressing outlook for the great nation of India if we do not see the abolishment of caste in this generation and the achievement of authentic Dalit Freedom.

Demolishing the Tyranny of Caste Hierarchy

It is a movement that seeks to end the oppression within Dalit and Backward Caste groups due to the notion of a superior/inferior caste hierarchy. It acknowledges that in some places, sections of the liberated Backward Castes oppress and discriminate the Dalit out of a mistaken sense of their "better" identity, or patently at the behest of the upper castes. It also acknowledges that the Dalit groups themselves need to unite to end the tyranny of the caste system and that the small number of liberated and well-to-do Dalit must not forget the plight of their brethren who continue to suffer.

POLITICS OF DALITISM: CREATING DALIT AMONG DALIT

The attempt of some of activists of Dalit movement in India to internationalise the issue in World Conference Against Racism (WCAR) concluded in the first week of September and follow up actions have created an impression that there is something basically wrong in the ideological orientation of the movement. The word Dalit was coined in post-colonial India by the disciples of Ambedkar. They did not accept the word Harijan (Men of God) used by Gandhi for the untouchables in Hindu social order because of their aversion against him. The word Dalit therefore, became the vernacular terminology for the oppressed classes, with a wider connotation for electoral sociology in the democratic polity of the country.

If we look to the history of Dalit movement, it is as old as the birth of the concept of untouchability, which was the darkest spot in Hindu social structure. Though, Hindu reformists tried their best to fight against this social evil right from the days untouchability was born, the real concern over it came to surface during the freedom struggle, when Mahatma Gandhi and Dr. B.R.Ambedkar fought against it in their own way. While Gandhi wanted complete eradication of untouchability for emotional integration of Hindu society, Ambedkar was for abolition of *Varna*shram structure of the Hindu social order.

The conceptual difference between the two messiahs of untouchables continues to affect the Dalit movement even after their death. While the disciples rejected Mahatma Gandhi for the sake of power and fulfillment of their personal ambitions, Ambedkar became a symbol of Dalit movement. A clue to understanding Ambedkar lies in his hatred of Gandhi.

The activists of Dalit movement adopted the same philosophy against the upper castes and are still found boiling in the anger generated by their messiah Ambedkar. Taking advantage of the violent landscape, which started emerging since the closing decades of twentieth century, the followers of Ambedkar adopted the sole agenda to create social disorder and capture power. In both the situations, the process of social transformation in Hindu society, which took off in positive direction just after independence got disturbed.

To understand the multi dimensional direction of the Dalit movement, we may briefly look into the difference between Gandhi and Ambedkar on this issue. During the first Round Table Conference, when Ambedkar favoured the move of the British Government to provide separate electorate for the oppressed classes, Gandhi strongly opposed it on the plea that the move would disintegrate the Hindu society. He went for an indefinite hunger strike from September 20, 1932 against the decision of the then British Prime Minister J.Ramsay MacDonald granting communal award to the depressed classes in the constitution for governance of British India.

In view of the mass upsurge generated in the country to save the life of Gandhi, Ambedkar was compelled to soften his stand. A compromise between the leaders of caste Hindu and the depressed classes was reached on September 24,1932, popularly known as Poona Pact. The resolution announced in a public meeting on September 25 in Bombay confirmed -" *henceforth, amongst Hindus no one shall be regarded as an untouchable by reason of his birth and they will have the same rights in all the social institutions as the other Hindus have*". This landmark resolution in the history of the Dalit movement in India subsequently formed the basis for giving due share to Dalit in the political empowerment of Indian people in a democratic Indian polity.

Even though Ambedkar was a party to Poona Pact, he was never reconciled to it. His contempt against Gandhi, which continued even after his assassination on January 30,1948. On the death of Gandhi he expressed, "*My real enemy has gone, thank goodness the eclipse is over*". He equated the assassination of Gandhi with that of Caesar and the remark of Cicero to the messenger - "*Tell the Romans, your hour of liberty has come*". He further remarked, "*While one regrets the assassination of Mahatma Gandhi, one cannot help finding in his heart the echo of the sentiments expressed by Cicero on the assassination of Caesar*". Considering Gandhi as a "*positive danger to this country*", he quoted from Bible that "*sometime good cometh out of evil, so also I think good will come out of the death of Mr. Gandhi*".

The reaction of Ambedkar over the death of Gandhi may be viewed as a politics of negation for vengeance against the caste Hindus and also for political power for Dalit. He felt, "the problem of depressed classes will never be solved unless they get political power in their own hand" (Thus spoke Ambedkar by Bhagwan Das). He however, did not clarify as to how in a democratic polity of pluralistic society, Dalit would be the sole custodians of power.

DALIT MOVEMENT AFTER AMBEDKAR

The post-Gandhian and post-Ambedkar Dalit activists re-invented the direction of their movement, which was by and large focussed towards developing the negative ideas in a dark room. They are yet to take the next step to focus their negatives in light for positive prints. In the absence of a scientific endeavour their movement lags in its march towards social reform, as it has more or less become a platform for the political empowerment of some individuals for their personal ambitions and vested interests. This is not only against the concept of equalitarian Hindu sociology of Vedic India but also against the concept of democracy.

The present clash for Dalit leadership has confirmed the theory of C.Rajagopalachari that many Dalit leaders are interested for continuance of the undesirable status of Dalit for the fulfillment of their personal ambitions. Disagreeing with Ambedkar on Dalit issue he said, "*...This is material explanation for the violent dislike of Gandhiji exhibited by Dr. Ambedkar, who looks upon this great and inspired reformer as the enemy of the untouchables, meaning thereby of the educated and ambitious among them who find that the depressed status furnishes short cut to position*".

It may be partially true that political empowerment is key to social and economic empowerment as suggested by Ambedkar but this cannot be the sole criteria for the social equality of Dalit. The representatives (122 -76 SC and 46 ST in parliament against its strength of 543 and 1085 -556 SC and 529 ST in state assemblies against their strength of 4370) of Dalit in parliament and state assemblies in sizeable strength have been sharing political power for last fifty years. But if they have failed to bring a desired social change and economic upliftment of Dalit, there is something wrong in the movement, which is yet to be identified. The students of the constituting history have therefore, a right to know from Dalit activists the reason behind the failure of their representatives sharing political power.

One may be amused to understand that how only160 Dalit delegates under the umbrella of National Campaign on Dalit Human Rights in WCAR would have fought for the cause of Dalit in India if the representatives of Dalit sharing political power could not assert and agitate for the cause of their community? An objective analysis of the prevailing social condition and sentiments in India may corroborate the theory of C. Rajagopalachari that Dalit movement has become a vehicle to promote the personal interest of some individuals or groups.

In the absence of an All India mind with a cohesive and unified perspective, Dalit movement has also failed to emerge as a strong political force. Dalit are divided into hundreds of castes and sub-castes. About 56 percent of Dalit population belong to about 20 dominant castes among them. These dominant castes are presently grabbing all the privileges provided to the Dalit constitutionally. Even Dr. Ambedkar failed to give an intellectual explanation to unify them together, as a result, his political influence during his life time also remained confined to only Mahar caste of his community in the Maharashtra region.

Dalit activists, due to lack of actual ideological direction are not clear whether they are interested to ensure the material prosperity of Dalit or equal status in Hindu social order. Untouchability has almost disappeared, as touch of Dalit is no more considered to have any polluting affect on caste Hindus. However, so long the Dalit enjoy the benefits of reservation in Government jobs and admission in academic institutions, they may have to bear the stigma of being considered unequal in merit to the caste Hindus. The objective of Dalit movements should be therefore, to erase such stigma, which is possible only if Dalit get a chance for their proper education befitting to the standard required for competitions.

Contrary to the objective of the movement discussed above, the managers of Dalit movement due to their vested interest do not want their people to be cleansed from the stigma of reservation and the agony of their past humiliation of being treated as untouchables. In stead of fighting for transformation of the Hindu social order, they are found more interested to promote themselves as Esperanto of United Nations politics. With weapon of hate, they are neither able to fight against the social inequality and injustice effectively nor in a position to contribute any significant social change.

In stead of looking on the growing consciousness among the educated caste Hindus against the social evil of caste discrimination against Dalit and appreciating this positive change, the Dalit activists ignore and understate the development. Their sole aim is now pointed towards personal ambitions at the cost of their community. This has created a new class of Brahmins among the Dalit, who are now exploiting the actual Dalit by grabbing the benefits meant for the latter. This may look like a paradox, but it is the hard reality.

The on going Dalit movement is gradually losing its track. Its multi-dimensional character based on the philosophy of love and hate is unfortunately turned into political theocracy, which is contrary to the basic concept of the total transformation of Hindu social order. Inciting the Dalit against the caste Hindus for historical agony without any honest effort for their emotional integration with rest of the Hindu social order is neither in the interest of this disadvantaged section of population nor in the interest of the nation.

The shrinking influence of the so called Brahminsm in electoral politics, social transformation, spiritual movement, or even other public affairs are enough indications of gradual changes in Hindu sociology. Dalit movements with a view to create social disorder by promoting caste hatred against the upper castes of ancient *Varna*shram system will simply halt the process of the on going social transformation. With their political empowerment by occupying the post of President, Union Cabinet ministers, Chief ministers, and bureaucrats, Dalit are gradually getting more opportunities for achieving social empowerment under democratic process. By gaining more confidence, Dalit are now found to be quite assertive of their rights. This however, does not mean that they have been acceptable in community dining or inter-caste marriage, which is not even prevalent within the various Dalit castes.

The objective of any social reform movement is to ensure a peaceful, decent and dignified life for every body without any social confrontation. But, unfortunately the Dalit activists are so obsessed and possessive in their approach towards the historical agony of their community that they have made the latter as prisoners of Dalitism, which hardly has any constructive plan for creation of a just social order. Their slogan for abolition of *Varna*shram (professional units) system and total abolition of caste is an utopian concept, which will never take root in the diverse and pluralistic Indian society.

Casteism is the bane of Indian society but the Indian people accept caste as a hard reality. Even the Christians and Muslims boast themselves of their upper caste heritage. In South India even Christians are maintaining visible distance from the Dalit Chritians as the latter continue to have separate church, separate burial ground and even separate places for social interactions. Similarly, even Muslims in India and Pakistan there is no inter- caste marriage among the Sheiks, Syed, Paithan and others because of their upper caste heritage before conversion.

As far as the present Dalit movement is concerned, it is in the hands of three vested interest groups of Dalit politicians, Dalt writers and Chrisian missionaries. Dalit political leaders like Kansi Ram and Ms Mayawati of Bahujan Samaj Party and Ram Vilas Paswan of Lok Jana Shakti are having their influence exclusively among the members of their own community. They can never come to power on their own due to their limited influence among the voters. For coming to power they are compelled to join some other parties dominated by caste Hindus. They are therefore, hardly in a position to bring any social change.

The second group, which claims to be the champion for the cause of Dalit is of Dalit writers. Their personal ambition and ego have kept them away from the common Dalit, who are illiterate and poor. They are more interested in their self-promotion than serving the cause of their community. Their possessiveness is often mistaken as love for Dalit. Since they do not get enough space in media to spit venom against the caste Hindus and are hardly in a position to play an effective role in electoral politics, they are always in search of the forces through which they could get national and international recognition. They have therefore, joined hand with forces (third group) determined to disintegrate the Hindu society.

The interest of the third group in Dalit movement is to de-Hinduise the Dalit and promote their proselytisational endeavour. The argument of this group that Christian society does not have any caste discrimination is not based on ground reality. The Dalit Christians are facing the problem of caste discrimination even in Christian society. Such discrimination is prevalent in Kerala even after the death of Dalit Christians, whose corpses do not find any place in the cemetery meant for upper caste convert Christians. T.V.Rajshekhar, a Dalit writer, while speaking in a seminar (Church and Dalit) organised by Christian leaders in Madras on June 14, 1986 said that Dalit Christians form about 80 percent Christian population in India but contrary to what Jesus Christ preached, the Dalit Christians are also the victim of caste discrimination as they have separate burial ground, separate churches and separate dwelling places.

Ever since the promulgation of presidential order No 19 of 1950 debarring the Dalit of non-Hindu and non-Sikh community to be included in the list of Scheduled castes, the Christian missionaries have been facing difficulty in alluring the Hindu Dalit for their conversion. For this they have already launched a movement for constitutional privileges for Dalit Christians. If they succeed in alienating the Dalit from Hindu social order, the entire Dalit community will get the benefit of constitutional provisions and it will help them in their mission for proselytisation.

Indian Social Institute(ISI), a Roman Catholic Mission outfit organised a meeting on "Durban and Dalit Discourse: Post Durban Scenario" on September 20. The meeting was organised with a view to forming a "broad alliance of disadvantaged section of society to battle the status quo that would prefer to keep them on the periphery of the country's social structure" (Hindu dated September 24). The move of the institute is to internationalise the issue. Had it not been so, it should first cleanse the Christian society in Kerala. In fact the Christian missionaries are also facing a dilemma of the isolation of Dalit from the affluent sections of the community. Dr. Prakash Luis, Executive Director of ISI said, "There is a sense of vertical divide within the community between the socially mobile 'Brahmanical Dalit' and the real Dalit among Dalit".

In the backdrop of the dialectics of Dalit movements, it appears that the Dalit have now become the victims of the politics of Dalitism being played by various groups. Instead of fighting the evils of caste discrimination in Hindu society, the Dalit movement has given birth to neo Dalitism, which hardly has any difference with the polluted Brahmanism.

The movement, which does not have the ingredients to bring about reconciliation among conflicting social groups and fails to accelerate the process of social harmony and human dignity, is bound to lose real direction. Dalit should therefore be very careful about the politics of Dalitism being played by vested interests not only at the cost of the disadvantaged community but also at the cost of social harmony, which is more dangerous for the nation.

7

Indian Constitution and Dalits

One of the more confusing mysteries of India is her caste system. The caste system, which has existed for more than 3,000 years, was developed by the Brahmin (priest) caste in order to maintain their superiority. Eventually, the caste system became formalized into four distinct classes (Varna).

The Brahmins are the highest Varna and are the priests and arbiters of what is right and wrong in matters of religion and society. Below them are the *Kshatriyas*, who served traditionally as soldiers and administrators. The Vaishyas are the artisan and commercial class, while the Shudras are the farmers and the peasants. It is said that the Brahmin has come from Brahma's mouth, *Kshatriyas* from his arms, Vaishyas from his thighs, and Shudras from his feet.

Beneath the four main castes is a fifth group, the Scheduled Castes. The people of the Scheduled Castes are not part of the Varna system. They are the untouchables, the Dalit.

A Dalit is not considered part of human society, but instead is considered something less than human. The Dalit generally perform the most menial and degrading jobs. Caste rules hold that Dalit pollute higher caste people with their presence. If higher caste Hindus touch an untouchable or even come within a Dalit's shadow, they must undergo rigorous series of cleansing rituals.

Approximately 250 million Indians (a full 25% of the population), are Dalit. In a country where everybody is supposed to have equal rights and opportunities, one out of four people is condemned to be untouchable.

Although the Indian Constitution guarantees fundamental rights and freedoms for all Indians, Dalits are systematically abused. Dalits are poor, deprived and socially backward. Their most basic needs of food, shelter, and safety are not fulfilled. They also cannot access decent education and employment. The systematic denial of their basic human rights results in a lack of education, food, healthcare, and economic opportunity, thereby keeping Dalit in perpetual bondage to the upper castes.

HIDDEN APARTHEID

More than 165 million people remain vulnerable to discrimination, exploitation and violence, says 'Hidden Apartheid: Caste Discrimination against India's 'Untouchables' because India has failed in its obligation to pursue, by all appropriate means, a policy of eliminating caste discrimination and ensuring that all public authorities and institutions do not engage in caste-based discrimination.

Using documents and data from India's own governmental and non-governmental agencies, the National Human Rights Commission, the National Commission for Scheduled Castes and Scheduled Tribes and media sources, the report, published inFebruary by the Centre for Human Rights and Global Justice (CHRGJ) and Human Rights Watch (HRW), documents India's systematic failure to respect, protect and ensure the fundamental human rights of Dalit.

CHRGJ-HRW's 'shadow report' is a response to India's recent submission of a report to the United Nations Committee on the Elimination of Racial Discrimination (CERD), which monitors implementation of the International Convention on the Elimination of All Forms of Racial Discrimination (ICERD), to which India is a party.

As party to the convention, India has an obligation to prohibit and bring to an end caste-based discrimination. Article 1 of the convention guarantees rights of non-discrimination on the basis of "race, colour, descent, or national or ethnic origin". In 1996, the committee concluded that the plight of Dalit falls under the prohibition of descent-based discrimination.

India's report to the committee was more than eight years overdue. Although it covers over a decade of India's compliance with the convention (from 1996 to 2006), it does not even mention Dalit abuse — something that India's own governmental agencies have documented and verified.

'Hidden Apartheid' fills this gap, presenting committee members with information that is essential to a fair assessment of India's record and, ultimately, to encouraging the government to live up to its domestic and international human rights obligations.

The report states that India has consistently cited its numerous legislations and policies as a measure of compliance with its obligations to end caste-based discrimination, choosing to ignore its failure to implement them, which has resulted in continued, and sometimes enhanced, brutality against Dalit.

The report focuses on the practice of 'untouchability' — the imposition of social disabilities on persons by reason of their birth in certain castes — which relegates a vast majority of India's 165 million Dalit (scheduled castes), to a lifetime of discrimination, exploitation and violence, including severe forms of torture perpetrated by State and private actors. All these acts are in violation of the rights guaranteed by the ICERD.

Entrenched discrimination violates Dalit' rights to education, health, housing, property, freedom of religion, free choice of employment and equal treatment before the law. The report says that Dalit also suffer routine violations of their right to life and security of person through State-sponsored or sanctioned acts of violence, including torture. Based on in-depth investigations by CHRGJ, Human Rights Watch, Indian non-governmental organisations, reports by Indian governmental agencies, including the National Human Rights Commission, the National Commission on Scheduled Castes and Scheduled Tribes and media sources, the report documents the pervasiveness of abuse against Dalit.

CONTINUOUS VIOLATION OF RIGHTS

Caste-motivated killings, rape and other abuses are a daily occurrence in India, says the report. Between 2001 and 2002, close to 58,000 cases were registered under the Scheduled Castes and Scheduled Tribes (Prevention of Atrocities) Act — legislation that criminalises particularly heinous forms of abuse against Dalit and tribals.

A 2005 government report states that a crime is committed against a Dalit every 20 minutes. Though staggering, this figure represents only a fraction of actual incidents since many Dalit do not register cases for fear of retaliation by the police and upper-caste individuals.

In the rare instance that a case does reach the courts, the most likely outcome is acquittal. Official data reveals that between 1999 and 2001 as many as 89% of trials involving offences against Dalit resulted in acquittals.

Sadly, the report notes, both State and non-State actors commit crimes against Dalit with impunity. The report cites the National Human Rights Commission's (NHRC's) observation that the law-enforcement machinery is the greatest violator of Dalit' human rights. According to the NHRC, India's apex national institution to protect human rights and redress grievances, police responsibility for the widespread torture of Dalit in custody, rape of Dalit women, and the looting of Dalit property "are condoned, or at best ignored".

Dalit, jurists and human rights groups claim that lack of political will and immunity laws that shield those responsible for human rights abuses from prosecution allow torture and other forms of custodial abuse to continue unchecked. Under a theory of collective punishment, the police often target entire Dalit communities in search of select individuals. Dalit women are particularly vulnerable to sexual violence by the police.

The open dissemination of propaganda targeting both Dalit and religious minorities by Hindu nationalist groups — whose members incite and engage in widespread violence — calls into question India's commitment to fulfilling its Article 4 obligations to condemn the promotion of hatred and discrimination in any form.

Innocuous treatment of the caste system in school textbooks and curricula, along with insufficient media attention towards Dalit issues all suggest that the Indian government is failing to take effective measures to counter caste prejudice, in contravention of Article 7 of the convention.

Dalit comprise the majority of agricultural, bonded and child labourers in India, says 'Hidden Apartheid', many surviving on less than US$ 1 a day, that is, by the UN and World Bank's definition, in extreme poverty.

Dalit are forced — through centuries-old tradition enforced by the hierarchical division of labour in the Hindu caste system — to perform tasks deemed too "polluting" or "degrading" for non-Dalit to carry out. According to unofficial estimates, more than 1.3 million Dalit — mostly women — are employed as manual scavengers to carry away human waste from dry pit latrines. In several cities, Dalit are lowered into manholes, without any protective gear, to clear sewage drains, resulting in more than 100 deaths each year from inhalation of toxic gases or from drowning in excrement.

Under Article 2 of the ICERD, India is bound to ensure the development and protection of particularly marginalised groups. India grants Dalit certain privileges, including 'reservations' (quotas) in education, government jobs and political posts. However, the report notes, like many of the protective measures adopted, the reservation policy has not been faithfully implemented.

Caste-based occupational distribution is often reinforced in government employment quotas, with Dalit assigned primarily to the post of sweeper. Reservations in higher education continue to be met with a great deal of resistance, leading to under-enforcement. Additionally, there has been widespread public opposition to reservations for Dalit in local government bodies, often leading to acts of violence against Dalit candidates.

According to government estimates, in 2000, the unemployment rate for Dalit and tribal groups was double that of non-Dalit/tribals. Public sector divestment is estimated to have left 200,000 Dalit employees jobless. Dalit continue to be significantly underrepresented in most professional strata.

Dalit representation in India's high-technology industries and service sectors is dismal. The National Commission for Scheduled Castes and Scheduled Tribes has stated that the private sector, which continues to enjoy government patronage, should also be brought under the purview of the reservation policy. 'Hidden Apartheid' also records the plight of Dalit women and the multiple forms of discrimination they face. In January 2007, the UN Committee on the Elimination of Discrimination against Women concluded that Dalit women in India suffer from "deeply-rooted structural discrimination".

Even as compared to Dalit men, Dalit women do not have equal access to employment opportunities or justice mechanisms. They must contend with threats to their personal security, including trafficking and sexual violence. "The Dalit woman faces triple discrimination because she is an untouchable, of a poor class and is a woman," the report quotes the National Campaign on Dalit Human Rights (NACDOR) as saying.

DALIT RIGHT TO EDUCATION

Literacy and enrollment rates among Dalit children in Bihar are alarmingly low, thus the conference sought to bring to light evidence and cases of the real challenges and discrimination faced by Dalit children in accessing and participating in education—including caste-based exclusion, segregation, humiliation, punishment and beatings. These factors, combined with poor quality of education and physical distance from schools, constitute the central reason Dalit children often drop out of school and get caught up in child labour. This conference brought together Dalit children, parents, activists, and teachers with administrators and other stakeholders in education to share their experiences and devise new strategies to achieve 100% enrollment, retention & effective learning among Dalit children.

Right to education is denied for Dalit and Backward classes for centuries in India. And it prevented their development in an unequal hierarchical social order. " Education provides the single and critical opportunity for all children in particular Dalit children for acquiring the social and intellectual skills they need to move out of the strictly hierarchical, segregated and stigmatized spaces of living, occupation and Special focuses and provisions are there for the weaker sections. But continuing disabilities, abuse, humiliation, violence, untouchablility, inaccessibility to educational institutions, poverty, caste based descriminations largely keep Dalit children from schools and caused their high drop out rates. Dalit children below eighteen years are 70 million people in India.

The National Policy on Education, 1986 aimed at the Universal enrolment of all Dalit children in the age group of 6-11 and 75 % enrolment in the 11-14 age groups. The 86th amendment of the constitution, 2002 promises free and compulsory education to all. Sarva Siksha Abhiyan (Education for All), 2000, focuses on marginalized children's eduactaion.

Despite all these the drop out rate of Dalit children is high."The national drop out rate among Dalit Children is 36.6% at primary,59.4% at middle and 73.1% at secondary level of education"(Report National Commission for SC&STs, Govt of India, 2000-2001).

According to NCERT (National Council fro Educational Research and Training) only 54.6% of schools and 10% Dalit students are covered by the free text book scheme.29.3 schools and 4.6 Dalit students are covered by free uniform. 13.9%schools and 3.9 % Dalit students were covered by the midday meal scheme.

Only 3.4% o f Dalit men over the age of 15 and I% of Dalit women had a post secondary education of any kind.The new education policies like privatization and huge cut in govt spending in education also affected them negatively.

Year	**ST**	**SC**	**others**
1991	29.6	37.41	57.69
2001	47.1	54.69	68.81

DALIT LAND RIGHTS

Most Dalit victims of violence and discrimination are landless agricultural labourers. In rural areas, where caste discrimination is most entrenched, land is the main asset determining an individual's social status and standard of living. Dalit' lack of access to land makes them economically vulnerable and dependent upon their upper- and middle-caste landlords. This economic dependency is often exploited by the landlords, allowing for many abuses against Dalit to go unpublished. Furthermore, the effects of globalization—namely, the large tracts of land being provided to multi-national corporations and projects funded by the World Bank—have meant that millions of small and marginal farmers, most of whom are Dalit, are losing their land or having their land alienated each year.

Laws and regulations exist that prohibit the alienation of Dalit lands, set ceilings on a single landowner's holdings, and allocate surplus government lands to be re-distributed to Scheduled Castes and Scheduled Tribes; however, most state governments have consistently failed to adequately implement this land reform legislation. Statistics show that government land reform policies are increasing the land holdings of non-SC households at a rate considerably higher than SC households. Perhaps most significantly, in cases where Dalit have been offered land under agrarian reform legislation, many have been forced to refuse it for fear of dominant-caste backlash. Since the dominant castes depend on the economic subjugation and exploitation of Dalit, and since Dalit land acquisition and ownership threatens this arrangement, land disputes often result in violence and abuse against the Dalit community (especially the destruction of their homes and property) as a means to "keep them in their place." Typically, in such disputes Dalit women are made the targets of violence in order to silence their male counterparts.

DISCRIMINATION AND EXPLOITATIVE FORMS OF LABOUR

Allocation of labour on the basis of caste is one of the fundamental tenets of the caste system. Within the caste system,

Dalit have been assigned tasks and occupations that are deemed ritually polluting for other caste communities. Throughout this report, Human Rights Watch has documented the exploitation of agricultural labourers who work for a few kilograms of rice or Rs. 15 to Rs. 35 a day. A sub-group of Dalit is condemned to labour even more exploitative. An estimated forty million people in India, among them fifteen million children, are bonded labourers. A majority of them are Dalit. According to government statistics, an estimated one million Dalit are manual scavengers who clean public latrines and dispose of dead animals; unofficial estimates are much higher. In India's southern states, thousands of Dalit girls are forced into prostitution before reaching the age of puberty.

Bondage is passed on from one generation to another. Scavenging and prostitution are hereditary occupations of "untouchable" castes. Dalit face discrimination when seeking other forms of employment and are largely unable to escape their designated occupation even when the practice itself has been abolished by law. In violation of their basic human rights, they are physically abused and threatened with economic and social ostracism from the community for refusing to carry out various caste-based tasks.

BONDED LABOUR

"Bonded labour" refers to work in slave-like conditions in order to pay off a debt. Due to the high interest rates charged and the abysmally low wages paid, the debts are seldom settled. Bonded labourers are frequently low-caste, illiterate, and extremely poor, while the creditors/employers are usually higher-caste, literate, comparatively wealthy, and relatively more powerful members of the community. The Bonded Labour System (Abolition) Act, 1976 abolishes all agreements and obligations arising out of the bonded labour system. It aims to release all labourers from bondage, cancel any outstanding debt, prohibit the creation of new bondage agreements, and order the economic rehabilitation offreed bonded labourers by the state. It also punishes attempts to compel persons into bondage with a maximum of three years in prison and a Rs. 2,000 fine. However, the extent to which bonded labourers have been identified, released, and rehabilitated in the country is negligible.

Most agricultural labourers interviewed for this report were paid between Rs. 15 and Rs. 25 (US$0.38 to $0.63), or two to three kilograms of rice, per day, well below the minimum wage prescribed in their state. Women were consistently paid less than men. Many labourers owed debts to their employers or other moneylenders. Under the Bonded Labour System (Abolition) Act, 1976, payment of less than minimum wage for the purposes of working off a debt amounts to bondage. The act's definition of the "bonded labour system" includes "any system of forced, or partly forced labour under which a debtor enters, or has, or is presumed to have, entered, into an agreement with the creditor to the effect that:

> by reason of his birth in any particular caste or community, he would render, by himself or through any member of his family, or any person dependent on him, labour or service to the creditor, or for the benefit of the creditor, for a specified period or for an unspecified period, either without wages or for nominal wages....
>
> Nominal wages are defined as wages which are less than
>
> (a) The minimum wages fixed by the Government, in relation to the same or similar labour, under any law for the time being in force; and
>
> (b) Where no such minimum wage has been fixed in relation to any form of labour, the wages that are normally paid, for the same or similar labour to the labourers working in the same locality.

The Strategy of Special Component Plan (SCP) for Scheduled Castes (SCs), now being renamed as Schedule Caste Sub Plan (SCSP) was evolved by the planning commission in 1979. It was introduced by the central government during the 6th plan and it was made mandatory for all State governments' departments as well as Central Government Ministries/ Departments. This Strategy entails targeted flow of funds and associated benefits from the annual plan of States/ Union Territories (UTs) at least in proportion to the SC population i.e. 16 % in total population of the State/ UTs and Central Government. The central objective of SCP is the economic development of SCs, it also intends to promote their educational and social development along with the fulfillment of their minimum needs and human resources development.

Evidences from the States such as Andhra Pradesh, Rajasthan & Tamil Nadu where civil society groups have been tracking the implementation of SCP in the State budgets, presents a very disturbing picture. Also the extent to which SCP has been implemented by the Central Government ministries/ departments, as measured in terms of the proportion of allocations earmarked for SCs in total plan allocations of the respective ministries/departments in union budget 2006-07 has been very low. Only Ministry of Social Justice and Empowerment, Ministry of Human Resource Development and Department of Science and Technology have shown plan allocation clearly earmarked for SCs.

However, except for Ministry of Social Justice and Empowerment, the proportion of Plan allocation for SCs is less than 16%. Moreover, in case of some of these ministries the allocations were only notional allocations. Also we find that almost all the schemes, under which there are clearly earmarked allocations for SCs, follow a conventional approach of placation instead of actual empowerment of SCs. One of the main arguments put forward in this respect is that their schemes are indivisible. Therefore it is not feasible for such mainstream ministries to implement SCP for SCs.

MANUAL SCAVENGING

Scavenging is the degrading and illegal task of cleaning human excrement from India's roads and dry latrines. Using little more than a broom, a tin plate, and a basket, they are made to clear feces from public and private latrines and carry them to dumping grounds and disposal sites. This is mainly a hereditary occupation reserved for Dalit. Dalit manual scavengers (known as Bhangis or Valmikis, among other caste names) are compelled to undertake their task, often being prevented from taking any other job. They are the worst victims of untouchability as they are considered unclean, impure and placed at the lowest level of the caste hierarchy. Even other Dalit often consider them as untouchables. Manual scavengers, or safai karmacharis, are considered to be the most oppressed and disadvantaged of any community in India. The practice has been long outlawed; however, it continues today in most Indian states.

Social discrimination against scavengers is rampant. Most live in segregated rural colonies and are unable to make use of common resources. As one scavenger in Ahmedabad District, Gujarat, stated: "When we are working, they ask us not to come near them. At tea canteens, they have separate tea tumblers and they make us clean them ourselves and make us put the dishes away ourselves. We cannot enter temples. We cannot use upper-caste water taps. We have to go one kilometer away to get water." There are three main types of scavengers: municipality workers, contract workers, and those working in private households.

The last two groups are the worst victims since they receive no health benefits. Government estimates suggest that there are about one million manual scavengers in India—95% are women—but unofficially the figures are much higher. They are given no protective gear (no gloves, masks, or instruments) to carry out their work. This work is extremely hazardous and scavengers often suffer from respiratory diseases, gastrointestinal disorders and trachoma, a disease often resulting in blindness. In many communities, in exchange for leftover food, scavengers are also expected to remove dead animal carcasses and deliver messages of death to the relatives of upper-caste neighbours. Their refusal to do so can result in physical abuse and ostracism from the community.

The Employment of Manual Scavengers and Construction of Dry Latrines (Prohibition) Act was enacted in 1993, but has proved ineffective in eliminating manual scavenging. The

Act prohibits the employment of manual scavengers or construction of dry latrines not connected to proper drainage channels and violations of the provisions of the Act can lead to imprisonment for up to one year and/or a fine of up to 2000 rupees. However, as the Comptroller and Auditor General (CAG) of India pointed out in a 2003 report, the law had only been adopted by 16 states as of 2003, and it had not been enforced in any state. Still today, the Act's penal sections are very rarely implemented.

Similarly, in March 1992, the Indian government enacted the National Scheme of Liberation and Rehabilitation of Scavengers and their Dependents; however, according to the CAG report, the scheme failed to achieve its objectives despite an investment of more than 600 crore ($60 billion). According to the National Commission for Safai Karmacharis (set up in 1993), the main reason for the unsatisfactory progress of the Scheme appears to be the inadequate attention (including misuse of funds and falsification of targets) given to it by State Governments and concerned agencies. State governments routinely deny the existence of manual scavengers altogether or claim that a lack of water supply prevents them from constructing flush latrines. Activists claim that the resources, including government funds, exist for construction and for the rehabilitation of scavengers; what is lacking is the political will to do so. Part of the reason why such rehabilitation schemes fail is clearly the state's complicity in the whole process. Many government offices and buildings still have dry latrines and municipalities employ manual scavengers to clean these latrines.

In fact, there is clear evidence that the number of both manual scavengers and dry latrines is actually increasing. In 1989 there were 600,000 scavengers while by 1995-96 the number had increased to 787,000 (a 31.6 % increase in less than a decade). Similarly, there were 720,500,000 dry latrines in 1989, but by January 2000 the number had increased by 9,600,000. With the increase of urbanization, manual scavenging is increasing. More and more Dalit are compelled to take the job as the changing economic scenario is offering less and less jobs for them.

UNTOUCHABILITY STILL REMAINS

Residential segregation of Dalit is prevalent across the country, in violation of India's obligations under Article 3 of the ICERD. Segregation is also seen in schools, in access to public services, and in access to services operated by the private sector. In his 1999 annual report, the UN special rapporteur on contemporary forms of racism, racial discrimination, xenophobia and related intolerance found "untouchability" to be "very much alive" in rural areas.

A recently published survey investigating the extent of 'untouchability' in 565 villages in 11 Indian states found that the practice continues to profoundly affect the lives and psyches of millions of Dalit. 'Untouchability' practices were documented in almost 80% of the villages surveyed.

Dalit are denied equal access to public places such as police stations, government ration shops, post offices, schools, water facilities and village council offices. More than 20% of Dalit do not have access to safe drinking water. Only 10% of Dalit households have access to sanitation (as compared to 27% for non-Dalit households), and the vast majority of Dalit depend on the 'goodwill' of upper-caste community members for access to water from public wells. Dalit are also excluded from, or receive discriminatory treatment at private businesses such as food stalls, barber shops and cinemas.

Strict prohibitions on marriage and other social interaction between Dalit and non-Dalit violate the rights of Dalit to marry and choose their spouses. Inter-caste marriages are frequently extra-judicially punished by acts of public lynching, murder, rape, beatings and other sanctions against the couple and their relatives. In one of the worst examples of this, on August 6, 2001, in Uttar Pradesh, an upper-caste boy and a lower-caste girl were publicly hanged by members of their own families for refusing to end an inter-caste relationship.

Dalit are routinely and frequently denied entry into places of worship. Some Dalit have responded to ill-treatment by upper-caste Hindus by converting *en masse* to Buddhism, Christianity and Islam. However, the loss of constitutional privileges upon conversion (to Christianity or Islam) is a serious impediment to Dalit' freedom to choose their religion. In recent times, the introduction of anti-conversion legislation in several states has made religious conversion extremely difficult, if not impossible. Tragically, even conversion does not guarantee escape since 'untouchability' is practised across all faiths in India.

Dalit are also systematically denied the right to own property. Landlessness — encompassing lack of access to land, inability to own land, and forced evictions — constitutes a crucial element in the subordination of Dalit, says the report. Land reform legislation is neither implemented nor properly enforced. When Dalit do manage to acquire land, access to it is often denied. In 2004, the Dalit of Kalapatti village, Tamil Nadu, were forced to flee after an attack in which upper-caste neighbours burned and destroyed over 100 Dalit homes.

Dalit children face consistent hurdles in their access to education. Ninety-nine per cent of Dalit students are enrolled in government schools that lack basic infrastructure, classrooms, teachers and teaching aids. They are made to sit in the back of the classroom and endure verbal and physical harassment by teachers and students. According to the UN special rapporteur on the right to education, teachers have been known to declare that Dalit pupils "cannot learn unless they are beaten". The effect of such abuse is borne out by the low literacy and high dropout rates for Dalit.

Upper-caste hostility toward Dalit' education is linked to the perception that Dalit are either incapable of being educated, or, if educated, will pose a threat to village hierarchies and power relations, says the report.

Attempts by members of the Dalit community to demand their rights, or to lay claim to land that is legally theirs are consistently met with economic boycotts or retaliatory violence. For example, in Punjab, on January 5, 2006, Dalit labourer and activist Bant Singh, seeking prosecution of the people who gang raped his daughter, was beaten so severely that both his arms and one leg had to be amputated.

In an incident that enraged Dalit all over India and shocked people across the country after it belatedly made national headlines on September 26, 2006, in Khairlanji village, Maharashtra, a Dalit family was killed by an upper-caste mob, after the mother and daughter were stripped, beaten and paraded through the village and the two brothers brutally beaten. They were attacked because they refused to let upper-caste farmers take away their land. After widespread protests at the police's failure to arrest the perpetrators, some of those accused in the killing were finally arrested and the policemen and medical officers who had failed to do their job were suspended from duty.

On February 1, 2007, the European Parliament found India's efforts to enforce laws protecting Dalit to be "grossly inadequate," adding that "atrocities, untouchability, illiteracy, [and] inequality of opportunity continue to blight the lives of India's Dalit".

"International scrutiny is growing and with it the condemnation of abuses resulting from the caste system and the government's failure to protect Dalit," said Brad Adams, Asia director at Human Rights Watch. "India needs to mobilise the entire government and make good on its paper commitments to end caste abuses. Otherwise it risks pariah status for its home-grown brand of apartheid."

"International outrage over the treatment of Dalit is matched by growing national discontent," says Professor Smita Narula, faculty director of CHRGJ at the New York University School of Law, and co-author of the report. "India can't ignore the voices of 165 million citizens."

Indeed, 'Hidden Apartheid's' scathing indictment echoes a statement made months earlier by India's prime minister. On December 27, 2006, Dr Manmohan Singh became the first serving Indian prime minister to openly acknowledge the parallel between the practice of 'untouchability' and the crime of apartheid.

RESERVATION POLICY

Reservation policy has been one of the corner stones of Dalit empowerment. But it has been implemented half heartedly from the beginning.The Dalit job force in the country concentrated largely either on the traditionally assigned degraded low paid jobs or to low class sweeper jobs in govt and supported services. 15% of the jobs in state and state supported departments to be reserved for the Dalit according to the existing rule considering the population strength 16.5% (Census report, 2001). But the vast private sector is excluded despite repeated and long demands from the Dalit organization to include it also within the purview of reservation.

Privatization of public sector units have already pushed majority of the Urban Dalit to casual labour with the decline of salaried jobs by sticking on formal methods of recruitments, the large private sector which opts for higher education and technical skills excludes the majority of the deprived sections.

This reinforcement of past job discrimination resulted in the over representation of Dalit in the poorly paid dead end jobs. Whenever they tried to shift to some better occupation were abused or beaten up by the uppercastes. The prescribed 15% of jobs in all classes of jobs falls short particularly in higher class jobs.

Dalit are over represented in low class jobs like sweepers in public sector indicating the caste based occupational allocation. The back log of SC/ST appointment in states service is 25,000 and 10,00,000 in central govt Some vacancies under reservation is not filled since 1978. About 54.30% in central govt departments, 45.10% in public sector banks and 88.18% in public sector enterprises. (National Commission for Scheduled Castes and Scheduled Tribes Report 1996-97 & 97-98, quoted in A Irudayam, Balck Paper 1999.)

Dalit women constitute 80.5 million people—8 out of every 100 citizens in the country—and approximately 48% of the total Dalit population, 16% of the total female population and 8% of the total Indian population. Vulnerably positioned at the bottom of the caste, class and gender hierarchies, Dalit women are India's worst victims of discrimination, deprivation, exploitation, and violence. Not only do Dalit women face endemic violence and discrimination (due to both caste and patriarchy), but the vast majority of crimes against them go unreported, unregistered and un-punished.

The available data on the situation of Dalit women presents quite a disturbing picture: An average of three Dalit women are raped everyday. A disproportionate number of the atrocities and human rights violations registered annually under the SC/ST (Prevention of Atrocities) Act are against women. The unemployment rate of Dalit women is 4.0% against 0.97% among non-Dalit in rural areas and 3.3% against 1.98% for non-Dalit in urban areas. The literacy rate of Dalit women is just 23.8% compared to that of 39.3% among non-Dalit. Due to discrimination, poverty, and gender role ideology, Dalit women have a drop out rate of 53.96% at the primary school level. The poverty rate among Dalit women is 36.2% against 21.6% among non-Dalit women. 94% of Dalit women are engaged in the unorganized, self-employed sector (farm/wage workers, domestic helpers, etc.), marked by overwork, low wages, non-payment of equal wages, and absence of social security or maternity benefits.

Dalit women face violence and exploitation not only from the dominant castes, but also at home within their own families and Dalit communities. Regardless of the context, when a Dalit woman defends her dignity and demands her basic human rights, if her position contradicts traditional caste, gender, and cultural norms, she is not given support and often becomes the target of violence. Statistics on Dalit women's access to justice show the extent of the problem. NCDHR's study and other reports show that perpetrators are punished in less than 1% of the cases.

In other words, the perpetrators of crimes against Dalit women go completely free in more than 99% of the crimes committed, and are even seen to further threaten and punish the same survivors. The study further reveals that in 39% of the instances of violence the survivors did not seek legal redress for fear of bringing dishonour to theier family, for lack of human or financial support, or because they did not trust that they would get justice. In 27% of the instances of violence, the victim's appeal for justice to the village panchayat or administration was thwarted by pressure and threats from the perpetrators. In 18% of the instances, the police thwarted justice by threatening, refusing to file the complaint, forcing an extra-legal compromise, or making false counter cases.

Despite the gravity of the situation, there are very little efforts or mechanisms by the Indian state or other movements or organizations to protect Dalit women or support their quest for justice. NCDHR aims in its work to create awareness among the national and international community regarding the unique plight of Dalit women and to expose the failure of the state to protect and promote Dalit women's rights. Our long term goal is to build effective monitoring and legal mechanisms to support women who face violence, to train and support Dalit women's rights defenders, to build alliances with other movements, and to ensure the effective functioning of the justice and administrative systems to destroy the culture of impunity.

MOVEMENT OF DALIT WOMEN

The interface of the severely imbalanced social, economic and political power equations in caste and patriarchy impacts Dalit women uniquely, very distinct from the experience of other women and even Dalit men. These forces combine to expose them to increased physical and sexual violence and increased exploitation of their labour. All these combined together keep Dalit women from having access and control over assets and resources. It does not recognize their social and economic contribution. It limits their choices and opportunities, placing them on the bottom rung in all development indicators. This process of exclusion and discrimination inculcates the disrespect and indignity of Dalit women at the hands of all men and also of non-Dalit women.

In recent years a sea of change has taken place and Dalit women have started asserting for their rightful place in Indian society. The role played by thousands of Dalit women in running the panchayats across the country has turned out to be an amazing success story of political awareness and mobilization beyond any conceivable imagination. It has dealt a striking blow to the caste system and the values of patriarchy. In this process of being empowered they have paid heavy prices too, but their resilience is tremendous and quite laudable. At every level of the caste hierarchy and patriarchal system, the Dalit Women's movement is quite active in mobilizing the unheard voices and in turning them into a powerful agent of change. NCDHR—via projects and platforms such as AIDMAM and DWAJ—has joined in and seeks to advance the vital concerns of this Movement for Dalit Women's Human Rights.

The All India Dalit Mahila Adhikar Manch (AIDMAM) is a common platform for Dalit women committed to challenging the nexus of patriarchy, caste, age-old social customs and traditions, class oppression, exploitation and, most of all, marginalization of Dalit women in the family, community, and nation they live in. AIDMAM is part of NCDHR's campaign for Dalit Women's Rights and has the membership and solidarity of non-Dalit Women, Dalit Men, social activists and other human rights defenders committed to the cause of protecting and promoting the rights of Dalit Women under the leadership of Dalit Women. AIDMAM's objective is to hold the state accountable for its failure to prevent violence against Dalit women and to take up advocacy at the state, national and international levels.

SPECIAL BUDGETING FOR DALITS

Special Component Plan(SCP) for the development of SCs is implemented from the 6th five year plan (1980-85).All the general planning in the country tended to exclude and marginalize Dalit. So "SCP is a policy instrument designed to ensure the fulfillment of constitutional guarantees and entitlements enjoined for the SC communities" (Planning Commission, Govt of India).

It is imperative for all the state govts and all their departments as well as the central govt to allocate plan funds in proportion to the SC population. And the Planning department is entrusted to ensure before the finalization of the budget proposals that all the departments concerned earmark the specific fund.

Lack of political will, castiesm, bureaucratic indifference or resistance led to the half hearted implementation of SCP. "It is disheartening to note that out of the total 62 Union ministries/ departments only 11 had formulated SCP so far" (The Ministry of Welfare of SC&STs speaking in the context of 9th five year plan.)

The usual practice is the heavy unspent funds are diverted to other purposes, leaving the earmarked /intended purposes unattended. Except for Ministry of social Justice and Empowerment, the proportion of plan allocation for SCs is less than 16%. And some of the ministries are only allocating notional amounts.

In 2006-07, Rs. 20,289,25 Crores (over 507 billion U.S. dollars) which by law should have been directed specifically towards the development of the Dalit community have instead been allocated for other purposes. To address this problem, researchers, Human Rights defenders, and Dalit activists from ten states assembled in New Delhi for a symposium on "Reclaiming the Scheduled Caste Sub-Plan." The Scheduled Castes Sub-Plan (SCSP) came into force in 1980 and made it mandatory for the Central Government and all State Governments to direct a targeted flow of their overall funds for the development of the Scheduled Castes (SC).

According to the plan, the amount allocated must minimally be in proportion to the SC population in the country and in each of the individual states. State-level research indicates that from its inception there has been failure to implement this plan and a widespread tendency to divert funds which should have been allocated for SCs. While Dalit make up at least 16% of the population in India, in 2007-08 the SCs were earmarked for only 6.1% of total allocations!

DALIT RIGHTS IN DISASTER MANAGEMENT

India is prone to natural disasters because of its peculiar geo-climatic conditions. Floods, landslides, droughts, cyclones, earthquakes are recurring phenomena. Dalit are invariably the most vulnerable section during any natural disaster and least likely to be able to access to aid when it become available.

Any disaster affects all sections of people across religions or castes. But the relief and rehabilitation programmes during any major disaster in India are beset with the evils of caste-based discrimination. The authority and agencies involved in relief and rehabilitation programme fail to provide relief with neutrality and impartially.

The Gujarat Earth Quake in 2001 brought to the fore how caste based discrimination in relief and rehabilitation programmes works. Against this experience NCDHR and other Dalit rights' organizations started to monitor closely relief and rehabilitation programmes during the wake of disasters.

CONSTITUTIONAL RIGHTS OF DALITS

General Rights in the Constitution

The Constitution of India, which came into force on 26 January 1950 provides the following fundamental rights to every citizen:-

WE, THE PEOPLE OF INDIA, having solemnly resolved to constitute India into a Sovereign Socialist Secular Democratic Republic and to secure to all its citizens

1. Justice, social, economic and political;
2. Liberty of thought, expression, belief, faith and worship;
3. Equality of status and of opportunity, and to promote among them all fraternity assuring the dignity of the individual and the unity of the nation.

Compensatory discrimination was one of the means chosen to achieve those ends. Its purpose is to promote equalization by offsetting historically accumulated inequalities. The Government of India has used compensatory discrimination as a means of achieving greater equality by deliberately overcoming some of those historically accumulated disabilities from which Dalit have long suffered.

The Constitution provides some preferential options to the Dalit who for so many centuries have been deprived of their rights in Indian society. It was Dr. Ambedkar, himself a Dalit and the chief architect of the Indian Constitution, who really formulated the provision of compensatory discrimination.

Article 14, Equality before the Law

The State shall not deny to any person equality before the law or the equal protection of the laws within the territory of India.

Article 15: Prohibition of Discrimination on grounds of religion, race, caste, sex or place of birth

1. The State shall not discriminate against any citizen on grounds only of religion, race, caste, sex, and place of birth or any of them.
2. No citizen shall, on ground only of religion, race, caste, sex, place of birth or any of them, be subject to any disability, liability, restriction or condition with regard to -
   a. Access to shops, public restaurants, hotels and places of public entertainment; or
   b. The use of wells, tanks, bathing ghats, roads and places of public resort maintained whole or partly out of State funds or dedicated to the use of the general public.
3. Nothing in this article shall prevent the State from making any special provision for women and children.
4. Nothing in this article or in clause (2) or article 29 shall prevent the State from making any special provision for the advancement of any socially and educationally backward classes of citizens or for the Scheduled Castes and the Scheduled Tribes.

Article 16, Equality of Opportunity in Matters of Public Employment

1. There shall be equality of opportunity for all citizens in matters relating to employment or appointment to any office under the State.

2. No citizen shall, on grounds only of religion, race, caste, sex, descent, place of birth, residence or any of them, be ineligible for, or discriminated against in respect of, any employment or office under the State.
3. Nothing in this article shall prevent Parliament from making any law prescribing, in regard to a class or classes of employment or appointment to an office under the Government of, or any local or other authority within, a State or Union territory, any requirement as to residence within that State or Union territory prior to such employment or appointment.
4. Nothing in this article shall prevent the State from making any provision for the reservation of appointments or posts in favour of any backward class of citizens which, in the opinion of the State, is not adequately represented in the services under the State.

4A Nothing in this article shall prevent the State from making any provision for reservation in matters of promotion to any class or classes of posts in the services under the State in favour of the Scheduled Castes and the Scheduled Tribes which, in the opinion of the State, are not adequately represented in the services under the State.

Article 17, Abolition of Untouchability

'Untouchability' is abolished and its practice in any form is forbidden. The enforcement of any disability arising out of 'Untouchability' shall be an offence punishable in accordance with law.

Article 25, Freedom of Conscience and Free Profession, Practice and Propagation of Religion

1. Subject to public order, morality and health and to the other provisions of this Part, all persons are equally entitled to freedom of conscience and the right freely to profess, practice and propagate religion.

2. Nothing in this article shall affect the operation of any existing law or prevent the State from making any law:
    a. Regulating or restricting any economic, financial, political or other secular activity which may be associated with religious practice;
    b. Providing for social welfare and reform or the throwing open of Hindu religious institutions of a public character to all classes and sections of Hindus. Explanation I: The wearing and carrying of kirpans shall be deemed to be included in the profession of the Sikh religion. Explanation II: In sub-Clause (b) of clause (2), the reference to Hindus shall be construed as including a reference to persons professing the Sikh, Jaina or Buddhist religion, and the reference to Hindu religious institutions shall be construed accordingly.
3. Special Rights Under the Presidential Order, 1950, known as the Constitution (SCHEDULED CASTE) Order, no.19, Aug.10, 1950

Political Rights and Privileges

Article 330, Reservation of seats for Scheduled Castes and Scheduled Tribes in the House of the People

1. Seats shall be reserved in the House of the People for -
    a. The Scheduled Castes;
    b. The Scheduled Tribes except the Scheduled Tribes in the autonomous districts of Assam; and
    c. The Scheduled Tribes in the autonomous districts of Assam.
2. The number of seats reserved in any State or Union territory for the Scheduled Castes or the Scheduled Tribes under clause (1) shall bear, as nearly as may be, the same proportion to the total number of seats allotted to that State or Union territory in the House

of the People as the population of the Scheduled Castes in the State or Union territory or of the Scheduled Tribes in the State or Union territory or part of the State or Union territory, as the case may be, in respect of which seats are so reserved, bears to the total population of the State or Union territory.

3. Notwithstanding anything contained in clause (2), the number of seats reserved in the House of the People for the Scheduled Tribes in the autonomous districts of Assam shall bear to the total number of seats allotted to that State a proportion not less than the population of the Scheduled Tribes in the said autonomous districts bears to the total population of the State.Explanation: In this article and in article 332, the expression "population" means the population as ascertained at the last preceding census of which the relevant figures have been published:Provided that the reference in this Explanation to the last preceding census of which the relevant figures have been published shall, until the relevant figures for the first census taken after the year 2000 have been published, be construed as a reference to the 1971 census.

Article 332, Reservation of seats for Scheduled Castes and Scheduled Tribes in the Legislative Assemblies of the States

1. Seats shall be reserved for the Scheduled Castes and the Scheduled Tribes, except the Scheduled Tribes in the autonomous districts of Assam, in the Legislative Assembly of every State.
2. Seats shall be reserved also for the autonomous districts in the Legislative Assembly of the State of Assam.
3. The number of seats reserved for the Scheduled Castes or the Scheduled Tribes in the Legislative Assembly of any State under clause (1) shall bear, as nearly as may be, the same proportion to the total number of seats in the Assembly as the population of the

Scheduled Castes in the State or of the Scheduled Tribes in the State or part of the State, as the case may be, in respect of which seats are so reserved, bears to the total population of the State.

3A. Notwithstanding anything contained in clause (3), until the taking effect, under article 170, of the re-adjustment, on the basis of the first census after the year 2000, of the number of seats in the Legislative Assemblies of the States of Arunachal Pradesh, Meghalaya, Mizoram and Nagaland, the seats which shall be reserved for the Scheduled Tribes in the Legislative Assembly of any such State shall be, -

a. If all the seats in the Legislative Assembly of such State in existence on the date of coming into force of the Constitution (Fifty-seventh Amendment) Act, 1987 (hereafter in this clause referred to as the existing Assembly) are held by members of the Scheduled Tribes, all the seats except one;

b. In any other case, such number of seats as bears to the total number of seats, a proportion not less than the number (as on the said date) of members belonging to the Scheduled Tribes in the existing Assembly bears to the total number of seats in the existing Assembly.

3B. Notwithstanding anything contained in clause (3), until the re-adjustment, under article 170, takes effect on the basis of the first census after the year 2000, of the number of seats in the Legislative Assembly of the State of Tripura, the seats which shall be reserved for the Scheduled Tribes in the Legislative Assembly shall be, such number of seats as bears to the total number of seats, a proportion not less than the number, as on the date of coming into force of the Constitution (Seventy-second Amendment) Act, 1992, of members belonging to the Scheduled Tribes in the Legislative Assembly in existence on the said date bears to the total number of seats in that Assembly.

4. The number of seats reserved for an autonomous district in the Legislative Assembly of the State of Assam shall bear to the total number of seats in that Assembly a proportion not less than the population of the district bears to the total population of the State.
5. The constituencies for the seats reserved for any autonomous district of Assam shall not comprise any area outside that district.
6. No person who is not a member of a Scheduled Tribe of any autonomous district of the State of Assam shall be eligible for election to the Legislative Assembly of the State from any constituency of that district.

The second important element in the compensatory discrimination is found in Article 335.

ECONOMIC AND SOCIAL RIGHTS AND PRIVILEGES

Article 335, Claims of Scheduled Castes and Scheduled Tribes to Services and Posts

The claims of the members of the Scheduled Castes and the Scheduled Tribes shall be taken into consideration, consistently with the maintenance of efficiency of administration, in the making of appointments to services and posts in connection with the affairs of the Union or of a State.

When taken with Article 16(4), this forms the basis for reserving jobs in government service for Dalit, Scheduled Tribes and "Other Backward Classes".

Article 46, Promotion of Educational and Economic Interests of Scheduled Castes, Scheduled Tribes and other Weaker Sections

The State shall promote with special care the educational and economic interests of the weaker sections of the people, and in particular, of the Scheduled Castes and the Scheduled Tribes, and shall protect them from social injustice and all forms of exploitation.

The Constitution also provided for a special officer (Article 338) for the Scheduled Castes and Scheduled Tribes as well as for a Commission to investigate the condition of the Backward Classes (Article 340). Both of these were appointed by and responsible to the President.

Article 338, National Commission for Scheduled Castes, Scheduled Tribes

There shall be a Special Officer for the Scheduled Castes and Scheduled Tribes to be Appointed by the President

1. It shall be the duty of the Special Officer to investigate all matters relating to the safeguards provided for the Scheduled Castes and Scheduled Tribes under the Constitution and report to the President upon the working of those safeguards at such intervals as the President may direct, and the President shall cause all such reports to be laid before each House of Parliament.

Article 340, Appointment of a Commission to Investigate the Conditions of Backward Classes

1. The President may by order appoint a Commission consisting of such persons as he thinks fit to investigate the conditions of socially and educationally backward classes within the territory of India and the difficulties under which they labour and to make recommendations as to the steps that should be taken by the Union or any State to remove such difficulties and to improve their condition and as to the grants that should be made for the purpose by the Union or any State and the conditions subject to which such grants should be made, and the order appointing such Commission shall define the procedure to be followed by the Commission.
2. A Commission so appointed shall investigate the matters referred to them and present to the President

a report setting out the facts as found by them and making such recommendations as they think proper.

3. The President shall cause a copy of the report so presented together with a memorandum explaining the action taken thereon to be laid before each House of Parliament.

The Constitution of India gave a special mandate to the President of India under Article 341 (1) to specify the castes, races under a Schedule. The castes as listed become eligible for the purposes of discriminatory protections and favours designed for that purpose. 3. The Exclusion of Christian Dalit from Special Rights and Protections. Article 341 (1) empowers the President of India, "...by public notification, (to) specify the castes, races or tribes or parts or of groups within castes, races or tribes which shall, for the purpose of this Constitution be deemed to be Scheduled Castes." But once the President has issued such an order, saying who can be included in the list or schedule, "Parliament may...include in or exclude from the list of Scheduled Castes... any... group..."

The third paragraph of this Order reads:

"Notwithstanding anything contained in paragraph 2, no person who professes a religion different from Hindu, shall be deemed to be a member of a Scheduled Caste."

In making this exclusion, the Indian Parliament had the excuse of following the Government of India (Scheduled Castes) Order of 1936 in which the British had excluded the Christian Dalit because these were already enjoying rights and protection as a minority community. This third paragraph was changed in 1956 by Parliament to "Hindu or Sikh" and again in May 1990 it was changed by the Parliament to "Hindu or Sikh or Buddhist."

Thus, Dalit who have converted to Christianity have lost the constitutional safeguards given to the Scheduled Castes of three other religions. This has increased their vulnerability.

Despite the Indian Constitution's special provisions and safeguards for the Dalit of the country, struggles of Dalit belonging to religious minorities prevailed. The number of people being affected is large: counting Dalit Christians alone, there are 18 million, which amounts to 65% of Christians in the country.

According to the Constitution (Scheduled Castes) Order 1950, only Dalit professing Hinduism, Buddhism and Sikhism are considered Scheduled Castes, the weaker section of society that enjoys special care from the State. Dalit of other religions cannot enjoy those protections. The legislation thus created discrimination and limited religious freedom.

In 1996, the Government prepared a draft amendment bill, Bill No. 17 of 1996, intending to include Dalit Christians in the list of Scheduled Castes by amending the Constitution (Scheduled Castes) Order 1950. However, the amendment bill could not be passed in the Parliament.

8

Contemporary Indian Politics Involving Dalits

Of late, some vested politicians in connivance with the anti-national forces started playing very dangerous political games. They have openly started instigating Indians to divide themselves on caste basis and making calculations accordingly. Reservation figures are muddled and misused to brainwash electorate, thereby, caste wars are created. The magic-combination of "BC-SC-ST-Minorities" is picking up and it has become a game-plan for them. For all such caste-conflicts, the "traditional enemy" is blamed and condemned. In the recent U. P elections, crores of Rupees were spent to experiment their conceived plan. In spite of the number game, extra-democratic means were adopted to capture power. After coming to power, unnecessarily, Mahatma Gandhi and Babasaheb Ambedkar have been pitted against each other drawing parallels. All Hindus should be very careful in such moves.

In urban areas and some villages the old concepts of a rigid caste system and untouchability usually no longer exist, though most Indians still voluntarily hold on to their caste origins, which is intended to reflect that their ancestors belonged to their castes with a sense of pride in the duties and responsibilities as required by the caste rules. In matrimonial matters, whether the wed coupie is Dalit or non-Dalit, caste identity is a practical near-must, although this also is changing.

Inter-caste couples may ignore the ignorance of caste prejudices due to an attraction on the basis of education, economic status, or, of course, romantic love.

While the Indian Constitution has duly made special provisions for the social and economic uplift of the Dalit, comprising the so-called scheduled castes and tribes in order to enable them to achieve upward social mobility, these concessions are limited to only those Dalit who remain Hindu. There is a demand among the Dalit who have converted to other religions that the statutory benefits should be extended to them as well, to "overcome" and bring closure to historical injustices.

Another major politically charged issue with the rise of Hindutva's role in Indian politics is that of religious conversion. This political movement alleges that conversions of Dalit are due not to any social or theological motivation but to allurements like education and jobs. Critics argue that the inverse is true with laws banning conversion, and the limiting of social relief for these backward sections of Indian society being revoked for those who convert. Bangaru Laxman, a Dalit politician, was a prominent member of the Hindutva movement.

Another political issue is over the affirmative action measures taken by the government towards the uplift of the Dalit by implementation of quotas in government jobs and university admissions aimed at improving Dalit representation. About 8% of the seats in the National and State Parliaments are reserved for Scheduled Caste and Tribe candidates, a measure sought by B.R. Ambedkar and other Dalit activists in order to ensure that Dalit would obtain a proportionate political voice.

Anti-Dalit prejudices exist in fringe groups, such as extremist far-right militia Ranvir Sena, largely run by upper-caste landlords in backward areas of the Indian state of Bihar. They oppose equal treatment of Dalit and have resorted to violent means to suppress them. The Ranvir Sena is considered a terrorist organization.

On the other side, extremist groups run by small minority of Dalit such as the "Dalit Panthers Movement" have committed violent acts against Brahmins and middle-caste people.

It is important to look at some of the reasons behind this. Firstly what were those internal and external situations that gave birth to the politics of Dalit identity. It's important to understand the rationale of this politics to understand this. After independence the rise of national bourgeoisie is not straightforward. This was made possible with a specific project. It is important to understand the five-year plans of Jawaharlal Nehru. What the backward sections get out of the development projects puts them on the way to economic prosperity and they inch towards the bigger issue of awareness and understanding of their rights also. This transforms into political consciousness of this section. Professional employees organizations organized on these lines are important in this regard. One other external reason is that the Communists could never understand these sections as consciously as it should have been. Instead they kept on believing in the pre-determined concept that class differences would eventually disappear. The ruling class could not recognize them as more than a votebank ever. This is a grotesque phenomenon of the democratic system of this weak capitalism that they take to using these identities in their fascistic and communal forms, instead of separate identity and self-determination of nationalities. This can not be ignored in the Indian politics of the last decade or so.

In the present times Dalit politics or the politics of Dalit identity is getting its all from this corrupt bourgeois value system. There is no project of the all round Dalit liberation in the programmes of the political parties associated with it. They lack any clear policy or political programme which can provide a parallel model of social justice for Dalit.

In fact in the name of Dalit, it is providing security to a section that is fundamentalist, comprising of fascist elements. By making caste politics the politics of identity it is following the way of present bourgeois political parties. Our society indulges in the politics of this political identity. This politics has done in the corridors of power exactly what bourgeois politics does.

Mainly there are three layers of the politics of Dalit identity in the present times. The political and ideological equation of the inner conflicts, struggles and tensions in these three layers is separate matter.

First layer is organizing the Dalit with political consciousness through the caste factor. It is present in almost whole country with minor differences. This is attracting ordinary Dalit by making an issue of the oppression and exploitation in the name of casteism in the past. This casteist politics is more dangerous and oppressive.

Second layer is of political section with Brahminical mentality whose main motive is to make Dalit serve their purpose by whipping up their desires. This section wants to keep Dalit won over through the assurance of security while keeping him tied to sub-conscious of insecurity. This is an issue of such an ideological knottiness that Dalit stays embroiled in the web of dependence on the other.

Third layer is that which does not use Dalit but links the politics of Dalit to his liberation. This liberation is, in fact, linked to all those deprived sections, which is not single layered. Though, this creates a paradigm by linking the discourse of human liberation with economics, it does not envision liberation of a Dalit human, unattached to proletariat. This third side is weak in the present scenario, but in future this can become the basis of authentic identity politics.

UNTOUCHABLE POLITICS DURING CONGRESS ERA

The attachment of Untouchables to Congress during the 1930s and 40s was far less than is sometimes assumed. In the years after Independence Untouchable support for Congress clearly strengthened. From 1952 until 1989, with the exception of the post-Emergency election of 1977, Untouchables tended to function in both national and State elections as a 'vote bank' for Congress. Their vote for Congress was a vote for the party of government, a party that had committed itself to a programme of action on Untouchability and poverty. In rational terms and here their situation was similar to that of the Muslims there was little electoral choice open to Untouchables in most parts of the country. If the Left had developed more strength outside what became its strongholds in West Bengal and Kerala, the Untouchable attachment to Congress might have been less. Thus in the very first post-Independence election of 1952 the Socialists won a good part of the Scheduled Caste vote. But this was the highpoint of their electoral experience in that State. It is only in the nineties that the logic of class (albeit often dressed in the garb of caste) is again being asserted across large parts of India, particularly the north.

While the Untouchables were a crucial Congress vote bank in India as a whole and in a majority of individual States, even before the recent flux they did not cling to Congress in regions where another party or movement rose to dominance. The major examples of long-term non-Congress dominance are West Bengal, Kerala, Tamil Nadu and Andhra Pradesh. Untouchables in the former two States have for a number of years had a strong identification with the Communist Party in its several divisions - in recent years predominantly with the dominant Communist Party of India (Marxist) (CPI (M)). A number of Ezhavas associated themselves with the fledgling Communist Party from the early 1940s, but with increasing prosperity the caste vote has been split along class lines between the Communists and Congress.

As to the other and poorer Untouchable castes of Kerala, these have been far less influential in the councils of the Communist movement. But in conformity with the class divisions of Kerala politics, the Scheduled Castes have tended to gravitate towards the parties of the Left. In West Bengal, the Communist movement was slower to gain control of the State: the first United Front Government came to power in 1967, a decade after the first such government in Kerala. Support for the CPI(M) in West Bengal has been broadly based and not confined to particular castes, but again the party has done particularly well among poorer voters and therefore among the Scheduled Castes. In short, the Untouchables of Kerala and West Bengal have behaved according to the logic of their class position within a political culture more directed to considerations of class than anywhere else in India. But from another perspective the Untouchables of these two States have been doing little different from their counterparts elsewhere in India. They have simply aligned themselves with the majority party - it is doubtful that most of these Untouchables have been affected with any special passion for Marxism.

In Tamil Nadu and Andhra Pradesh regional parties have come to dominate State politics. The non-Brahmin movement of Tamil Nadu spawned a succession of parties - first the Justice Party and after Independence the Dravida Munnetra Kazhagam (DMK) and Anna DMK. Anti-Brahminism has been joined with Dravidian nationalism to produce a highly distinctive political and popular culture. For Decades State elections have largely been fought out between the DMK and Anna DMK, each of which lays claim to the common culture. The Untouchables were relatively slow to embrace the culture, given their break with the non-Brahmin movement in the early 1920s and their subsequent attraction to Congress. But with the dominance asserted by the DMK and then the Anna DMK from the late 1960s, the Untouchables have been rolled up into the prevailing politics of the State. But since Congress has often been able to engineer electoral accommodations with one or other of the three dominant leaders over the last three decades -Karunanidhi and the film star politicians M. Ramachandran (MGR) and Jayalalitha - many Tamil Untouchables have voted for the DMK or Anna DMK at State elections and for Congress in national elections. If we turn to Andhra, the emergence of a dominant regional party is more recent.

The Telegu Desam party of Andhra has been built around N. I Rama Rao, the charismatic Telegu movie star. NTR's style, like that of the Tamil leaders, was best described as populist, and his party attracted Untouchable voters as it moved into a position of dominance. But Telegu Desam has not been so dominant even in State elections as have successive regional parties in Tamil Nadu. In short, and unlike the position in the Communist States, in both Tamil Nadu and Andhra the Untouchables have not been wholly lost to Congress.

Within Congress the importance of the Untouchable vote did not translate itself into great influence for individual Untouchables in either the organisation or the ministry. In particular, the building of the compensatory discrimination system arose more from the arithmetic of elections and the goodwill of sections of the elite than from the efforts of Dalit parliamentarians. Jagjivan Ram was alone as a Scheduled Caste politician in becoming a genuinely national figure through Congress. There have been a couple of Chief Ministers - one of them was Bhole Paswan Shastri, who three times held this position in Bihar for very brief periods in the 1950s. Bhole Paswan was respected for his modesty, dignity and probity, but he made no deep mark on even State politics: his life and career are discussed in the next chapter.

A small number of other State and national politicians have gained a measure of ministerial seniority, but none has had either a long period at the apex of ministerial service or any substantial political base. Just why this is the case may require an answer at several levels. Perhaps it is to be expected that a collection of castes distinguished by their overall subordination would not produce the highest crop of educated, experienced and generally talented politicians. Over time the gap in education and sophistication between Untouchables and, say, Brahmins has diminished, and the depth of talent among Untouchable aspirants for high office is no doubt growing. But it will not help the Untouchable cause to deny that there has been a gap at all. On the other hand, issues of talent and preparation for public office can scarcely constitute the primary explanation for the low representation of Untouchables at the highest political levels.

There are persistent suggestions that Dalit politicians have not thrived within Congress if they have too strenuously promoted the cause of their own people. This is an explanation sometimes offered in relation to Yogendra Makwana, a talented and energetic Minister of the early 1980 whose career did not prosper under either Indira or Rajiv Gandhi. Makwana can be contrasted with Buta Singh, a Mazhabi Sikh (converted from a Sweeper caste) who rose to the position of Home Minister under the same Prime Ministers. Buta Singh (later relegated to a junior portfolio under Narasimha Rao) was known for his political savoir-faire and his loyalty to the Nehru family, rather than for any particular zeal for the problems of the Scheduled Castes. Of course, as a category Prime Ministers tend to distrust colleagues of whatever community if they have a political base or agenda independent of their own. Yet it remains an important truth that the ideological and social makeup of Congress has made it less than welcoming to highly assertive advocates of the Untouchable cause. Low social standing has also made individual Untouchable spokesmen relatively easy targets for political demolition. Untouchables have therefore tended to construct their political careers as dependants within factions led by high-caste politicians. It is impossible to think of a single example of a substantial multi-caste faction leader who is/was himself a Dalit.

Something more needs to be said here about the career of Jagjivan Ram. Under the patronage of the Nehrus Jagjivan Ram rose to the position of Defence Minister. He climbed a rung higher to the post of Deputy Prime Minister under Charan Singh in 1979, a position that rewarded him for ostensibly having delivered the Untouchable vote to the Janata coalition in the extraordinary election of 1977. Jagjivan Ram's career is notable for its extraordinary longevity, a consequence of both his competence and also his carefulness not to engage in dissent and controversy. On both counts he was the ideal Untouchable for Congress to promote through its ranks.

Jagjivan Ram was the only significant Untouchable to have played a strong part in Gandhi's Harijan movement of the 1930s. He became President of the All India Depressed Classes League formed in 1935, and was elected to the Bihar Assembly for Congress in the election of 1937. In 1946 he was appointed Labour Minister in the Viceroy's Executive Council, and from then (with a short interregnum during the Kamaraj Plan) he held Cabinet positions in successive Congress Governments and later the

Janata Government until its electoral defeat in 1980. Once he became a Minister he seems not to have made Untouchability a central preoccupation in either speech or action.

His most extensive public comment is to be found in a small book published in 1980, Caste Challenge in India. This book is neither novel in its analysis nor specially hard-hitting, though clearly its author believed that he could be more expansive now that his career had come to an end. Thus despite the book's mild tone, the preface contains the propitiatory remark that his views are offered 'not to hurt any class or caste but to provide a brief historical account of the Hindu social system and the miserable condition of the Scheduled Castes and Tribes'.

It is difficult to estimate the power that Jagjivan Ram wielded within Congress. He played an important role at several critical moments in the post-Nehru era: he supported Indira Gandhi's candidacy for Prime Minister in 1966, stayed with her when Congress split in 1969, and quit the party in 1977. Paul Brass observes that he was 'always thought to be able to control 40 to 60 votes in Parliament and was deferred to in the Congress for that reason'. But the quality of this 'control' is not self-evident. It seems likely that he had more power than anyone else in selecting Scheduled Caste candidates for Congress from the reserved seats in Bihar, and he may have exercised some power in neighbouring Uttar Pradesh and perhaps other States too; his qualifica-tion was not only his long career but also the fact that his own Chamar caste was by far the largest Scheduled Caste of north India.

Presumably Ram's role in the selection of candidates invested him with some influence in relation to the MPs who depended upon his continued support. Thus it is possible that he was able to deliver votes to Indira Gandhi in the succession contest after the death of Prime Minister Shastri and in the Congress split of 1969. But when he left Congress in 1977 he failed to persuade any of the Party's other Scheduled Caste MPs to accompany him. And more importantly, there is no evidence that he either sought or was able to mobilise a bloc of MPs in order to make policy gains for the Scheduled Castes within Cabinet. Any part he may have played in either the development or maintenance of programmes and policies favourable to Untouchables was for the most part hidden.

It is suggested that when he was Minister for Railways he was successful in rapidly building up the Scheduled Caste component of the railways workforce. And in his other portfolios too he may have exerted pressure for the legal quotas to be filled. But by far his most potent moment came when he left Congress on the eve of the post-Emergency election in 1977, since his departure seemed to crystallise the first large anti-Congress vote among north Indian Untouchables. This vote was of major significance to the outcome of the election. But the limits of Jagjivan Ram's electoral appeal and the special nature of the 1977 election were revealed when he failed to prevent the return of these same voters to Congress in 1980.

There is no single set of characteristics common to the leadership of Congress over the last half century, but a glance at the background of those at the very apex of Indian politics is instructive. All five Congress Prime Ministers have been Brahmins, including three from the Nehru family. In the non-Congress Governments of 1977-79 and 1989-91 two of the Prime Ministers were Rajputs, one was a Brahmin and the third was Charan Singh, a Jat, and till then the only Prime Minister from a background other than that of a twice-born (upper) caste. Now Deve Gowda, short-lived Prime Minister after the 1996 election, shares that status with Charan Singh. While it is not possible to extrapolate from the caste background of Prime Ministers to the background of Congress leaders in general, high-caste and particularly Brahmin domination of the most senior positions has been characteristic of Congress throughout its long history. Nor is this phenomenon confined to Congress. Atul Kohli has produced figures to show that both Congress and Communist Party dominated Governments in West Bengal have had a strikingly skewed caste composition.

The caste of Ministers in Congress Governments in West Bengal between 1952 and 1962 was 23 per cent Brahmin, 31 per cent Kayastha, 24 per cent Vaishya, and only 2 per cent Scheduled Caste. In the case of Governments led by the

Communist Party of India (Marxist) between 1977 and 1982 there were even more Brahmins than in the Congress Governments, over 35 per cent; the number of Kayasthas (3 per cent) and Vaishyas (23 per cent) was almost the same as in Congress Governments, while Scheduled Caste representation was marginally lower at 1.5 per cent. These figures must be read in the context of a State which has the highest concentration of Scheduled Caste people in the country - now almost 24 per cent (Census 1991). Demonstrably, the many Scheduled Caste members of the West Bengal Assembly have almost no chance of rising to the position of Minister. Their representation is even lower if inferior Ministers - Ministers of State and Deputy Ministers - are left out. In the Governments formed after the elections of 1952, 1957, 1962, 1977 and 1982 there was not a single Scheduled Caste member of the Council of Ministers, Of course, it is not merely the Scheduled Castes that have been grossly underrepresented in West Bengali Cabinets - the same is true for Scheduled Tribes, Muslims and lower-caste Hindus.

A similar, if less pronounced, pattern is true of the organisational wing of the Communist Party of India (Marxist), and given the ideological orientation of the party it is worth attending to this phenomenon more closely. In both Kerala and West Bengal Untouchables are scarcely represented at the highest levels of the Party. In Kerala, those who have risen to leading Party positions from poor backgrounds have almost always come from 'proletarian' unions of the towns. The Ezhava dominated bidi workers union is one such example. Scheduled Caste workers in Kerala still tend to be agricultural labourers, and they have found it impossible to rise to the top of the Party hierarchy. In West Bengal, until the late sixties the Party was essentially an urban and high-caste organisation. With the later focus on agrarian problems there has been a growing membership drawn from the villages. Scheduled Caste membership is now in double figures, most of it rural in origin (though not usually drawn from the ranks of agricultural labourers, the lowest agrarian category). But even if such people are as likely as anyone else to rise to the top of the Party - a questionable assumption - it would take considerable time before their presence might be felt.

It is not open to infer the whole character of a government or a political party from the caste composition of its senior members. The Communist governments of West Bengal and Kerala have been among the best State governments in India in terms of both probity and service to their poorer citizens. But even these governments are vulnerable to criticism for their insufficient attention to those at the very bottom of the social hierarchy. For example, both governments have frequently been attacked for their failure to meet job reservation quotas. Presumably this failure can be said to arise from an ideological antipathy to programmes constructed on the basis of social primordialism (caste). But it can also scarcely be irrelevant that reservation is adverse to the interests of large proportions of the castes that predominate within the government. Even in less intensely caste conscious West Bengal it cannot be assumed that Communist Ministers are effectively without caste (or class). This is not to propose the existence of a caste conspiracy or even a lack of goodwill towards the underprivileged. It is merely to recognise that it is difficult to induce and sustain a sense of urgency about the claims of out-groups in the absence of their own advocates.

A deeper criticism of the Communist governments can be levelled at their agrarian programmes. Thus Kerala has one of the poorer records of land reform among the various States. There has been only a slight amount of redistribution of agricultural land, and agricultural labourers (many of them Untouchables) have had to be content with gaining ownership of the land on which their 'hutment' is built within the village. Kerala has done far better in the matter of fixing minimum wages for its agricultural labourers, though here there have been some unfortunate consequences. Partly because of the resulting high cost of labour there has been a radical reduction in the amount of work available to Kerala labourers: mechanisation, leaving land fallow, and employment of out-of-State workers have been options preferred by many employers. The West Bengal experience on the same two issues has been the reverse of that of Kerala.

West Bengal has done much better in the area of land redistribution, and it has also accomplished significant reforms for sharecroppers. But the CPI(M) Government has paid little attention to the interests of the army of agricultural labourers in the State. A large proportion of these labourers are, of course, from the Scheduled Castes, and their rates of pay and general living conditions are at the poorer end of the national scale. Nor is Operation Barga beyond criticism. These reforms were abandoned at the highly incomplete point when further action would have directly injured the interests of small, usually absentee, landlords.

Many of these mainly high-caste people have been supporters of the CPI(M) regime, and the decision can therefore be painted in tones of political pragmatism. Moreover, in an 'encircled' polity such as West Bengal there are undoubtedly limits to just how much redistribution is a possibility. Clearly we must be careful not to repackage the whole huge problem of Indian poverty and inequality into the receptacle of caste - this will make no analytical sense, nor indicate a way out of the practical condition. Nonetheless, we doubt it can be said that ties of caste and community, wrapped up in positions of class, are of no relevance to the policy and performance of the Government of West Bengal.

The above question can be crystallised by reference to Ambedkar's description of Indian Communists as 'a bunch of Brahman boys'. He was referring not only to the number of Brahmins within the Party, but also to discriminatory attitudes and blindness to the problems of the Untouchables. If we discount the hyperbole, the observation contains a (slippery) grain of truth. On the one hand we should not subscribe to the false proposition that only the representatives of a particular community are capable of working for the good of that community. But we must also recognise that a community or a people needs to speak for itself if its interests and potential are to be realised to any great degree.

This is the dialectic embedded in the issue of Untouchable representation in contemporary politics. Thus it is reasonable to assume that greater Untouchable representation at the highest levels would produce outcomes more favourable to their own people than occurs through government dominated by the high castes. The benefits would no doubt range from individual allocations (such as jobs, licences, contracts) to broader policy. To give one small but important example of possible policy, greater Untouchable presence in government could conceivably lead to the application of more pressure towards the exten-sion of affirmative action into private- and not merely public-sector enterprises. This is exactly the sort of non-revolutionary but quite far-reaching change that is potentially within the realm of government action in India.

DALIT POLITICS AFTER AMBEDKAR

Until the recent emergence of the Bahujana Samaj Party, the only post-Independence example of a party centred on Untouchables was the Republican Party of India (RPI). This was the final political vehicle devised by Ambedkar, though its formation in reached fruition only some months after his death. The Republican Party was a transformation of the Scheduled Castes Federation, electorally unsuccessful and also judged to be an inappropriate organisational form for Buddhists who had sloughed off caste by the act of abandoning Hinduism. Again, as in the days of the Independent Labour Party, Ambedkar planned a party along class rather than caste lines. But almost from the beginning the RPI ran into ideological, organisational and factional problems. The first major division was between an old guard more deeply rooted in the village world of the majority of Mahars, and a younger and more highly educated leadership that increasingly focussed on the opportunities inherent in urban life and the scheme of compensatory discrimination.

This generational conflict was connected to a split between those who saw the future of Mahar politics in terms of broader economic and class struggle - some of these were the older village-based activists - and an emerging leadership less committed to working with caste Hindus and even other Untouchable communities. While Ambedkar himself had been far less concerned with agrarian problems than with broader questions of political and constitu-tional principle, his stature had been such as to engender loyalty right across Mahar society and thus to blur the divergence of interest within it. After Ambedkar, and in the context of growing social and economic diversity among the Mahars, there was no one who could command this general loyalty. By 1959 division in the RPI was so deep that the two major factions held separate conventions. Inevitably it was the younger, better-educated and more prosperous faction based in the cities that became the more energetic element of the party.

The RPI carried its divisions into the election of 1962, and failed to win a single Lok Sabha seat from the new linguistic state of Maharashtra. It did somewhat better in the State Assembly election of that year, but after that it won only a handful of Assembly seats in Maharashtra. The RPI also put down roots in several States where Atnbedkar's influence had been relatively strong - particularly Uttar Pradesh (notably the cities of Agra and Aligarh) and Punjab, but also Haryana, Andhra Pradesh and Karnataka. Extraordinarily, the RPI was electorally more successful in Uttar Pradesh than in Maharashtra. Its success in UP was built around a substantial Buddhist politician of Chamar origins, B. P. Maurya, who drew votes away from Congress by engineering a local coalition of Untouchables and Muslims in the city and District of Aligarh. But the inherent instability of this alliance - there had been no historical sympathy between Chamars and Muslims - and the Congress split of 1969 quickly changed the electoral equation for the RPI in Uttar Pradesh. By 1971 B. P. Maurya and his major opponent within the party, Ramji Ram, were both returned to the Lok Sabha under the banner of Indira Gandhi's ostensibly left-orientated branch of the Congress. This was the effective end of the Republican Party as a force in Uttar Pradesh.

In Maharashtra, the death or eclipse of one Ambedkarite form has been a prelude to the rise of another. Thus in the early 1970 an organisation calling itself the Dalit Panthers was formed with the project of reinstating class-based Dalit politics following the Republican Party's perceived lapse into narrow self-interest. The name, with its insurrectionist symbolism, was borrowed from the Black Panthers of the United States. At the time India was marked by widespread famine, pervasive student activism and a non-party oppositional politics which later developed into Jayaprakash Narayan's direct confrontation of Indira Gandhi. But the Dalit Panthers proved unable to connect up with broader leftist politics.

They were also no more attuned to the Dalit 'masses' - a majority of Mahars were still illiterate villagers - than was the Republican Party, and within a couple of years they were even more riven by ideological and personality differences. The core ideological split was publicly evident by 1974 and was personified in the two pre-eminent leaders of the movement, Namdeo Dhasal and Raja Dhale. For Dhale's faction, the defining moment in Dalit history was the mass conversion to Buddhism under the leadership of Ambedkar; future gains were to be made primarily through a deepening and widening of Buddhist consciousness rather than through secular political action. Namdeo Dhasal, on the other hand, represented a more orthodox leftist, indeed Marxist, position, which gave both Ambedkar and the conversion movement less of a defining role. Abolition of Untouchability was an issue of class and economics more than of caste, religion and consciousness, and the natural allies of the Untouchables were the poor classes of whatever religious or caste community.

Consistent with this view Dhasal had seen the CPI as the appropriate overall leader of the Dalit. But within a few years Indira Gandhi's anti-poverty programmes of the Emergency period persuaded Dhasal that here was a leader genuinely committed to the poor, and his faction supported Congress in the 1977 election. By then the Panthers were divided into a number of geographically centred factions of little potency, and it was only the riots in 1978 surrounding the Maharashtra Government's decision to add the prefix 'Dr Babasaheb Ambedkar' to 'Marathwada University' that brought them into some prominence again. The Dalit Panthers had failed to define a durable role for themselves - they were political activists without a political party or a clear strategy agreed among themselves. Moreover, they had become scarcely more radical, and certainly no more connected to ordinary Mahars, than the Republican Party. And, of course, they had demonstrated little capacity to reach out to other Untouchable castes.

The void left by the demise of the Panthers has been filled not by another party or other directly political organisation of the Mahar Daltts but, extraordinarily, by a literary movement. A whole new literature has sprung up on the common basis of rejection of varna. The lives and interior world of Untouchables have been explored by a profusion of writers, some of them highly talented. It is tempting, and indeed legitimate, to see this new literature as heir to the great tradition of bhakti, though many of its exponents reject this tradition, Chokha Mela in particular, for its acceptance of inequality in the expectation of a better world in the life-to-come. The resort to literary means of communicating Dalit anger has been consciously adopted in disgust at what is perceived to be the failure of orthodox politics to transform the lives of the Dalit. Clearly the Dalit literature is an intensely political body of writing, some of it infused more with passion than with concern for literary effect. But the best Dalit writers are widely recognised as having created a literature of genuine merit.

Nor is this Dalit literature confined to Maharashtra. There is now a vigorous assembly of Dalit writers in Karnataka too. The immediate origins of this movement can be located in a speech delivered in 1974 by a Minister in the Congress Government of Karnataka. Basavalingappa, an Untouchable, was moved to describe the literature of Kannada, the language of the region, as little more than boosa or cattle fodder. He had in mind this literature's lack of attention to the lives of ordinary people, among them the Untouchables (still usually called Adi-Karnataka). It was as if Basavalingappa had put a torch to a pile of tinder, so great was the explosion of both acclamation and repudiation.

To the orthodox custodians of Kannada literature the Untouchable Minister had defamed their cultural heritage in the service of a mindless radicalism. But to an astonishingly large number of actual or aspiring Dalit writers, Basavalingappa had opened the door to a palace of opportunity to express their rejection of their own place in Karnataka society. A conference of Dalit writers was held in 1974, and some hundreds are said to have attended. In subsequent years this Dalit literary movement has moved in a number of directions. For example, one group of young Dalit has established a popular weekly magazine, Sugathi, which combines the transmission of popular culture (film features and so on) with political and social comment on Dalit affairs. Its readership is mostly drawn from Adi-Karnatakas themselves, and in 1988 circulation was some 65,000 copies.

The literary movement preceded any narrow political expression of Dalit radicalism in Karnataka, and subsequent institutional forms have not followed the pattern of Maharashtra. Without the direct legacy of Ambedkar, the Karnataka Dalit have not sought to establish a Dalit political party. Rather, the Dalit Sangharsh Samiti has been set up as something of an umbrella organisation for the various Dalit groups within the State. Dalit activities have been directed to educating the consciousness of Adi-Karnataka adults and children, and staging agitations and demonstrations on matters of particular concern. A special focus has been on Harijan atrocities. Within particular industries - the nationalised banks, for example - there are organisations of Dalit workers. Many of the Dalit activists have embraced Buddhism and are engaged in increasing their knowledge of the literature of this religion and proselytising among the unconverted. But while the Karnataka movement has derived its inspiration from Ambedkar and from the Maharashtra movement in general, there is also a concern to avoid what is seen to be the Maharashtra defect of being too inward-looking and exclusive.

Some of these activists have gone so far as to reject reservation of jobs and parliamentary seats as a trap which cuts them off from other progressive elements and also fails to do anything for the larger Dalit community. And there is special scorn for the occupants of reserved seats in legislatures. While there have been no intense ideological splits in Karnataka, there is evidence of the same tensions that have so destructively affected the Ambedkarite movement in

Maharashtra. The recurrent choice for radical Untouchables everywhere is between cultivating a separate Untouchable identity or constructing alliances with all oppressed people who are prepared to listen.

Even more than in Maharashtra, the Dalit movement of Karnataka has been an urban phenomenon. The Untouchable castes of village Karnataka have not been drawn into a movement whose main preoccupations have been literary, cultural and religious. During a visit to his ancestral village, one of our Dalit guides - a leader among Dalit bank employees and a Buddhist - spoke scornfully of the backwardness of the Adi-Karnataka there. They lacked ambition and remained locked into a world of drudgery, alcohol and attachment to what he called 'some non-veg god'. To this man there was no point in trying to rouse the consciousness of his caste fellows and relatives in the village. His time was better spent working with young men studying in schools and colleges in the towns, and in staging demonstrations that would catch the eye of the media.

The lack of mobilisation of village Untouchables in Karnataka and even Maharashtra serves to point up the distinctiveness of the rural revolt in Bihar. In so far as there has been an ideological guide to the activity in Bihar, it has been a derivative of revolutionary Marxism. This should not lead us to conclude that Marxism is the appropriate ideology for the Dalit of Karnataka and Maharashtra, or that Ambedkarite principles are inherently incapable of attracting widespread support in rural India. As we shall see, Kanshi Ram has skilfully used the figure of Ambedkar to build a following among rural as well as urban Chamars in Uttar Pradesh. But it is notable that the Bihar mobilisation has proceeded primarily on demonstrations on matters of particular concern.

A special focus has been on Harijan atrocities. Within particular industries - the nationalised banks, for example - there are organisations of Dalit workers. Many of the Dalit activists have embraced Buddhism and are engaged in increasing their knowledge of the literature of this religion and proselytising among the unconverted. But while the

Karnataka movement has derived its inspiration from Ambedkar and from the Maharashtra movement in general, there is also a concern to avoid what is seen to be the Maharashtra defect of being too inward-looking and exclusive. Some of these activists have gone so far as to reject reservation of jobs and parliamentary seats as a trap which cuts them off from other progressive ele-ments and also fails to do anything for the larger Dalit community. And there is special scorn for the occupants of reserved seats in legislatures. While there have been no intense ideological splits in Karnataka, there is evidence of the same tensions that have so destructively affected the Ambedkarite movement in Maharashtra. The recurrent choice for radical Untouchables everywhere is between cultivating a separate Untouchable identity or constructing alliances with all oppressed people who are pre-pared to listen.

These are the same broad issues that were the core of the programme of Ambedkar's Independent Labour Party from 1937 to 1942, and in somewhat variant form they were also the foundation of the later Republican Party and Dalit Panthers. But none of these bodies actually pursued their programme with any determination, and the post-Independence organisations fell seriously out of step with village Mahars at the same time as they became further isolated from communities other than the Mahars. Part of the problem has been Buddhism: despite its merits as a wellspring of personal empowerment, Buddhism scarcely speaks to the issues that are of immediate concern to poor villagers of Mahar or any other Untouchable caste. In so far as the Dalit leadership of Maharashtra has concentrated on the project of Buddhism, they have tended to abdicate from a position where mobilisation of village and less educated Untouchables is a possibility. Even worse, preoccupation with another religious system has driven a positive wedge between the Mahar Buddhists and Hindus from other poor and subordinated communities.

But despite the limitations of the Ambedkarite movement as an electoral and mobilising force in western India, the thought and life of Babasaheb Ambedkar enjoy a tremendous and indeed fast-growing potency across large parts of India. Within Maharashtra itself one of the recent expressions of this was the demonstrations and counter-demonstrations surrounding the publication of Ambedkar's work Riddles in Hinduism. This work is part of a multi-volume set of Ambedkar's writings being published, or usually republished, by the Government of Maharashtra under the direction of Dalit scholars. That the project has gone forward at all is testimony to the weight of Ambedkar's writing and the political passion of his followers. Riddles in Hinduism had been considered too inflammatory a work to be published during Ambedkar's lifetime, and tens of years after it was written the work had scarcely become less controversial.

While Maharashtra and neighbouring Karnataka remain the centres where Ambedkar's legacy is taken most seriously, the physical image of the historical figure is now to be found on posters and in the form of statues in countless locations throughout India. The propagation of Babasaheb's image has become both a sacred duty to his followers and also an easily available means for politicians and political hopefuls to position themselves as radical champions of their own communities. Juxtaposition of one's own image beside that of Ambedkar can now be an alternative to statement of a clear political position. But more positively, through the politics of iconography Dalit have been busy reclaiming their own twentieth-century history. The great loser in this struggle of images is Gandhi. Whereas once Gandhi could be portrayed as the great champion of the 'Harijan', now Dalit themselves prefer to ignore or even castigate him for condescension and adherence to subordinating orthdoxy. Now it is Ambedkar who shows the way in thousands of out-of-the-way locations to which his writ did not run during his own lifetime.

DALIT POLITICS IN NORTHERN INDIA

North Indian politics are presently in a state of great flux. Whereas the Hindi-speaking region was once the basis of Congress rule of the nation, now the Congress vote has quite disintegrated there. Uttar Pradesh is the most dramatic case.

In the general election of 1984 Congress won eighty-three out of eighty-five UP seats with 5 per cent of the total vote. But five years later the party won only fifteen seats with 32 per cent of the vote. In 1991 the Congress vote slipped further to 18 per cent, and it won five seats. This was also its tally of seats in 1996. Congress' dominance had been built on a strong command of the Brahmin, Muslim and Untouchable 'vote banks', together with considerable but variable support from the other upper castes and also the Backward Castes. The latter were the first to desert the party, and since the mid-eighties it has also suffered the fatal blow of having lost its three stable vote banks.

The waning of Congress has coincided with the rise of two other parties - the Janata Dal and its offshoots, including Mulayam Singh's Samajwadi Party, and the Bharatiya Janata Party (BJP). These parties have risen to prominence partly because of the vacuum caused by the waning of Congress, and partly because of their own attractiveness. Thus the leading party in 1989 was Janata Dal, with fifty-four seats and 36 per cent of the vote. But in the next election of 1991 the largest party was the BJP with fifty-one seats and 33 per cent of the vote. The Janata Dal and the Samajwadi Party draw their major strength from the Backward Castes, whereas the BJP has traditionally been strongest among the upper castes of the towns. But each of these two political forces picked up other groups as they gathered momentum. Thus the Janata Dal and Samajwadi parties attracted a large share of the Muslim vote disenchanted with Congress after the destruction of the Babri Masjid. And the BJP has picked up considerable Backward Caste support, partly because it has had a strong Backward Caste (Lodhi) leader in Kalyan Singh.

Another development of the first importance in Uttar Pradesh has been the rise of Kanshi Ram's Bahujana Samaj Party to the point where it was able to form the State government in 1995 and 1997. Although Kanshi Ram has benefited crucially from the collapse of Congress, his rise is not to be attributed simply to the vacuum effect. Kanshi Ram has spoken directly to the aspirations of the Chamars, and he has also had a radicalising impact on a wider constituency of Backward and other Scheduled Caste communities. Kanshi Ram's mode of operation has been to yoke an aggressive Ambedkarite ideology to hard-headed manipulation of the vote banks of Uttar Pradesh.

The indispensable basis of his power is his own community, the Chamars. These constitute not only the largest Untouchable caste in India, but almost certainly the largest single caste in Uttar Pradesh.' Kanshi Ram has not had the total support of the Chamars - until recently the Jatavs of western UP have been an important hold-out but his command in eastern UP has been overwhelming. Kanshi Ram's strategy has been to join his bank of Chamar voters to other Scheduled Caste and Backward Caste voters (particularly the Kurmis) and also the Muslims. He has been careful to cede the non-Chamar communities a majority of Bahujana Samaj candidates - there has been a specially large number of Muslim candidates - in the knowledge that voters will often be attracted by a candidate of their own community. The Bahujana Samaj could offer these communities the prospect that the large Chamar vote would be added to theirs, since the Chamars believed that the party was above all theirs. But before we consider the contemporary situation in some detail, something must be said about the origins of Kanshi Ram and the Bahujana Samaj Party.

RISE OF KANSHI RAM

Kanshi Ram was born in 1934 as a Raedasi Sikh, a community of Punjabi Chamars converted to Sikhism. The family had 4 or 5 acres of land, some of it inherited and the rest acquired through government allocation after Independence, a small landed background is characteristic of many Scheduled Caste legislators but remains a comparative rarity for Dalit in general. Kanshi Ram's father was himself 'slightly' literate, and he managed to educate all his four daughters and three sons. Kanshi Ram, the eldest, is the only graduate. He was given a reserved position in the Survey of

India after completing his BSc degree, and in 1958 he transferred to the Department of Defence Production as a scientific assistant in a munitions factory in Poona.

Kanshi Ram had encountered no Untouchability as a child, and overt discrimination was not a phenomenon within the educated circles of his adult life. But his outlook underwent a sudden change in 1965 when he became caught up in a struggle initiated by other Scheduled Caste employees to prevent the abolition of a holiday commemorating Dr Anibedkar's birthday.' During this conflict Kanshi Ram encountered a depth of high-caste prejudice and hostility towards Dalit that was a revelation to him. His almost instant radicalisation was completed soon after by a reading of Ambedkar's Annihilation of Caste: he read the book three times in one night, going entirely without sleep.

Kanshi Ram's introduction to the political ideas of Ambedkar - he has never been attracted to Buddhism - was through his Mahar Buddhist colleague and friend at the munitions factory, D. K. Khaparde. Together the two of them began formulating ideas for an organisation to be built by educated employees from the Scheduled and Backward castes. Such an organisation would work against harassment and oppression by high-caste officers, and also enable the often inward-looking occupants of reserved postions to give something back to their own communities. So Kanshi Ram and Khaparde began to contact likely recruits in Poona. At about this time Kanshi Ram abandoned any thought of marriage, largely because it did not fit into a life he now wanted to dedicate to public concerns. He had also quite lost interest in his career, though he continued in the job until about 1971. He finally left after a severe conflict over the non-appointment of an apparently qualified Scheduled Caste young woman. During this conflict he had gone so far as to strike a senior official, and he did not even bother attending most of the ensuing disciplinary proceedings. He had already made up his mind to become a full-time activist, and the movement was by then strong enough to meet his modest needs.

In 1971 Kanshi Ram and his colleagues established the Scheduled Castes, Scheduled Tribes, Other Backward Classes and Minorities Employees Welfare Association, which was duly registered under the Poona Charity Commissioner. Their primary object was: To subject our problems to close scrutiny and find out quick and equitable solutions to the problems of injustice and harassment of our employees in general and the educated employees in particular.

Despite the Association's inclusive reach, its aggressively Ambedkarite stance ensured that most of its members were Mahar Buddhists. Within a year of its establishment there were more than one thousand members and it was able to open an office in Poona: many of the members were from the Defence and Post and Telegraph Departments, and their first annual conference was addressed by the then Defence Minister, Jagjivan Ram. Kanshi Ram's next organisational step was to create the basis of a national association of Scheduled Caste government servants. As early as 1973 he and his colleagues established the All India Backward and Minority Employees Federation (BAMCEF), and a functioning office was established in Delhi in 1976. BAMCEF was relaunched with greater fanfare on 6 December 1978, the anniversary of Ambedkar's death, with claims of two thousand delegates joining a procession to the Boat Club Lawns in New Delhi (BAMCEF Bulletin April 1979). Although the stated objects of the new organisation were essentially the same as those of the earlier body, the rhetoric had grown bolder. It was not merely the oppressors who came in the line of fire, but also many of the reserved office holders too:

As all the avenues of advance are closed to them in the field of agriculture, trade, commerce and industry almost all the educated persons from these [oppressed] communities are trapped in Govt. services. About 2 million educated oppressed Indians have already joined various types of sobs during the last 26 years. Civil Service Conduct rules put some restrictions on them. But their inherent timidity, cowardice, selfishness and lack of desire for Social Service to their own creed have made them exceptionally useless to the general mass of the oppressed Indians.The only ray of hope is that almost everywhere in the country there are some educated employees who feel deeply agitated about the miserable existence of their brethren. (BAMCEF Bulletin 2 1974)

By the mid-1970s Kanshi Ram had established a broad if not dense network of contacts throughout Maharashtra and adjacent regions. During his frequent train trips from Poona to Delhi, he adopted the habit of getting down at major stations along the way - Nagpur, Jabalpur and Bhopal, among others - to contact likely sympathisers and to try to recruit them to the organisation (Kanshi Ram Interview: 1996). Once he had moved to Delhi he pushed into Punjab, Haryana and Uttar Pradesh, as well as further into Madhya Pradesh. Parallel to his work among educated employees Kanshi Ram was also contacting a wider audience with simple presentations of Ambedkar's teachings. Thus in 1980 he put together a roadshow called 'Ambedkar Mela on Wheels'. This was an oral and pictorial account of Ambedkar's life and views, together with contemporary material on oppression, atrocities and poverty. Between April and June 1980 the show was carted to thirty-four destinations.

STATES OF THE NORTH

Jang Bahadur Patel, a Kurmi (Backward Caste) and President of the Uttar Pradesh Branch of the Bahujana Samaj Party until late 1995, recalls meeting Kanshi Ram for the first time when he brought his roadshow to Lucknow. Kanshi Ram talked persuasively about how Ambedkar had struggled for all the downtrodden classes, and how the Scheduled Castes, Tribes and also the Backwards and Minorities were all victims of Brahminism. Because of their weight of numbers, these people had the potential to convert themselves from 'beggars to rulers'. It was all a matter of organisation. Patel immediately joined BAMCEF, though he was in a distinct minority as a non-Untouchable: Untouchables constituted about 90 per cent of the membership, with the other 10 per cent being split between tribals and Backward Caste people.

BAMCEF's motto, 'Educate, Organise and Agitate', was adopted from Ambedkar, and its activities were formally divided into a number of welfare and proselytising objects. But increasingly Kanshi Ram's agitational activities were leading him into politics. By the late 70s he was no longer content with being the leader of reserved office holders, a class for whom he had less than complete respect. Kanshi Ram's first attempt to create a radical political vehicle capable of mobilising the larger body of Dalit was the Dalit Soshit Samaj Sangharsh Samiti (DS4) formed in 1981. This was conceived as a political organisation parallel to BAMCEF: it shared the same President in Kanshi Ram, the same office, and many of the same members. DS4 was a quasi rather than fully fledged political party, partly because government servants were forbidden to take part in electoral politics. But DS4 made little concrete progress, and late in 1984 Kanshi Ram took the plunge and formed the Bahujana Samaj Party (a variant on the name of Phule's nineteenth-century organisation).

Inevitably, this caused major strains in BAMCEF ranks. Their agitational activities had placed many of his colleagues from the Poona and early Delhi periods in a delicate position as government servants and, in any case, the political loyalty of many of them was to the several strands of the Republican Party. There were also strains arising from Kanshi Ram's will to total domination of all three organisations. And the need for money was rising with the push into politics: one of the Maharashtra workers recalls delivering Kanshi Ram a purse of forty thousand rupees collected from Maharashtra in 1984. These several strains grew more severe over the next two years, and early in 1986 a major split took place. Kanshi Ram announced at that time that he was no longer willing to work for any organisation other than the Bahujana Samaj Party. His transition from social worker to politician was complete.

Kanshi Ram is more an organiser and political strategist than an innovative thinker or charismatic public speaker. While his Ambedkarite ideology has remained constant and lacking in any innovation, there has been a progressive sharpening of his rhetoric. The early issues of BAMCEF's monthly magazine, The Oppressed Indian, were full of his didactic expositions of Ambedkar's views on Indian society. These have now given way to simpler formulations, repeated in numerous newspaper accounts and both public and private speech.

The central proposition is that Indian society is characterised by the self-interested rule of io per cent over the other 90 per cent (the bahujan samaj or common people). Although the ruling io per cent is composed of several castes, they derive their legitimacy and ruling ideology from Brahminism. All the institutions of society reflect this ruling ideology and distortion, including the press. These institutions can therefore be termed Manuwadi (after the great Brahmin-inspired text) or Brahminwadi. In the marketplace of elections, such simplicity has been further reduced to crudeness and epithet. A slogan coined after the formation of DS4 was, 'Brahmin, Bania, Thakur Chor, Baki Sab Hem DS-Four'. Loosely translated, this rhyme states that Brahmins, Banias and Rajputs are thieves, while the rest of society are their victims.

The epithets reached their height during the election campaign for the UP Assembly in 1993, the most notorious being: 'Tilak, Taraju, Talwar. Maaro Unko Joote Char'. This slogan, with its insistent rhythm in Hindi, advocates that Brahmins, Banias and Rajputs, each identified by a slighting term, be beaten four times with a shoe - a traditionally demeaning form of punishment because of the ritual impurity of leather. While Kanshi Ram and Mayawati denied authorship of such slogans, they served as a simple and dramatically offensive marker of the party's ideological position.

Kanshi Ram's strategy and his larger understanding of social change are now considerably evolved. He no longer believes in the primacy of social reform. Rather, expenditure of effort on any object other than the capture of government is seen to be superfluous. It is administrative power that will bring about desired social change, not vice versa. So he declines to spell out policies on basic issues such as the liberalisation of the Indian economy or on land reforms. His view is that such issues are irrelevant to the project of gaining power, and that the appropriate policies will fall into place once power is attained. His picture of India is of a kind of holy war on the part of the bahujan samaj against their Brahminwadi oppressors. In the context of this war debates about policy are almost frivolities. This is a stance of pure fundamentalism, but it also frees him to engage in the most ruthless pragmatism in the name of capturing power.

Consistent with this stance, Kanshi Ram has become increasingly critical of the institution of reservation in government employment. Reservation is a 'crutch' - useful for a cripple, but a positive handicap for someone who wants to run on his own two feet. He now throws off the line that once the bahujan samaj get to power throughout India, it will be they who can condescend to the Brahmins by giving them reservation proportional to their own meagre population.

There is more than a little bravado in this, but there is no doubt that Kanshi Ram is now hostile to the system of institutional preference that was the indispensable basis of his own personal and political career. It seems that he believes that reservation has now done enough for the Scheduled Castes. He notes that of some 500 Indian Administrative Service (IAS) Officers in Uttar Pradesh, 137 are from the Scheduled Castes. By comparison, there are only seven IAS officers from the Backward Castes, six of them Yadavs. His point is not that there are now too many Scheduled Caste officers -their number conforms strictly to the legal quota - but too few from the Backward Castes. He apparently assumes that the capture of political power will automatically transform the composition of the bureaucratic elite.

The Bahujana Samaj Party first made headway in Punjab, Kanshi Ram's home State, but his primary political task was to wean the Chamars of Uttar Pradesh from Congress. It was Kanshi Ram's fortune that he built the party at the historical moment that the long-term Congress decline became a landslide. The formal entry of his party into Uttar Pradesh was in a by-election in 1985 for the Lok Sabha seat of Bijinor, in which its candidate was Mayawati. She is a Jatav (or

Chamar), the daughter of a minor government official in Delhi, and had completed a BA and LLB from the University of Delhi.

Mayawati had made contact with Kanshi Ram in 1977 while she was a student, and had gradually been drawn into his organisation. Her opponents in Bijinor included Ram Vilas Paswan - the two have had poor relations since this contest - and Meira Kumar, Jagjivan Ram's daughter, representing Congress. Rajiv Gandhi was at the height of his popularity at the time, and Meira Kumar won the seat easily. But by 1989 the Bahujana Samaj Party had put in five years of solid organising work in UP and also in the neighbouring regions of Madhya Pradesh, Punjab, Delhi, and parts of Haryana. And meanwhile the Congress Party had slumped in popularity. Kanshi Ram had prepared the ground carefully. He had selected organisers and candidates from a variety of social backgrounds. One of his organisers was Dr Mahsood Ahmed, a temporary lecturer in history at Aligarh Muslim University. Mahsood had become disillusioned with Congress when Indira Gandhi made her infamous tilt towards the Hindus in the early 1980s. He joined BAMCEF and then switched to DS4 in 1983 as a full-time organiser and fund raiser. Mahsood was later put in charge of the whole of eastern Uttar Pradesh for the Bahujana Samaj Party.

The years of organisation bore fruit in 1989 and 1991. In the four State Assembly and Parliamentary (Lok Sabha) polls for Uttar Pradesh between 1989 and 1991 the Bahujana Samaj Party's share of the vote varied only marginally between 8.7 and 9.4 per cent. But this impressive vote produced a disappointing number of seats - in 1989 the party won thirteen out of 425 State Assembly seats, and in 1991 it won twelve. The party won only two Parliamentary seats in 1989, and one in 1991; Kanshi Ram himself subsequently won a by-election from UP in 1992. Both the strength and the weakness of the party is that its primary 'vote bank', the Chamars, are relatively evenly spread across the State. This spread gives the Bahujana Samaj a chance in a large number of seats, but also make it logically impossible to win even a single seat without strong support from other communities. Although it has attracted a measure of Muslim, Backward Caste and other Scheduled Caste support, it has encountered considerable resistance in these target communities. We need to look more closely at this problem.

First, there is the question of why the majority of Jatavs of western UP deviated from their kinfolk in the eastern part of the State, and continued to vote Congress in 1989 and 1991. The answer to this question is not entirely clear. Some have blamed the result on the poor organising capacities of Mayawati - she was in charge of this region - but the deeper reason may be the Jatavs' historical association with B. P. Maurya. In a move of some desperation, Congress resurrected the 70-year-old Maurya as one of four national Vice-Presidents in the run-up to the 1996 elections. But by then Mayawati had become an electorally popular figure in eastern UP. As to the Scheduled Castes other than the Chamars/Jatavs, only Pasis appear to have voted for Kanshi Ram's party in large numbers.

The Valmikis (formerly known as Bhangis) voted solidly for the BJP in the 1993 Assembly elections, and the sole Valmiki in the Lok Sabha elected in 1991 represented the BJP (though in 1980 he had been elected for the Janata Party). Mangal Ram Premi MP accounts for the Valmiki support of the BJP by simply adverting to the community's dislike of the Chamars. The Chamars are more numerous, better educated and more successful in acquiring reserved positions than the Valmikis, and this tends to produce resentment. Many of the Dhobis too have recently voted for the BJP. In short, Kanshi Ram's party has not solved the problem of how to mobilise all or even most of the Scheduled Castes. The problem that dogged Ambedkar has thus repeated itself in Uttar Pradesh, though Kanshi Ram's Chamars are both more numerous and numerically more dominant among the Untouchables than were Ambedkar's Mahars in the western part of the country.

Among Backward Castes, Kanshi Ram's strongest support has come from the Kurmis. In Bihar, this is an upwardly mobile peasant community responsible for several of the worst atrocities against Dalit. But in Uttar Pradesh the

Kurmis are comparatively low on the scale of prosperity. Moreover, they have had a history of anti-Brahmin radicalism - Shahu Maharaj of Kolhapur remains a source of inspiration to some of them. And a sprinkling of them had been members of the Republican Party. The Kurmis could see advantage in being associated with a party that was not dominated by the more numerous Yadavs (whose firm affiliation is with Mulayam Singh's Samajwadi Party). As to the large number of other Backward Castes in UP, over the last several years there has been an intense three-way tussle between the BJP, the Bahujana Samaj Party and the Samajwadi Party to capture their support. All three have had some success, but perhaps the larger part of this vote is a floating one that will flow with the main political current of the time.

The last community to consider is the Muslims. In the aftermath of the destruction of the Babri Masjid the Muslims have been politically leaderless. They have shunned Congress for what they see to have been its culpable failure to prevent the demolition of the mosque, and have given considerable support to Mulayam Singh's Samajwadi Party and some support to Kanshi Ram. Thus in the municipal elections of Uttar Pradesh in November 1995 and in the national and UP elections of 1996 it seems that UP Muslims were prepared to vote for whichever party was locally the strongest anti-BJP force. In short, the politics of post-Congress Uttar Pradesh are currently cast largely in terms of community vote banks. Political strategy is a matter of positioning one's party so as to retain one s core vote bank and also attract others at the margins. At least as much as any other player, Kanshi Ram has adapted to this game with calculating skill.

MAYAWATI IN GOVERNMENT

Before the UP Assembly election (held after the dismissal of the BJP Government), Kanshi Ram entered into an alliance with Mulayam Singh. The primary vote banks of the two men were complementary the Yadavs and the Chamars. This was by no means a 'natural' alliance, since the two communities had engaged in perennial and sometimes violent conflict in the villages. Indeed, the Yadavs had frequently captured voting booths in eastern UP and prevented the Chamars from voting. But each of the leaders could now see that his prospects were poor without the other, and they agreed on a division of seats so as to combine their vote. The alliance produced a dramatically enhanced increase in seats for the Bahujana Samaj Party (67), but its vote rose less dramatically to 11 per cent (achieved admittedly in a sharply reduced number of contests).

Meanwhile the Samajwadi Party won 109 seats and 25.83 per cent of the vote, making it second to the BJP with its 177 seats and 33.3 per cent of the vote. The Samajwadi Party and the Bahujana Samaj Party were able to form a coalition Government, with Mulayam Singh as Chief Minister. But Kanshi Ram and Mayawati soon came to believe that their party's interests were being infringed by Mulayam - one issue was the alleged kidnapping of one of their candidates during panchayat elections. There was also concern at the number of 'atrocities' perpetrated against Scheduled Caste people, some of them by Yadavs; the belief was that Mulayam was deliberately failing to control his own followers in this matter. But above all Mulayam had brought about the defection of a number of the Bahujana Samaj legislators to his own party - some of them were Kurmis and was daily seeking to whittle away his coalition partner from above. Accordingly, in June 1995 Kanshi Ram and Mayawati brought the Government down.

Given the overwhelming importance that Kanshi Ram now places on the acquisition of administrative power, his willingness to form a new Government with the support of the 'Manuwadi' BJP becomes more comprehensible. He took the view that so long as he did not have to take orders from the BJP then he was prepared to put up with the odium of being propped up by the party hated by the whole of progressive India. Perhaps conveniently, he argued that the Congress, the Janata Dal and the Communists were as much 'Manuwadi' parties as was the BJP.

But there was still an enormous cultural and ideological gulf between his party and the BJP, and it was left to an outsider to play a perhaps crucial role in bridging the gap. Jayant Malhoutra, a prominent industrialist and Member of the Rajya Sabha, did much of the diplomatic negotiation between the leaders of the two parties. He and Kanshi Ram had formed an unlikely friendship several years earlier, and Malhoutra claims that his assistance to Kanshi Ram was motivated by concern to help bring about a 'soft landing' for India after the inevitable clash between the haves and have-nots. For its part the BJP knew that neither of the other two large legislative parties would support a minority Government of its own. Since the HIP leaders had come to have a special antipathy to Mulayam's rule, their best option was to allow the third and seemingly less threatening party to form a Government - they saw more to fear from the Yadavs than the Dalit. The HIP leadership had in mind the longer-term goal of permanently splitting the vote banks commanded by the Samajwadi Party and the Bahujana Samaj Party, thereby opening up a path to their own domination of Uttar Pradesh.

In June 1995 Kanshi Ram ceded to Mayawati the task of leading the new Government in Uttar Pradesh, and her period as Chief Minister has been a platform upon which Mayawati has built a now considerable political presence in Uttar Pradesh. Early on the much younger Mayawati was properly regarded as a mere lieutenant of Kanshi Ram, to whom popular accounts suggest she is romantically as well as politically linked. But Mayawati has been able to bring a charisma and liveliness to the hustings that Kanshi Ram himself has lacked. She has represented a novelty - a direct and forthright Dalit woman with courage sufficient to run hard against the powerful institutions that so oppress poor Indians. In short, Mayawati has become both considerably popular and also a force to reckon with.

The Government of 1995 is properly regarded as a joint Kanshi Ram-Mayawati Government - Kanshi Ram continued to reside primarily in Delhi but made frequent trips to Lucknow, the capital of Uttar Pradesh, and was consulted on all major decisions. In terms of new policies or administrative programmes, there was little to be seen from the four months of their rule. But this is by no means to say that this was not a signficant or a distinctive administration. Part of its significance resides in the intrusion of a different culture into the machinery of government of the State. Mayawati demonstrated that the Bahujana Samaj's antipathy to 'Brahminwadi' culture was no mere abstraction but was to serve as a guide to the identity of the actual bureaucrats who could be trusted to direct the administration. In a word, Mayawati chose to promote and work through a small coterie of Scheduled Caste officers. For example, the high-caste incumbents in the Chief Secretary and Chief Minister's Principal Private Secretary positions were both replaced by Scheduled Caste officers. Even more controversially, a number of more junior Scheduled Caste officers were favoured with accelerated promotion and positions at the centre of the administration. This change inevitably provoked resentment and the claim that merit had been replaced by casteism.

Within the larger administration of the State Maywati made energetic resort to the device of transfers and disciplinary action against officers found delinquent in one aspect or another. The transfer of senior officials for reasons other than completion of a normal term has become commonplace in a number of States of India, but by common consent Mayawati engaged in the practice more richly than before in Uttar Pradesh. Quite deliberately she created a climate of fear in order to motivate officials to work to her agenda. She dealt particularly severely with officials judged to have failed to protect the most vulnerable people in a particular District, the Dalit above all. Overwhelmingly condemned in the press, her actions appear to have evoked a sense of satisfaction among common people routinely subjected to official arrogance and callousness. And a number of commentators both within the administration and outside believed that Mayawati had administered a powerful and long overdue lesson to bureaucrats that their place was as servant, not master, of the people.'

The most persistent complaint about the Bahujana Samaj Government was the degree of illicit money it exacted, particularly in the matter of obliging individual bureaucrats regarding their transfer or non-transfer. Given the habitual misuse of public office to derive funds for party if not personal purposes, it would be surprising indeed if some of these stories were not true. What cannot be established is whether such official wrong-doing was conducted on a scale greater than that of earlier administrations in Uttar Pradesh. Perhaps a good deal of the problem arose from the callowness of Mayawati and her lieutenants - some of the stories suggest that their insufficient knowledge of the system, and also the hurry they were in, made it difficult for them to derive funds efficiently and quietly. Official corruption is something of an acquired art.

It is clear that Mayawati was not an accessible Chief Minister. Apart from the question of the tightness of her bureaucratic team, she was inaccessible to many of her own Ministers and to representatives of the BJP who felt entitled to a hearing in return for their support of the Government. Some of this inaccessibility may have arisen from motives that were not unreasonable. Thus Mayawati and Kanshi Ram were determined not to run a Government that freely granted favours to people for reasons other than the welfare of the party itself. They were particularly suspicious of requests from politicians where the request seemed to arise from personal pecuniary interest. The problem of inaccessibility was compounded by Kanshi Ram's continuing to reside in Delhi rather than Lucknow throughout the life of the Government.

There were also issues of personal style. Mayawati's reputation is one of meting out harshness and even humiliation to those with whom she finds fault, though it is also true that many informants report having experienced no such treatment. On the other side, the practice of showing elabourate respect to the leaders became something of a culture within party circles. This sometimes took the form of touching the feet of Mayawati and Kanshi Ram, a ritual form of respect that now tends to be seen as demeaning and 'feudal' in origin. The complaint is that the two leaders encouraged this practice. In short, there were problems of both process and style that gave rise to considerable resentment and disaffection in

Lucknow. This is one, but only one, reason for the largc number of defections from the legislative party that took place after the Government fell.

The public style of the Mayawati Government was more abrasive than radical. Indeed, Mayawati's own most provocative gesture was enacted even before she formed her own Government. In March 1994, during the Mulayam Singh government, Mayawati had somewhat casually condemned Gandhi as 'an enemy of the Dalit and the Bahujan samaj at large' (The Telegraph: in March 1994). Despite the frequency of previous Ambedkarite attacks on the Mahatma, Mayawati's remarks occasioned a storm of protest in the pages of the press.

The extravagance of this reaction was a pointer to the sensitivities aroused by the Dalit' proximity to power in Uttar Pradesh. During her own Government Mayawati curbed her rhetoric - indeed, she felt constrained to lay the customary wreath on the occasion of Gandhi's birth celebration. The most flamboyant gesture of her Government - and here Kanshi Ram's hand is clearly evident - was to build a Pariwartan Chowk or Revolution Square in Lucknow that was to have huge statues of the great figures of anti-Brahmin activism: Phule, Periyar, Ambedkar, Shahu Maharaj.

In the event, the Government fell before the statues could be completed. Construction of the Chowk proceeded around the clock in order to coincide with the staging of a Periyar Mela: this was a celebration of the life and works of the great figure of the Tamil non-Brahmin movement, Periyar E. V. Ramaswamy Naicker. The event was less than a resounding success in Lucknow, where Periyar is almost unknown, but the symbolism was probably directed more to Dalit in the south of India.

After the fall of the Bahujana Samaj Government it became fashionable to declare that a great opportunity had been lost by Kanshi Ram and Mayawati: they could have struck a blow for the liberation of the Dalit but they squandered their opportunity in corruption, crassness and the politics of business-as-usual. This is a dubious interpretation. Throughout their brief perio i of power Kanshi Ram and Mayawati had little room to manceuvre. They had a small minority of MLAs, and they knew they existed on borrowed time from the beginning. At best they could have had about a year in power before elections in mid-1996. There was simply no time to initiate solid administrative or development programme even if they had the capacity to formulate such initiatives.

In these circumstances the politics of symbolism was bound to be the most effective way to encourage their own constituency. But strong symbolism breeds savage reactions in contemporary India, and the New Delhi leadership of the BJP found it increasingly difficult to hold State leaders to the bargain of supporting Mayawati in the name of strategic electoral gain. It surprised no one when this leadership bowed to the pressures welling up in Uttar Pradesh and decided to end the life of the minority Government. President's rule intervened until a new Government could be formed after the general election of April 1996; in the event it was not until March 1997 that a new Government took office.

THE RULING OF BAHUJANA SAMAJ PARTY

The last several years have been an exhilarating roller coaster ride for Kanshi Ram, replete with towering peaks and deep troughs. His ambition has been to become the kind of national leader the Dalit have never had. In 1994 he made his most concerted bid to build a national movement by conducting rallies and meetings in Kerala, Karnataka, Maharashtra, West Bengal and Andhra Pradesh. The Bahujana Samaj had contested seats in a number of these States as early as 1989, but Kanshi Ram was now more serious about taking his message throughout the country. But these efforts came to little, particularly in the strong Communist States of Kerala and West Bengal.

There, his caste-based analysis failed to cut into the prevailing ideology constructed out of the language of class. Kanshi Ram developed a considerable following in Andhra, where he staged a number of impressive rallies. It seemed for a time that he could have entered into a governing alliance with NTR's Telegu Desam Party, but negotiations broke down and the Bahujana Samaj was soon a spent force in Andhra. After the fall of Mayawati's Government in Lucknow it became clear that the national and provincial elections of 1996 would be crucial to the very survival of the party.

Although candidates were to be put up in a number of States, Uttar Pradesh was by far the most important arena. Given the close competition between the three leading political forces - Congress, the BJP and the 'Third Front' of leftist and regional parties - Kanshi Ram hoped to be in a position to dictate outcomes at both State and national levels. But the whole history of his party suggested that there could be little electoral success without an alliance with another major force. The logical partner was the Janata Dal, but Kanshi Ram declared himself against any new alliance that included Mulayam. This stand appeared tantamount to political suicide. It was clear that Kanshi Ram's movement could not easily survive a poor resuit in Uttar Pradesh in 1996. Unlike the figure of Ram Vilas Paswan, Kanshi Ram had set his sights on great and rapid victories. His age and ill health seem to have intensified the sense of urgency that had succeeded the patience of his earlier years in politics.

Considering its lack of strategic alliances, the Bahujana Samaj Party did surprisingly well in the Lok Sabha election of 1996. It won a total of eleven seats, six of them in Uttar Pradesh, three in Punjab and two in Madhya Pradesh. (In the previous Parliament its only UP seat was the one occupied by Kanshi Ram himself.) It was clear that Mayawati had become something of a cult figure in Uttar Pradesh. And in order to compensate for its lack of partners the party had energetically sought to woo communities other than its own vote bank of Chamars. The still leaderless Muslims were a particular target, and about one-quarter of the party's tickets in Uttar Pradesh had been conceded to Muslims. There were also a number of Backward Caste candidates.

In the subsequent UP Assembly election in 1996 Kanshi Ram and Mayawati reverted to the approach of constructing a strategic alliance. This time their ally was Congress. Amazingly, given its glorious past, Congress was relegated to the position of junior partner, and it was agreed that the combination's candidate for Chief Minister would be Mayawati. Kanshi Ram was reported to have asked Congress to field 100 Brahmins in the 125 seats allotted to it, so as to wean the upper castes from the BJP and attract them back to Congress. Again Kanshi Ram was playing the caste game with ruthless application. His own list of candidates was carefully mixed according to the appropriate communitarian formula: of his sixty-seven successful candidates, nine are upper caste representatives, twelve are Muslims, twenty-six from the Backward Castes and twenty Dalit.

The overall result of the 1996 Uttar Pradesh Assembly election was strikingly similar to the previous Assembly election: the BJP won 174 seats in the Assembly of 425 seats; Mulayam Singh's Samajwadi Party won 110 seats; and the Bahujana Samaj (67) and Congress (33) jointly won 100. Again there was a stalemate. For a time it appeared that Mulayam Singh, now installed as Defence Minister in New Delhi, would be forced by his coalition partners at the centre to back a Bahujana Samaj-Congress Government in Uttar Pradesh. This plan ultimately collapsed under the weight of multiple rivalries and suspicions. President's rule from the centre persisted until finally a Bahujana Samaj-BJP coalition Government took office in Lucknow in March 1997.

This time the agreement was that Mayawati would serve as Chief Minister for six months and then give way to Kalyan Singh from the BJP for the same period. Again Kanshi Ram and Mayawati could argue that it did not matter which of the 'Manuwadi' parties they made an alliance with Congress or the BJP. Their task was simply to get into government and remake the system from the inside. And second time around their abrasiveness has been even greater.

During the drawn-out struggle to form a Government Mayawati was so fearful of her Assemblymen defecting to other parties that she locked them up in the Party headquarters in Lucknow for a period of weeks. They were not allowed out of the building, not even for Diwali, and visitors could see them for no more than fifteen minutes at a time (The Asian Age: 1 November 1996). During this same period Kanshi Ram's always strained relations with the 'Manuwadi' media deteriorated to the point that he ordered an attack on a group of journalists outside his official residence in New Delhi. He personally assaulted one of the journalists, and criminal charges are pending.

It is far too early to make a mature assessment of the Kanshi Ram- Mayawati phenomenon. Early on it might have been thought that the two leaders had achieved little more than the transfer of Congress Chamars to their own party in the context of the overall collapse of Congress in the north. It is certainly true that their only stable 'vote bank' is the Chamars, and no doubt a principal reason for the Chamars' support is their understanding that this is 'their' party. The Chamars have also responded favourably to Kanshi Ram and Mayawati's arrogant disdain for orthodoxy and their denunciation of the large and petty oppressions that still characterise the lives of many Chamars.

This community is now richer, better educated and bolder than when it gave its support to Jagjivan Ram. But Kanshi Ram and more recently Mayawati have also worked hard to dispel the notion that their party represents only the Dalit, let alone simply the Chamars. They have had considerable success in attracting other groups, including Muslims, to their cause, despite their willingness to cultivate relations with the anti-Muslim BJP.

To what extent their approach is more than opportunistic exploitation of the multiple divisions of contemporary Uttar Pradesh society remains a question. Perhaps this question will partly be answered by the impact Mayawati can make on the apparatus of government in Uttar Pradesh, such that a culture of governance less hostile to those at the bottom of the social hierarchy begins to emerge. Undoubtedly Kanshi Ram and Mayawati have their faults, but they do represent a more aggressive attack on the order of social orthodoxy than has previously been seen from participants in the mainstream of Indian electoral politics. Kanshi Ram has shown that a person of Dalit origins can lead a party that wins seats at the ballot box and is not afraid to form a Government that puts the interests of the most subordinated Indians at its very centre. Throughout India it will now be more difficult to ignore the interests of Dalit.

PROMINENT DALIT LEADERS

MAYAWATI

Mayawati, a Jatav (Chamar) woman, became Chief Minister of Uttar Pradesh (UP) in 1995. She is the first Dalit woman to have acceded to the highest office in an Indian state, but gender is not the most remarkable aspect of this accession. Its special importance arises from the uniqueness of a Dalit becoming Chief Minister through the vehicle of a political party centred on Untouchables themselves. The Bahujana Samaj Party, founded and still dominated by Kanshi Ram, seized its unlikely opportunity in UP after the collapse of a Government in which it was junior partner.

Mayawati's minority Government was backed for strategic reasons by the right-wing Bharatiya Janata Party (BJP), and it lasted a mere four months. But the very advent of such a Government had an electrifying effect on Untouchables across India. It was as if the world had been stood on its head, so that the bottom ruled over the top. When Mayawati again came to power in April 1997, this time in actual coalition with the BJP, the event was improbable without being unimaginable. The earlier accession had established, perhaps for the very first time that the Dalit were a central and not merely a marginal political force.

Installation of two Mayawati Governments is not the only event of recent political significance to the Dalit. At the national level a powerful Dalit leader has emerged within the Janata Dal, the party that formed Governments after the elections of 1989 and 1996. Ram Vilas Paswan was Minister for Labour and Welfare in V. P. Singh's Government of 1989-90, and he was one of the driving forces behind the immensely controversial decision to adopt the Mandal Report and thus extend reservation of public employment to a new class of 'Backward' elements. The intention was to try to create an historic coalition of the downtrodden by joining together the Dalit, the Backward Castes and, after the destruction of the Babri Masjid, the Muslims too.

While no such secure coalition is yet in sight, its very possibility continues to have political potency. So this aspiration was something of an ideological rationale for the formation of the coalition Government led by Deve Gowda after the inconclusive election of 1996. Ram Vilas Paswan was Minister for Railways in that Government - he retained the post after the Prime Ministerial change-over of 1997 - and he was widely regarded as the politician most relied upon by Prime Minister Gowda. Kanshi Ram and Ram Vilas Paswan, bitterly opposed though they are to each other, represent a new Untouchable politics that is radical and assertive but also ruthlessly pragmatic. For the first time across large parts of India the Dalit have to be taken seriously rather than viewed as a vote bank to be exploited by their social superiors.

Still another indication of the new radicalism is the so-called Naxalite activity that has persisted for a number of years in regions of Bihar and also Andhra Pradesh. In Andhra, the violent activity is centred in the same Telengana region that produced a major insurrection at the time of Independence. Untouchable labourers were at the centre of that insurrection (Harrison 1960: 2 15-16).The Madigas and also the Mangs have been a key constituent of the new agrarian resistance, though the movement has tended to be led by high-caste figures. While the Naxalite activities of Andhra and Bihar cannot be portrayed as the likely future of Untouchable politics in India as a whole, nor can these movements be dismissed as phenomena relevant only to the most backward regions of India. Like the more widespread and articulate Dalit movement, the insurrectionary labourers of Bihar and Andhra reflect a deep Untouchable resistance. But for the rest of this chapter we are concerned with more mainstream political life.

RAM VILAS PASWAN

Ram Vilas Paswan was elected to the Bihar State Assembly in 1969 as a member of die Samyukta Socialist Party. At the time he had considerable attraction to the Naxalite movement and no faith whatsoever in non-violence.' In 1970 Paswan's confrontationist tactics led to his imprisonment for seven months in Bhagalpur jail (later infamous for the deliberate blinding of a number of prisoners). It was only with the advent of the 'JP Movement' that he came to accept the superiority of non-violence. Paswan became a close colleague of Jayaprakash in 1974, and he was of some importance m the movement by virtue of being both an MLA and also a Harijan (the term still used in Bihar).

He was arrested at the beginning of the Emergency in 1975, and spent the whole of the Emergency in jail. In the election of 1977 he won a reserved Parliamentary seat for the Janata Party, and with the exception of the period from 1984 to 1989 has been a member of the Lok Sabha ever since. His party affiliation has changed with the many recompositions of the secular anti-Congress parties - he has variously been a member of the Janata Party, Lok Dal and the Janata Dal. The three leaders he has acknowledged in this time are Charan Singh, Karpoori Thakur and V. P. Singh.

Ram Vilas Paswan had a tumultuous period as Minister for Labour and Welfare in the V. P. Singh Government of 1989-90. He says that this was the portfolio he wanted, because he could simultaneously do work for the Dalit and the Backward Castes. One of his accomplishments was implementation of the long-standing Dalit demand that Dr Ambedkar's portrait be placed in the main hall of Parliament alongside the other greats of the national struggle for Independence. He was also able to persuade the Government to extend reservation in employment to Scheduled Caste persons who had become Buddhists; rite primary beneficiary of this change is the Mahars.' But, of course, Paswan's most notorious action was to be intimately involved in the decision to adopt the Mandal Report that had lain on the table throughout the 1980s - it was commissioned by the previous Janata Government. This measure was of no value to the Scheduled Castes but of immense symbolic importance to the Backward Castes, particularly those of Uttar Pradesh and Bihar. The backlash it created among the upper castes was a major factor in the disintegration of the Government.

Paswan's strategy in opposition remained essentially the same as it was in Government. His object was to be seen as the national leader of the Dalit, while simultaneously promoting himself as a strong leader of other out-groups - the Backwards and also the Muslims, from whom he claims to have particularly strong personal support. To augment his appeal to the Dalit he established a separate organisation called the Dalit Sena. Apparently this was established as early as 1983, but Paswan invested more energy in it after Congress lost its hold on the north Indian Untouchable vote. Of course, the key image placed alongside Paswan on the posters and promotional material of the Dalit Sena is that of Ambedkar. On the walls of the public rooms of his New Delhi residence there are now more likenesses of Ambedkar than of anyone else. But Paswan has come late to Ambedkar. The influences on him have mostly derived from the Lohia socialist movement and from Jayaprakash Narayan. But clearly Ambedkar has become the key symbol for building any all India Dalit constituency. Paswan cannot afford to surrender any part of the Ambedkar legacy to his principal rival, Kanshi Ram.

There have always been formidable obstacles in front of Ram Vilas Paswan. His own power base is limited: he is the pre-eminent leader of the Paswans, the second Untouchable community (behind the Chamars) of one State, Bihar. For the rest, since clearly he wishes to be Prime Minister, he has to stake his claim to be the overall leader of the disadvantaged. One practical obstacle is that his spoken English is sufficient only for limited private conversation, and he therefore has no real capacity to build a mass following outside the Hindi belt. And, of course, there are a number of other competitors for the same constituency of the disadvantaged. Finally, there remain deep questions as to whether an Untouchable will be acceptable as Prime Minister of India.

Paswan's party, Janata Dal, has done badly in electoral terms since its triumph in 1989. Its results in the 1996 poll were also poor, but events played into Paswan's hands. After the failure of the BJP to gain defections from other parties, Deve Gowda was able to cobble together an unlikely coalition of leftist, centrist and regional parties to form a Government in 1996. Deve Gowda installed his Janata Dal partyman Ram Vilas as his principal political lieutenant. Always energetic, as Minister for Railways Paswan rapidly turned this classic source of patronage into an instrument to promote the interests of Dalit. He claims, for example, that he has been able to regularise the position of thousands of temporary sweepers in the railways. When Congress brought down Gowda's Government at the end of March 1997, Paswan was one of the names mentioned as a possible replacement Prime Minister. But the position went to an establishment politician, the then Foreign Minister I.K. Gujral.

In terms of actual policy Ram Vilas does not stand for a programme greatly different from that of any of the other parties putting up for the Scheduled Caste vote. Despite his inclination towards radicalism, he recognises that structural change will now be difficult to bring about in the short run. It is too late for radical land reform, and the reforms that are possible have to be conducted with due regard to the stance of the courts. The major way ahead is to train Dalit so that they have marketable skills. He sees it as important to extend the principle of reservation to the developing private sector. Whatever his youthful origins, Paswan is now far from a social revolutionary. He is against the assertion of any animus against the upper castes - his second wife is an upper-caste Sikh - and Brahmins in particular. Rather, his overall goal is to work towards ensuring that Dalit and other out-groups get their fair share of social goods.

The great change in the politics of the Untouchables is that over large parts of India they can no longer be taken for granted as a dumb vote bank. To a much greater extent than even a decade ago they have begun to shape their own politics. The biggest change has been in the north, and the single most potent factor has been Kanshi Ram. He has given encouragement to Dalit across India, even though he has failed to have a major electoral impact outside a few States of the north. But Kanshi Ram did not fabricate his own political success from nothing.

The times have eminently suited him. While the V. P. Singh Government's adoption of the Mandal principles of reservation initially served to displace Kanshi Ram as a strong advocate of the oppressed, the Mandal factor later worked in his favour. The Mandal decision served to create and legitimate a new politics of the disadvantaged, and Kanshi Ram's later electoral alliances were creatures of this new political environment. Meanwhile, the rise of the BJP has obligingly sapped the capacity of Congress to compete for the Dalit vote.

While Kanshi Ram and Mayawati have been spectacularly successful in Uttar Pradesh, the success has been built on dubious foundations and has appeared in danger of collapse at every point. His strategy has been to build an organisation of his own, and to use this body to draw votes and even active support from social groupings beyond his own caste. But major electoral success has depended on the construction of alliances with other parties, and these alliances have lacked both principle and stability.

Ram Vilas Paswan, by contrast, has pursued the more cautious route of climbing the ladder in a broader, socially more heterogeneous, party on the mild left of Indian politics. He has projected himself as the special leader of Dalit within this national party. Paswan's fortunes have risen and fallen with the position of his party, but his strategy is eminently more risk averse than that of Kanshi Ram. Like Ambedkar before him, Kanshi Ram has plotted a difficult route to power.

More generally, it is now abundantly clear that there can be no single political strategy for Dalit throughout India. If India had developed a dominant national politics constructed on the basis of class and relative disadvantage, the situation might be different. But it is also a mistake to assume that such a politics would necessarily have taken a form advantageous to the Dalit. In this chapter we have found that considerations of caste have obstinately clung to its processes (as well, for that matter, to those of the similarly egalitarian faiths of Christianity and Sikhism).

The current fragmentation of party politics means that no party can realistically hope to command a national majority of the Dalit vote. But this too is not necessarily unfavourable for the Dalit. It will be recalled that in the era when they voted overwhelmingly for Congress their political and social power was considerably less than it is today. The common political task of the Dalit is to add to their collective power, but there can be no single strategy that will deliver this objective.

Bibliography

Ashok Kumar, E.N. 1998a. Upward mobility or class formation. pp 240-62, in Simon R. Charsley & G.K. Karanth eds *Challenging Untouchability. Dalit initiative and experience from Karnataka*. New Delhi: Sage Publications Publications.

Assayag, Jackie 1992. *La colère de la déesse décapitée. Traditions, cultes et pouvoir dans le sud de l'Inde*. Paris: CNRS Éditions.

Bapat, Gururao V. 1998. *Yakshagaana performance and meaning - a semiotic study*. Udupi, Karnataka: Regional Resources Centre for Folk Performing Arts.

Briggs, G.W. 1920. *The Chamars*. Calcutta: Association Press.

Brouwer, Jan 1995. *The Makers of the World. Caste, craft and mind of South Asian artisans*. New Delhi: Oxford University Press.

Buchanan, Francis 1807. *A journey from Madras through the countries of Mysore,* Canara, and Malabar .... 3 vols. London: T. Cadell & W. Davies.

Chaitanya Deva, B. nd. Indian musical instruments. http://www.4to40.com/discoverindia/. Download 04.07.2006.

Charsley, Simon R. 1996 'Untouchable': what is in a name? *Journal of the Royal Anthropological Institute* (n.s.) 2, 1, pp 1-23.

Charsley, Simon 2002. Evaluating Dalit leadership: P.R. Venkatswamy and the Hyderabad example, *Economic and Political Weekly* , Vol 37, No. 52, pp 5237-43.

Charsley, Simon R. & G.K. Karanth 1998. Dalits and state action: the 'SCs'. In *Challenging Untouchability. Dalit initiative and experience from Karnataka*, ed. Simon R. Charsley & G.K. Karanth. New Delhi: Sage Publications.

Coburn, Thomas B. 1984. *Dçvi-mâhâtmya. The crystallization of the goddess tradition*. Delhi: Motilal Banarsidas.

Cohn, Bernard S. 1990. *An anthropologist among the historians and other essays*. Delhi: Oxford University Press.

Das, Veena 1968. A sociological approach to the caste puranas: a case study, *Sociological Bulletin* 1: 141-64

Desai, P.B. 1968. *Basavesvara and his times*. Dharwar: Karnatak University, Kannada Research Institute.

Dube, S.C. 1955. *Indian Village*. London: Routledge & Kegan Paul.

Dumont, Louis 1980. *Homo hierarchicus. The caste system and its implications*. 2nd ed. Trans M. Sainsbury, L. Dumont & B. Gulati. Chicago: University of Chicago Press.

Elliott, Walter (compiler) pre-1890. 'Aboriginal Caste Book', made in South India in 3 vols, included in Johnston Papers, British Library.

Elmore, Wilber Theodore 1915. *Dravidian Gods in Modern Hinduism. A study of the local and village deities of Southern India*. Hamilton, NY: The Author.

Epstein, T. Scarlett 1962. *Economic development and social change in South India*. Manchester: Manchester university Press.

Fawcett, F. 1890. On some festivals to village goddesses, *Journal of the Anthropological Society of Bombay* 2, pp 261-82.

Fox, George Townsend 1850. *A Memoir of the Rev. Henry Watson Fox, missionary to the Teloogoo people, South India*. London: Religious Tract Society.

Geertz, Clifford 1966. Religion as a cultural system, pp 1-46 in Michael Banton ed. *Anthropological approaches to the study of religion*. London: Tavistock Publications

Gribble, J.D.B. 1875. *A Manual of the District of Cuddapah*. Madras: Government Press.

Gurumurthy, K.G. 1977. *Kallapura: a South Indian village*. Dharwar: Karnatak University.

Hanchett, Suzanne 1988. *Coloured rice. Symbolic structure in Hindu family festivals*. Delhi: Hindustan Publishing Corporation.

Hewitt, Garth & Paul Field 2001.*The Dalit Drum* [audio CD with video extra]. ICC, Eastbourne, UK, for Christian Aid.

Hiebert, P.G. 1971. *Konduru: structure and integration in a South Indian village*. Minneapolis: University of Minneapolis Press.

Ilaiah, Kancha 1996. *Why I am not a Hindu*. Calcutta: Samya (Bhatkal & Sen).

Ishwaran, K. 1992. *Speaking of Basava. Lingayat religion and culture in South Asia*. Boulder: Westview Press.

Jana Natya Mandali (JNM) 1995. *Kâramcçdu pôrâta katha'* (Story of the Karamchedu struggle). Vijayawada: Pragati Book House.

Karanth, G.K. 1981. *Rural youth. A sociological study of a Karnataka village*. New Delhi: Concept Publishing Company.

Khare, R.S. 1985. *The Untouchable as himself. Identity and pragmatism among the Lucknow Chamars*. Cambridge: Cambridge University Press.

Lele, Suresh & Sabrina Francis dir. 2004. *Mahadiga The man descending from above* (film: 43 mins.) Hyderabad: Chindu Cultural Resource Centre.

Luke, P.Y. & John B. Carman 1968. *Village Christians and village culture. Study of a rural church in Andhra Pradesh, South India*. London: Lutterworth Press.

McCormack, William 1959. The forms of communication in Vi ras aiva religion. In *Traditional India. Structure and change*, ed. Milton Singer, pp 119-29. Austin: University of Texas Press.

Mackenzie, J.S.F. 1879. Customs of the Komti caste, *Indian Antiquary*, Vol. 8, p. 36.

Madaviah, A. 1905/06. The Matangi, *Christian College Magazine* 23 (NS Vol 5), pp 301-03

Martin, H.V. [1937]. *Among the Madigas* (pp. 30). London: Livingstone Press.

Mitchiner, John E. *Traditions of the seven Rsis.* Delhi: Motilal Banarsidas 1982.

Nanjundayya, H.V. & Ananthakrishna Iyer, L.K. 1928-35. *Mysore Tribes and Castes.* 4 vols. + Appendix vol. 5, 1936. Mysore: University Press.

Nair, Janaki 1994. The devadasi, dharma and the state, *Economic & Political Weekly* vol. 29, No. 50, pp 3157-67.

Narayana Rao, Velcheru & David Shulman (eds & trans.) 2002a. *Classical Telugu poetry. An Anthology.* New Delhi: Oxford University Press.

Oppert, Gustav 1893. *The original inhabitants of Bharatavarsa or India.* Westminster: Constable.

Parry, Jonathan P. 1994. *Death in Banaras.* Cambridge: Cambridge University Press.

Parvathamma, C. 1971. *Politics and religion. A study of historical interaction between socio-political relationships in a Mysore village.* New Delhi: Sterling Publishers.

Prasad, Chandrabhan 2004. Despair and hope of the Mahadiga, *The Pioneer* 08.09.04.

Ramaiah, Kotaganahalli 1993. *Sindh Madiga Sanskruti.* Bangalore: Karnataka Sahitya Academy.

Rao, V.V.L. Narasimha [1989]. *Swami Sri Veerabrahmendra. A monograph on Potuluri Veerabrahmam.* Hyderabad: Viswarshi Publication.

Reddi, N. Subha 1950. Community conflict among the depressed castes of Andhra, *Man in India* 30, 4, pp 1-12.

Reddy, D. Narasimha 1985. Karamchedu: A dialectic without development, *Economic and Political Weekly,* Vol. 20, No. 37: 1546–49.

Sackett, F. Colyer 1951. *Posnett of Medak.* London: The Cargate Press.

Sarma, M. Nagbushana 1995. *Folk Performing Arts of Andhra Pradesh.* Hyderabad: Telugu University.

Satyanarayana, K. 1983. *A study of the history and culture of the Andhras,* Vol. 2. New Delhi: People's Publishing House.

Shah, A.M. & R.G. Shroff 1959. The Vahîvanca Bârots of Gujarat: a caste of genealogists and mythographers. In *Traditional India. Structure and change.* Milton Singer ed. pp 40-70. Austin: University of Texas Press.

Shankar, Jogan 1990. *Devadasi cult: a sociological analysis.* New Delhi: Ashish Publishing House.

Singh, T.R. 1969. *The Madiga: a study of social structure and change.* Lucknow: Ethnography and Folk Culture Society.

Singh, Yogendra 1973. *the modernity of Indian tradition: a systematic study of social change.* Delhi: Thomson Press.

Siraj ul Hassan, Syed 1920. *The castes and tribes of H.E.H. the Nizam's Dominions.* (Madigas. 409-20). Bombay: The Times Press.

Srinivas, M.N. 1976. *The remembered village.* New Delhi: Oxford University Press.

Stein, Burton 1980. *Peasant state and society in medieval South India.* Delhi: Oxford University Press.

Subbachary, Pulikonda 2000 *Telugulô kulapûrânâlu âsrita vyavastha. A study of caste myths and dependent caste system of Telugus.* Hyderabad: Prajashakti Book House.

Subbarao, T.V. 2001. The ballad-cycle of Katama Raju: a Telugu folk epic. pp189-98 in B. Ramakrishna Reddy ed. *Dravidian folk and tribal lore.* Kuppam: Dravidian University.

Sudhakar, Yendluri (Endluri) 2004. *Vargeekaraneeyam (A Long Dalit Poem).* Rajahmundry: Manasa & Manogna Publishers. 2nd ed. 2005

Thurston , Edgar & K. Rangachari 1909. *Castes and tribes of Southern India.* 9 vols. Madras: Government Press.

Tirumala Rao, Jayadheer 1996. Hidden culture of

dependent castes – a case study of Dakkali, a Dalit community. pp 190-93 in R. Soma reddy et al. eds *Castes, communities and culture in Andhra Desa. 17th and 18th centuries, AD*. Hyderabad: Osmania University (Department of History).

Umaheshwari R. 2001. Chindu, pillar of Dalit art forms, *Deccan Chronicle*, 17 September, p. 3.

Venkateswarlu, Bittu 1997. *Jâmba purânam (Mâdiga kula sâmskritika chitram)*. Hyderabad: Janapada Kala Parishodhana Vedika.

Vijaishri, K. Priyadarshini 2003. Transcending the devadasi: reform and pattern of sacred prsotitution in colonial Andhra. pp 177-95 in Manas Ray, ed. *Space, sexuality and postcolonial cultures*. Calcutta: Centre for Studies in Social Sciences.

Whitehead, Henry 1921. *The village gods of South India*. 2nd ed. Calcutta: Association Press.

Ziegenbalg, B. [1713] 1869. *Genealogy of the South-Indian gods: a manual of the mythology and religion of the people of southern India: including a description of popular Hinduism*. (Orig. German *Genealogie der malabarishen Götter*:) English trans. G.W. Metzger. Madras: Higginbotham. Reprint: New Delhi: Unity Book Service 1984.

Index

I

J

K

L

M

O

P

R

S

T

U

V

❑❑❑